Integrative theory and practice in psychological therapies

Integrative theory and practice in psychological therapies

New directions

Maria Luca, Claire Marshall and John Nuttall

 Open University Press

Open University Press
McGraw-Hill
8th Floor, 338 Euston Road
London
England
NW1 3BH

and Two Penn Plaza, New York, NY 10121-2289, USA

First published 2019

Senior Commissioning Editor: Hannah Kenner
Development Editor: Tom Payne
Editorial Assistant: Karen Harris
Content Product Manager: Ali Davis

A catalogue record of this book is available from the British Library

ISBN-13: 9780335262489
ISBN-10: 0335226825
eISBN: 9780335248414

Library of Congress Cataloging-in-Publication Data
CIP data applied for

Typeset by Transforma Pvt. Ltd., Chennai, India

Praise for this book

'In a time of seemingly intractable and widening divisions and extremisms, voices expressing the virtues of integration and dialogue are increasingly necessary. This is no less true in the fields of psychotherapy and counselling. Luca, Marshall and Nuttall have produced a text that clearly demonstrates the benefits of an integrative approach to theory and practice. The heart of this text is the necessity for each therapist, regardless of their initial training and preferred model(s), to develop their own personal integrative and embodied way of working. In my view, both experienced therapists and those in training will want this book ready to hand. Highly recommended!'

Professor Michael Worrell, Consultant Clinical Psychologist and Head of Department, Postgraduate CBT Training, Royal Holloway, University of London, UK

'Integrative theory and practice in psychological therapies offers wide-ranging explorations of diverse facets of integrative psychotherapy including dissecting our theoretical base; interrogating the nature of practice and relationship building with clients; assessment; supervision; training; ethics; and our wider professional context. The strength of this book is the scholarly, academic approach taken where the epistemological underpinnings of psychotherapy are capably unpacked. The authors, Maria Luca, Claire Marshall and John Nuttall, dedicate particular chapters to their specialist interests. This text should be a "go-to" companion for any doctoral student on a reflective–reflexive quest to find their own personal model of integrative psychotherapy.'

Dr Linda Finlay, Integrative Psychotherapist and Academic Consultant

'I deeply regret that I did not have access to such a brilliant and forward-thinking book when I first entered the psychotherapy field. [The authors] have produced the gold-standard textbook on integration in psychotherapy, providing us not only with solid theoretical models but, also, with moving personal testimonies about the ways in which practitioners can benefit from the best theories and practices in our profession, without having to become too secularised and segmented. I applaud the authors for their creative work, which will help to train a whole new generation.'

Professor Brett Kahr, Senior Fellow, Tavistock Institute of Medical Psychology, London, UK and Trustee, United Kingdom Council for Psychotherapy

'Supported by the outcome research into effective psychotherapy, this book argues that searching for a new integrative system would be pointless and instead "we should seek to enhance and develop effective integrative therapists". Thereafter, the three accomplished authors take the reader on a personal "integrative quest" – an ongoing process of finding one's own integrative approach in a post-modern world – accounting for every aspect of reflection, from the philosophical and sociological to the poetic and the deeply personal, by way of the history of thought, politics, the story of the integrative project, psychology, theory and much more. The book is erudite, informative, challenging, exciting, sometimes frustrating, sometimes moving, always engaging. Each chapter is a plateau, a rhizome and a rupture. What an education."

Professor Charlotte Sills, Integrative Psychotherapist,
Coach, Supervisor and Trainer

'The book places the integrative therapy movement within the context of the development of psychological therapy in a way that is accessible both to psychological therapy beginners and experienced psychological therapists. It is contemporary and leading edge, keeping abreast of current developments within the profession. The knowledge and expertise of the authors does not just encompass clinical integration but also a range of modalities and philosophical outlooks. It shows that there are many variants of integration, including individualised approaches, which makes its range of applications almost infinite. But it also shows that the authors are well-versed in many aspects of the psychological therapy profession, demonstrating their comprehensive grasp of the fields of psychological therapy practice, training, research and supervision and the history and development of the profession.

The book has breadth and depth. It places integrative therapy within the broad context of the history of ideas going back to ancient times but then zooms forward to contemporary thinking and incorporates many key developments in-between including the Enlightenment and the development of scientific thought. In addition to its academic expertise, the book is also practical since it includes what I would refer to as the 'core conditions' and client-focussed nature of integrative therapy and also several case vignettes, both in depth and brief.

The book is not only about integrative therapy and clinical practice but also about many other things – philosophy, science, society and being human. The authors do not shy away from sharing their own journeys. We need to 'reflect upon our being and doing to gain self-knowledge' – a process that must include 'our shadow and our dark side'.

Dr John Lees, Psychotherapist in private practice and
Associate Professor of Psychotherapy and
Counselling, University of Leeds, UK

Contents

List of figures and tables

Figures

Tables

About the authors

Maria Luca is a Reader in Psychotherapy and Counselling Psychology and the Director of the Regent's Centre for Relational Studies and Psychological Wellbeing (RCRSPW) at Regent's University London. She is the leader of the PhD Programme and Editor in Chief of the *Journal of Psychological Therapies Reflections*. She was previously the Head of the School of Psychotherapy & Psychology. As an accredited integrative psychotherapist and supervisor with the UKCP and the MBACP, Maria has 22 years' post-qualification clinical experience in the NHS and in private practice. Among other publications, such as book chapters and articles in peer-reviewed journals, she is editor of: *Sexual Attraction in Therapy* (2014) and *The Therapeutic Frame in the Clinical Context* (2012). Her special interests include psychotherapy integration, working with sexual attraction and sexuality in therapy, sexual bullying, grounded theory and working with medically unexplained symptoms.

Claire Marshall is a counselling psychologist with more than ten years' experience in private health care, third sector and organisational management. Previously, Claire was the clinical manager of services in North and Central London. Claire has worked as a counselling psychologist within: private practice, supporting adults with a range of issues; therapeutic homes for young people in care; a specialist service for developmental trauma; a forensic unit; and an addictions service. As a supervisor, Claire has run group and one-to-one supervision in various private and public sector settings, as well as for United Nations psychosocial workers stationed in North African refugee camps. As an academic, Claire is currently a member of faculty of the Professional Doctorate in Counselling Psychology at the University of East London, as well as at the New School of Psychotherapy and Counselling. Her special interests include: forced migration; social narratives around humanitarian aid; humanitarian operations in conflict and post-conflict settings; responses to forced migration from state and non-state actors, with a particular focus on trauma policy and interventions; community development initiatives; critical psychology; social justice issues; language and ontology; and social epistemology.

John Nuttall is Head of School of Psychotherapy and Psychology and Assistant Dean for Research at Regent's University London. John is also a Professor of Integrative Psychotherapy, teaching theory, skills and research methods in the field, and a professional psychotherapist in private practice. John has had an extensive career in senior management in multinational industry and commerce and is a Certified Management Consultant and Chartered Marketer. He has written widely on management and psychotherapy, and his special interests include psychotherapy integration, organisation theory, and the provision of counselling and psychotherapy in the community. He is also an honorary psychotherapist and Chair of the charity, West London Centre for Counselling (WLCC), a major provider of therapeutic counselling in primary care.

Acknowledgements

We wish to acknowledge the support we have received from our friends and families during this process. Much of the material in this book has evolved from our training work at the School of Psychotherapy & Psychology at Regent's University London and the University of East London.

We wish to thank all our students, supervisees and colleagues, as well as our clients who have indirectly contributed to our own personal development and evolution. Writing this book has been a collaborative endeavour for us, one that has proved both rewarding and challenging. We also wish to extend our thanks to the editorial team of Open University Press, especially Tom Payne for his valuable feedback and collegial support on the manuscript and Hannah Kenner for her support throughout the production and publication of this book.

Preface

This book has been a collaborative endeavour, with each author offering their unique perspective on integration. There is also a thread running through the book. We all hold the view that integration is a personal quest, something that is informed by a social constructivist perspective that taps into the wealth of different concepts, theories and clinical approaches concerning what it is to be human, something that distils the essence of human beings and draws on perspectives from engagement in pre-reflection, reflection and meta-reflection.

As therapists and academics, we are mindful of our ethical responsibility. In order to illustrate our perspectives and how these apply in practice, we have shared scenarios from our practice. However, these scenarios are not case studies. They are situations that take place in clinical practice but do not convey or represent any particular client. Further, the material used is in the spirit of exploring the integration of theory and practice and making situations more accessible for our readers.

1   Introduction

Maria Luca

Throughout this book, we argue for an individualised and personal approach to therapeutic work, anchored in the particular psychological needs of clients, identified through integrative assessments and formulations. Personal integration does not adopt rigid adherence to any particular pre-existing modality; rather, it pulls together strands of knowledge, skills and techniques that are applied by each of us and have been found to be effective. The book also aims to develop new directions in integration, rooted in the notion that each integrative therapist embarks on a journey of knowledge and experience from practice, one that shapes their theoretical and clinical approach. The aim is to demystify as well as develop elastic, flexible processes that are conducive to effective therapeutic work and embrace the notion that the subjectivities of every client–therapist couple interact and create what we describe as a *relational dynamic*.

We encourage clinicians to use rigorously reflected and clinically relevant knowledge to help them shape and revise their understandings of clients and think through what would work best for the individual. To assist practitioners in achieving their unique integrative model, we provide clinical examples and share our personal journeys to integration. We also present principles of good practice for engaged therapeutic relationships, with the aim of providing rigorous assessments and psychological formulations. We believe that clinically derived knowledge is fundamental in conceptualising, in making sense, and in deciding on the most appropriate treatment options for each client, informed by theory and practice.

We recognise that different modalities (for example, humanistic/existential or psychoanalytic) each hold value and therapeutic effectiveness in themselves. We therefore espouse the principle that modality 'wars', in terms of claims regarding which modality is the superior approach, can only reinforce separations within the professions of psychotherapy and counselling psychology that instead could benefit from embracing the evidence that all modalities have value (Hubble et al. 1999). For instance, Wampold (2011) argued that there are negligible differences among treatment effectiveness, but certain therapist qualities make some treatments more effective than others.

This book has been designed to explore what we have learned through practice experience, linking this to theory and critically evaluating its effectiveness. Each chapter has been written by a scholar with expertise in integration. John Nuttall presents a quest and a framework for personal integration; Claire Marshall conceptualises integration within a postmodern context; and Maria Luca explores the challenges in becoming an integrative therapist, sharing her own personal journey and teasing out the qualities of relational therapists. She argues that embodied, integrative therapists and supervisors use their intuition, affective bodily responses, cognitive thinking, and, most importantly, practice experience to understand and engage with clients genuinely, transparently, ethically and professionally.

One of our principal objectives in the book is to explore how integrative informed therapy can be applied in practice and how practice can inform integrative conceptualised therapy. Our core belief is that modality 'wars' reinforce separation among colleagues who share the same objective: to work towards effective therapy that is helpful to clients. The position of psychological maturity in professionals is the cornerstone of collaboration and respect of difference, not just with clients but also with colleagues. Theoretical and conceptual differences are neither equated with conflict nor with superiority or inferiority.

We invite the reader to think critically about the theories, modalities and scenarios we present in order to develop their own model. In the spirit of reflection, we hope that in developing their own model, the readers will also think critically about theories and psychological interventions so they can grow, develop and prevail with the test of time and practice.

References

Hubble, M.A., Duncan, B.L. and Miller, S.D (eds) (1999) *The Heart and Soul of Change: What Works in Therapy*. Washington, DC: American Psychological Association.

Wampold, B.E. (2011) *Qualities and Actions of Effective Therapists*. American Psychological Association Education Directorate. Available at: http://www.apa .org/education/ce/effective-therapists.pdf (accessed 17 December 2018).

2 The history of the integrative quest

John Nuttall

Introduction: integrative origins in the ancient world and antiquity

> Graspings: wholes and not wholes, convergent, divergent, consonant, disso-
> nant, from all things one and from one thing all.
>
> (Heraclitus, Fragment DK. B10)

Much of today's diversity in psychotherapy can be traced to and identified in the ideas and controversies posed by the philosophers of Ancient Greece. The issues of what is 'real' and stable as opposed to what is 'sensed' and changing, and the corollary investigations of how or in what sense we can know the world and view it as interacting, were of major concern to these early philosophers. Parmenides (b. circa 520 BCE), for example, was traditionally read as believing in a permanent or unchanging reality, while others like Xenophanes (b. circa 570 BCE) can be read as positing that the reality to which we have access is in a constant state of flux. Therefore, our experiences of reality ought to be subject to some scepticism – we are limited to critically analysing what we observe and debating with others what they observe.

These ancient debates about the fundamental nature of reality may seem at great remove from the current dynamics of counselling and psychotherapy. But the connection between how we see the world or what view we take regarding what reality is (i.e. metaphysics) and how we understand reality to interact (i.e. natural science) is of great importance for our field. We can see this in the later writings of another ancient thinker, Hippocrates. Hippocrates (b. circa 470 BCE), and other associated writers whose works are archived under his name, espoused a rationalist and secular approach to health care that challenged the prevailing view that disease, especially mental disease, had supernatural causes. They were therefore the first in the western tradition to ascribe mental illness to physical states and the malfunctioning of the brain and were credited with the first classification of mental illness, identifying such mental states as paranoia, melancholia, mania and hysteria. According to Hippocrates, the imbalance of the four humours (black bile, blood, phlegm and yellow bile), each of which has corresponding mental states, causes physical and mental ailments. Hence, re-balancing the humours, through treatments based on clinical observation – either by direct intervention or lifestyle change – is key to a person's well-being. If Hippocrates laid the foundations of a new approach to medicine, Galen (b. 130 BCE) developed the corresponding practice. This became the dominant paradigm in the Roman Empire, no doubt helped by his position as philosopher physician to the Stoic Emperor Marcus Aurelius.

The way that Hippocrates approached medicine was steeped in an intellectual history of viewing the world as consisting of interacting physical things, a view of the world as sensible and in flux. He integrated these views into his care and, as a result, believed that mental ailments and helping clients get well were things that were subject to empirical, quantifiable methods. Had he viewed the workings of the world as part-Divine, he might have believed that mental ailments required quite different therapeutic processes. We will explore this process of moulding our own unique practices by bringing together various approaches and insights throughout this book.

Hippocrates's humourism and Galenic practice remained the prevailing approach until the Renaissance, despite a resurgence of the belief in the supernatural origins of mental illness espoused by the growth of Christianity and, in part, the prevailing philosophy of Neoplatonism. However, in the Islamic world, a more progressive approach seems to have developed from the syncretism of the eighth-century Translation Movement of the growing Islamic Empire. By the tenth century, Islamic scholars had explained a range of emotional disorders, including anxiety, paranoia, depression and obsession (Haque 2004), the treatment for which seems to have been a kind of cognitive therapy. In the West, it was Paracelsus (1493–1541) who challenged Galenic orthodoxy by incorporating alchemical beliefs and knowledge into the art of healing. He believed many diseases were caused by environmental agents and introduced the principle of treating the underlying nature of disease rather than its symptoms. Accordingly, he believed mental illness should be treated with compassion and understanding, and Carl Jung wrote of him: 'We see in Paracelsus not only a pioneer in the domain of chemical medicine, but also in those of an empirical psychological healing science' (Hargreaves 2019). It took over two hundred years for this approach to be taken seriously against the backdrop of a rapidly growing population and increasing urbanisation. In Europe, the general civic and medical policy response was incarceration of the mentally ill in huge asylums, exemplified by the notorious Bethlem Hospital in London.

The emergence of psychotherapy

Despite the theoretical roots of integration sinking deep into the ancient world, the term 'psychotherapy' seems to have emerged only around the 1850s (Shamdasani 2005) in relation to the contemporaneous interest in the use of hypnosis as a treatment option. Psychotherapy, as the empirical-clinical discipline we know today, has existed for little more than a hundred years (Ehrenwald 1976; Frank 1986). Its origins arguably date from the coincidental innovative work, at the *fin de siècle* of the nineteenth century and turn of the twentieth century, of Freud, Pavlov and Moreno (Corsini 1995: 12). These pioneers fathered three distinct foundational schools of psychotherapy (Clarkson 1992a; Nelson-Jones 2001) now recognised as psychoanalysis, cognitive–behaviourism and humanistic psychotherapy, respectively. However, to this must be added a more recently acknowledged fourth school of transpersonal psychotherapy (Boorstein 1996: 2), which, paradoxically, has much deeper roots in what Frank (1986) called the religio-magical traditions of shamanism, mysticism and spiritual belief. These schools form the basis of one grouping of the current psychotherapy profession, although a range of categorisations abound (Beutler, Bongar and Shurkin 1997; Roth and Fonagy 1996; UKCP 2016). For example, the United Kingdom Council for Psychotherapy (UKCP) currently recognises 11 colleges purportedly representing different theoretical and philosophical approaches, whereas Roth and Fonagy identified only six 'major classes' (1996: 3). In our view, these additional colleges or classes can be readily amalgamated within the four foundational schools we discuss here.

The foundational schools of psychotherapy

Twentieth-century psychology, in all its varieties, was determined by a modernist *Weltanschauung* that was 'centrally concerned with locating foundational forms' (Gergen 1990: 23). Such forms are characteristic of the schools previously enumerated. Psychoanalysis posits a structure to the mind consisting of three internal psychic organs (the id, ego and superego), cathected by an inherent psychic energy derived from instinctual strivings. These function within the three mental domains of the unconscious, preconscious and conscious. Further elaborations of psychoanalysis by the object relations and intersubjective approaches have not fundamentally challenged the intrapersonal dynamics this structure engenders, with the menacing corollary of psychological distress and mental illness. The term 'psychodynamic' has therefore become the generic title used to encompass those systems of psychotherapy using these or similar structural propositions.

The cognitive–behavioural school is based on behaviourist theories of operant conditioning and stimulus-response processes combined with cognitive developmental theories of social learning. The basic premise is that we are instinctual biological beings who respond to, and are conditioned by, the environment and context in which we grow up and live. The cognitive–behavioural school of psychotherapy has recently made claim to a 'third wave' of approaches that, nevertheless, struggle for integration (David and Hoffman 2013) by encompassing techniques, such as mindfulness and meditation, that might be otherwise considered as belonging more to the transpersonal tradition. A further 'fourth wave' has incorporated ideas from positive psychology – arguably in an attempt to embrace the principles of the earlier human potential movement and humanistic psychology.

Humanistic psychotherapy is much more concerned with human motivation and aspiration and posits a teleological organismic force that manifests as a driver for human aspiration, called the actualising tendency. These ideas stem from the US human potential movement of the 1950s and 1960s, although the later incorporation of European existential philosophy brought the limitations of being human within its perspective. The advent of postmodernism and cybernetics in the 1970s and 1980s resulted in the growth of Systemic Therapy, which seeks to understand the individual in relationship with others as part of a larger system, such as a partnership, family, organisation or community. We consider this to be part of the humanistic turn, although Roth and Fonagy (1996) argue that it has a unique theoretical underpinning. Alongside this, emerging from within the humanistic movement, the fourth school of transpersonal psychotherapy encouraged recognition of states of consciousness that are 'beyond individuality, beyond the development of the individual person into something which is more elusive than the individual person' (Grof, quoted in Boorstein 1996: 2). This school attempts to reconcile the influence of internal dynamics, developmental conditioning and organismic aspiration with spiritual and mystical experience by positing a continuum of consciousness within which all states of mind can be placed (Wilber 1993).

The proliferation of psychotherapeutic approaches

Within and across these four schools, a wide range of systems of psychotherapy have developed. The number of these has been estimated at various times to be as high as 400 (Karasu 1986; Corsini 1995). This proliferation has continued, although many of the new approaches are derivatives of these foundational schools mentioned earlier, each of which has a distinct theoretical underpinning. Nobody has yet discovered the definitive truth of how psychotherapy works, and the research quoted earlier suggests no one approach is universally more effective than another.

Psychotherapy integration

Integration is defined by the *Collins English Dictionary* as 'the act of combining or adding parts to make a unified whole'. In psychotherapy, integration is about bringing together disparate theories, techniques and practices to construct ways of and a rationale for blending them, with the intention of improving the therapeutic outcome.

As Polkinghorne asserted, the variety of psychotherapeutic approaches, as seen in our discussion of the foundational schools, would 'provide *prima facie* evidence that no one therapy is correct' (1992: 158). However, there has been a growing consensus that 'there is no significant evidence that a theoretical approach is relevant to the outcome of Eurocentric psychotherapies – no matter how measured' (Clarkson 2003: 4). Such a view suggests that the quest to integrate the various foundational forms should not concentrate on a search for new effective integrative systems of therapy. Instead, we argue, we should seek to enhance and develop effective integrative *therapists*. Such practitioners would have within their capability and understanding a variety of skills and techniques, along with a broad view of the human condition. This might be achieved by undertaking a reflective and reflexive process of determining their own integrative approach to therapy and what works. As a number of prominent integrationists assert, 'The survival of the mental health professions, in other words, will be better ensured by identifying empirically validated treaters rather than empirically validated treatments' (Hubble et al. 1999: 439).

As an aside, it is disappointing that in the UK, the NHS has chosen to ignore this admonition in its introduction of the scheme for Improving Access to Psychological Therapies (IAPT), deciding instead to adopt what it considers to be empirically validated approaches. A policy promoting such access might have better captured the many empirically validated therapists already trained and experienced in the provision of counselling and psychotherapy (Nuttall 2016).

But let us return to integration. 'Integration as a point of view has probably existed as long as philosophy and psychotherapy' (Prochaska and Norcross 1999: 459) and the iterative and circular process they highlight was probably first espoused by Heraclitus, whose writing opens this chapter and who suggested that transformation (in this case, *integration*) is characterised by such a recursive process (Fragment 60). To write a full history of what has become known as the 'integration movement' would need more than this chapter, and the topic is worthy of a book in its own right. Freud arguably began the integrative quest in his *Project for a Scientific Psychology* (1895), as his theories seem to have emerged from the combination of his knowledge of neuroscience, academic psychology, psychiatry and contemporaneous theories on neurotic disorders. As Adam Phillips poignantly asks, 'If psychoanalysis wasn't a science, or wasn't only a science, what was it? These were the questions that haunted Freud, and the profession he invented; and that emerged gradually out of his early training' (2014: 76). However, it is only since around the 1980s that a significant move towards integration of the different psychotherapeutic schools has developed as the factors that maintained segregation have broken down. The exponential advances in communications, increased resources in social and mental health provision, and the growth in the number of training schools, especially in higher education, have led to a proliferation in the exchange of ideas and learning. The ascendancy of 'globalisation' has also led to the incorporation of philosophies and beliefs from a wider range of cultures and areas of the world. The consequent mélange has been linked to the advent of postmodernism and the challenge to single truth ideologies that underpin the foundational schools. In the early 1990s, Jerry Gold wrote that we had entered an era in which 'developments in psychotherapy almost always are integrative in the broadest sense of the word' (1993: 5–6).

The integration movement

A number of names have been given to the integration movement, the abiding characteristic of which has been, 'a dissatisfaction with single-school approaches and a concomitant desire to look across and beyond school boundaries to see what can be learned from other ways of thinking about psychotherapy and behaviour change' (Norcross and Arkowitz 1992: 1). One of these early names was the 'eclectic movement', but the generally accepted term for this professional lobby is now the 'integration movement' (Hollanders 2000: 34) and 'integrative psychotherapist' soon became one of the most popular titles used in the profession (Norcross 1997). These trends were crystallised by the formation in the USA of the Society for the Exploration of Psychotherapy Integration (SEPI) in 1982, by the British Society for Integrative Psychotherapy in 1987 (now succeeded by the UK Association of Psychotherapy Integration [UKAPI]), and by the European Association for Integrative Psychotherapy (EAIP) in 1993. Recent studies indicate that in Great Britain and the USA, 87 per cent (Hollanders and McLeod 1999) and 90 per cent (Norcross et al. 2005) of counsellors and psychotherapists, respectively, now consider they provide some form of integrative practice. In its mission statement, SEPI proclaims that it is an 'interdisciplinary organization whose aim is to promote the exploration and development of approaches to psychotherapy that integrate across theoretical orientations, clinical practices, and diverse methods of inquiry' (SEPI 2017).

Similarly, the UK integration movement, represented by UKAPI, views 'integrative psychotherapy as an approach to the psychotherapeutic endeavour which acknowledges the resonances between different schools of therapeutic thought, draws on concepts from various models, and explores client relationships both inside and outside the therapy room' (UKAPI 2017a).

Importantly, neither of these professional associations offers a prescription for psychotherapy integration, nor do they describe what might comprise integration. Instead, and very significantly, at its recent annual conference, UKAPI (2017b) promoted integration as a *personal* quest and not just a *profession-wide* activity. Prior to this, several of the leading members of SEPI had described the 'three most frequently employed strategies for psychotherapy integration as technical eclecticism, common factors and theoretical integration' (Safran and Messer 1997: 143). These strategies were originally specified by Arkowitz (1989) and are more aptly referred to as 'routes' by Norcross and Newman (1992: 10), who pointed out 'integration, as is now evident, comes in many guises and manifestations' (1992: 15). A similar idea was put forward by Fear and Woolfe (2000: 337), saying there is now a 'proliferation of integrative theories'. Despite this proliferation, one could argue that most, if not all, are probably 'approximate models of the same phenomenon: the human mind in distress' (Roth and Fonagy 1996: 12).

A number of pragmatic ways of integrating have been suggested, such as 'assimilation', the addition of a variety of techniques into an existing core system (Messer 1992), and 'complementarity' (Goldfried 1995), the combining of complementary techniques from different systems. However, the integrative quest, or the search for a coherently organised 'grand theory' (McLeod and Wheeler 1995: 287), might never be fulfilled. The incommensurate nature of the four foundational schools, the multitude of approaches and the lack of consensus on what is therapeutically mutative make the concept of a grand theory elusive. However, Clarkson

(1992b: 290) has argued that the integrative quest should be viewed as a process rather than the search for a position, and stated 'sometimes one must stop in order to catch one's breath and commit some fraction of an ongoing dynamic process to the constraints of words on paper'. This book represents such a commitment of words on paper.

The early integrationists

The first integrationist might be considered to have been Freud, the father of psychoanalysis (Frances 1988; Javel 1999). Javel contends that classical psychoanalysis diverged from Freud's actual techniques and writings, arguing that 'in certain ways, CBT is closer to Freud than classical psychoanalysis' (1999: 397), so he exhorts cognitive–behaviourists 'to look at the works of Freud for insight, inspiration and answers' (1999: 406). For example, he points to similarities between Freud's (1904) concept of involuntary thoughts and transference and cognitive therapy's automatic thoughts and expectations of others (Beck 1976). This view has some history, as the first recognised attempt to integrate behaviourism and psychoanalysis was presented to the American Psychiatric Association by French (1933) and again by Kubie (1934), although their perspectives were not appreciated at the time. Subsequently, others, such as Dollard and Miller (1950), Alexander (1963), Marks and Gelder (1966), and Brady (1968), have developed these links further.

One key figure in the US integration movement was Hal Arkowitz (1992). He suggested that one of the most influential books on the integration of psychoanalysis– and cognitive–behavioural therapy is Wachtel's (1977) *Psychoanalysis and Behaviour Therapy: Towards an Integration*, which argues that the psychoanalytic theories of Sullivan and Erikson explain problematic behaviour as a conditioned response to interpersonal relations. Wachtel called this approach 'cyclical psychodynamics', a novel merging of psychoanalysis and cognitive–behaviourism, which he later developed into an approach called 'integrative psychodynamic therapy' (Wachtel et al. 2005). These integrative developments seem to have been the precursors of what emerged in the UK as cognitive analytic therapy (Ryle 1990).

Alongside these developments, in a seminal article on integration, Rosenzweig (1936) introduced the concept of 'common factors' and posited that, as all approaches appear equally efficacious, there must be common factors operating that override any presumed differences among approaches. Anticipating future outcome studies and treatment approaches, he believed that factors common within all therapies would explain the comparable outcomes of different approaches.

As humanistic psychology developed in the 1960s (Moss 1999), a greater willingness emerged among the psychotherapy schools to share and accept each other's understanding. This was vividly demonstrated by the production of the Gloria Films (Rogers et al. 1965), but was also exemplified by the influence of two prominent authors of that decade. First, Jerome Frank, who wrote *Persuasion and Healing* (1961), identified a number of features common to the psychological healing traditions of different cultures. Second, Arnold Lazarus introduced the concept of technical eclecticism in 1967 and developed the approach called multimodal therapy (Lazarus 1989). The integration of humanistic and behavioural approaches was encouraged further by Martin (1972) and Thoreson (1973). However, probably the most acknowledged integrative system developed in this period incorporating humanistic values is Egan's skilled helper model (1975), which combines aspects of the cognitive–behavioural school while being grounded in the core conditions of the person-centred approach.

Transactional analysis, which also developed in the 1960s, has been similarly described by one leading integrative practitioner and transactional analyst as 'a multi-faceted system of psychotherapy' that 'integrates intrapsychic dynamics with interpersonal behaviours . . . within a humanistic/existential framework of values' (Clarkson 1992a: 1). Eric Berne, the founder of transactional analysis, hinted at these integrative links himself when he wrote, in a footnote, that he considered the object relations theory of Fairbairn to be 'one of the best heuristic bridges between transactional analysis and psychoanalysis' (1975: 134). More recent therapies that, arguably, combine techniques from different schools with the cognitive–behaviour approach are evident in mindfulness-based cognitive therapy (Segal et al. 2012) and acceptance and commitment therapy, systems of psychotherapy claimed as members of the so-called third wave of the cognitive–behavioural school (Hofmann et al. 2010).

The causal factors for integrationism

These developments raise questions about the current state of psychotherapy integration and the influence of the postmodern *Zeitgeist*, which Clarkson suggested encouraged a growing realisation that the so-called 'truths' or meta-narratives represented by the four foundational schools are 'fundamentally flawed as singular definitions of reality' (1995: vii). There was a tendency in the postmodernism of the late twentieth century to question the truth and efficacy of the prevailing group of foundational schools – schools with a defined set of psychotherapeutic theories and techniques – and move towards a more flexible approach to individual care. Palmer and Woolfe (2000), for instance, suggest that it 'has led to a growing interest in flexibility of response and bringing together ideas from disparate schools' in both counselling and psychotherapy. Several professional and economic factors have also encouraged integration. Gold described a trend to stop 'looking for the "best" therapy to a more pragmatic search for the best of many therapies in order to survive economically and professionally' (1993: 6), and Newman and Goldfried (1996) highlighted the pressure to improve the cost effectiveness of treatments from insurance companies and government health services.

Paradoxically, this pressure towards integration, whether from a postmodern or economic stance, has led to two slightly competing paradigms of provision: those of evidence-based *practice* (EBP) and evidence-based *treatment* (EBT). The former would seem to support integration in so far as it promulgates effective practice by considering the totality of an approach's integrity, ethics and coherence, whereas the latter would seem to engender segregation in that it validates specific treatments for specific conditions – such treatments often identified with only one of the traditional schools. In the USA, this dichotomy consequent to EBT was promulgated by the American Psychological Association setting up the Standing Committee on Science and Practice, which developed a somewhat controversial list of 'validated treatments'. In the UK, this role has been taken up by the National Institute for Health and Care Excellence (NICE) and has resulted in the national IAPT scheme. IAPT's staged approach, which attempts to prioritise mild to severe psychological distress, has resulted in the validation of a small number of very specific manualised treatment regimes, a process that seems anathema to the aims of psychotherapy integration. Within this context, it is disappointing that the IAPT scheme, although necessary and laudable, has undermined the rich and varied provision of therapeutic services that had already grown to meet the UK's community needs. The requirement, determined by NICE, to provide therapies that meet the criteria of EBT has led to a new generation of approaches being developed that purport to treat the dominant presenting problems in primary care of depression and anxiety, and their manualised delivery and apparent predictable outcomes made the economic objectives of reduced unemployment and social benefit payments seem attainable (Layard 2006).

In her seminal exposition of the therapeutic relationship, in which she develops a new framework for psychotherapy integration, Clarkson draws on a range of research evidence to conclude, 'the [therapeutic] relationship is consistently being shown in research investigations as more significant than theoretical orientation' to clinical outcomes (2003: 5). Roth and Fonagy (1996) presented a similar conclusion in their review of psychotherapy outcome research by type of illness and client group, adding to Asay and Lambert's (1999) work on the common factors in psychotherapeutic practices. This view, combined with the postmodern perspective, has resulted in the emergence of what might be considered higher-order models of integration that eschew deference to psychological theories in favour of emphasising the quality of the therapeutic relationship *per se*. Prochaska and DiClemente's transtheoretical model (1984), Hobson's conversational model (1985) and Clarkson's five-relationship framework (1995) are pioneering developments in this vein. More recent attempts to reify this perspective have, paradoxically, led to the nebulous growth of a range of 'new' approaches under the umbrella of relational psychotherapy (Lowenthal and Samuels 2014). Despite these influences, there is, potentially, a more personal imperative seeking resolution in the quest for integration. Sussman (1992) and Bager-Charleson (2010) have concluded that a significant motive for people choosing to become psychotherapists can be the resolution of their personal dilemmas. As a corollary, it is possible that the quest for an integrative approach to psychotherapy has a deeper psychological meaning for the integrative practitioner and might be part of an advance towards a personal sense of wholeness. Horton also sees it as a personal development that reflects 'the thinking and practice of the individual therapist' (2000: 326).

Conclusion

Integration has become a professional necessity as the need to prove cost effectiveness and efficacy, to either private insurance companies or government health services, increases. As Gold suggested, there was an imperative to stop 'looking for the "best" therapy to a more pragmatic search for the best of many therapies in order to survive economically and professionally' (1993: 6). There now seems to be a proliferation of integrative approaches (Hollanders 2000; Palmer and Woolfe 2000; Norcross and Beutler 2014), with some arguing that integration is a process that can never be completed (Clarkson 1992b: 290) and that it should be based on a dialectic process that recognises context and plurality (Safran and Messer 1997). In support of such personal integrating journeys, Goldfried's *How Therapists Change* (2001) brings together 15 autobiographical accounts of prominent integrationists.

Developing a personal integrative approach seems to be the means by which therapists gain emancipation from the dogma of the single school and move towards a state of individuation. Few research studies have focused on the personal process underlying psychotherapy integration but the work of Rihacek, Danelova and Cermak (2012) suggests the tension between what they call 'autonomous' (internal congruence) and 'heteronomous' (external influences) criteria is a significant factor. Notwithstanding the philosophical backdrop presented here, even if we consider the origins of psychotherapy integration to have its seeds in Freud's early works, the concerted quest for an integrative approach is a relatively recent phenomenon. Faced with the huge variety of approaches and systems of therapy available, both the individual therapist and institutional service providers seek coherence and concerted thinking from leading academic, clinical and professional bodies. However, the perspective championed by this book is that psychotherapy integration needs to be a *personal construction by the individual therapist* and that health institutions would be better seeking effective *therapists* rather than specific effective *treatments*. The search for an efficacious integrative approach has many diverse contributors, and so far has proved elusive. Organisations such as SEPI and UKAPI are bringing some coherence to the quest, but as Norcross and Beutler sum up the current state of integration: 'to put it differently, integrative psychotherapy has a long past but a short history as a systematic movement' (2014: 505).

References

Alexander, F. (1963) The dynamics of psychotherapy in the light of learning theory. *American Journal of Psychiatry*, 120: 440–8.

Arkowitz, H. (1989) The role of theory in psychotherapy integration. *Journal of Integrative and Eclectic Psychotherapy*, 8(1): 8–16.

Arkowitz, H. (1992) Integrative theories of therapy. In D.K. Freedheim (ed.), *History of Psychotherapy: A Century of Change*. Washington, DC: American Psychological Association.

Asay, T.P. and Lambert, M.J. (1999) The empirical case for the common factors in therapy: Quantitative findings. In M.A. Hubble, B.L. Duncan and S.D. Miller (eds), *The Heart & Soul of Change: What Works in Therapy* (pp. 33–56). Washington, DC: American Psychological Association.

Bager-Charleson, S. (2010) *Why Therapists Choose to Become Therapists: A Practice-Based Enquiry*. London: UKCP Karnac.

Beck, A.T. (1976) *Cognitive Therapy and the Emotional Disorders*. New York: International Universities Press.

Beutler, L.E., Bongar, B. and Shurkin, J.N. (1997) *A Consumer's Guide to Psychotherapy*. New York: Oxford University Press.

Berne, E. (1975) *What Do You Say After You Say Hello?* Ealing: Corgi Books.

Boorstein, S. (1996) Introduction. In S. Boorstein (ed.), *Transpersonal Psychotherapy* (pp. 1–8). New York: New York University Press.

Brady, J.P. (1968) Psychotherapy by combined behavioural and dynamic approaches. *Comprehensive Psychiatry*, 9: 536–43.

Clarkson, P. (1992a) *Transactional Analysis Psychotherapy: An Integrated Approach*. London: Routledge.

Clarkson, P. (1992b) Systematic integrative psychotherapy training. In W. Dryden (ed.), *Integrative and Eclectic Psychotherapy: A Handbook* (pp. 269–95). Buckingham: Open University Press.

Clarkson, P. (1995) *The Therapeutic Relationship in Psychoanalysis, Counselling Psychology and Psychotherapy*. London: Whurr.

Clarkson, P. (2003) *The Therapeutic Relationship*, 2nd edn. London: Whurr.

Collins English Dictionary (1999) Integration. London: HarperCollins.

Corsini, R.J. (1995) Introduction. In R.J. Corsini and D. Wedding (eds), *Current Psychotherapies* (5th edn) (pp. 1–14). Itasca, IL: F.E. Peacock.

David, D. and Hoffman, S.G. (2013) Another error of Descartes? Implications for the 'third wave' cognitive behaviour therapy. *Journal of Cognitive and Behavioral Psychotherapies*, 13(1): 111–21.

Dollard, J. and Miller, N.E. (1950) *Personality and Psychotherapy: An Analysis in Terms of Learning, Thinking and Culture*. New York: McGraw-Hill.

Egan, G. (1975) *The Skilled Helper*. Pacific Grove, CA: Brooks/Cole.

Ehrenwald, J. (1976) *The History of Psychotherapy: From Healing Magic to Encounter*. New York: Jason Aronson.

Fear, R. and Woolfe, R. (2000) The personal, the professional and the basis of integrative practice. In S. Palmer and R. Woolfe (eds), *Integrative and Eclectic Counselling and Psychotherapy* (pp. 329–40). London: SAGE.

Frances, A. (1988) Sigmund Freud: The first integrative therapist. Address to the Fourth Annual Convention of SEPI, Boston, MA, May.

Frank, J.D. (1961) *Persuasion and Healing*. Baltimore, MD: Johns Hopkins University Press.

Frank, J.D. (1986) What is psychotherapy? In S. Bloch (ed.), *An Introduction to the Psychotherapies* (pp. 1–23). Oxford: Oxford University Press.

French, T.M. (1933) Interrelations between psychoanalysis and the experimental work of Pavlov. *American Journal of Psychiatry*, 89: 1165–203.

Freud, S. (1966 [1895]) *Project for a Scientific Psychology* (Standard Ed., Vol. 1, pp. 283–94). London: Hogarth Press.

Gergen, K.J. (1990) Towards a postmodern psychology. *The Humanistic Psychologist*, 18: 23–34.

Gold, J.R. (1993) The sociological context of psychotherapy integration. In G. Stricker and J.R. Gold (eds), *Comprehensive Handbook of Psychotherapy Integration* (pp. 3–8). New York: Plenum Press.

Goldfried, M.R. (1995) *From Cognitive-behaviour Therapy to Psychotherapy Integration: An Evolving View*. New York: Springer.

Goldfried, M.R. (ed.) (2001) *How Therapists Change: Personal and Professional Reflections*. Washington, DC: APA Books.

Haque, A. (2004) Psychology from an Islamic perspective. *Journal of Religion and Health*, 43(4): 357–77.

Hargreaves, J.G. (2019) Paracelsus. In *Encylopaedia Britannica*. www.britannica.com/biography/Paracelsus (accessed 4 March 2019).

Hobson, R.F. (1985) *Forms of Feeling: The Heart of Psychotherapy*. London: Routledge.

Hoffman, S.G., Sawyer, A.T. and Fang, A. (2010) The empirical status of the 'new wave' cognitive behavioural therapy. *Psychiatric Clinics of North America*, 33(3): 701–10.

Hollanders, H. (2000) Eclecticism/integration: Some key issues and research. In S. Palmer and R. Woolfe (eds), *Integrative and Eclectic Counselling and Psychotherapy* (pp. 31–56). London: SAGE.

Hollanders, H. and McLeod, M. (1999) Theoretical orientation and reported practice: A survey of eclecticism among counsellors in Britain. *British Journal of Guidance & Counselling*, 27: 405–14.

Horton, I. (2000) Principles and practice of a personal integration. In S. Palmer and R. Woolfe (eds), *Integrative and Eclectic Counselling and Psychotherapy* (pp. 315–28). London: SAGE.

Hubble, M.A., Duncan, B.L. and Miller, S.D. (1999) Directing attention to what works. In M.A. Hubble, B.L. Duncan, and S.D. Miller (eds), *The Heart & Soul of Change: What Works in Therapy* (pp. 407–47). Washington, DC: American Psychological Association.

Javel, A.F. (1999) The Freudian antecedents of cognitive behavioural therapy. *Journal of Psychotherapy Integration*, 9(4): 392–402.

Kahn, C. (1981) *The Art and Thought of Heraclitus*. Cambridge: Cambridge University Press.

Karasu, T.B. (1986) The psychotherapies: Benefits and limitations. *American Journal of Psychotherapy*, 40(3): 324–43.

Kubie, L.S. (1934) Relation of the conditioned reflex to psychoanalytic technique. *Archives of Neurology and Psychiatry*, 32: 1137–42.

Layard, R. (2006) *The Depression Report: A New Deal for Depression and Anxiety Disorders*. London: LSE.

Lazarus, A.A. (1989) *The Practice of Multimodal Therapy: Systematic, Comprehensive and Effective Psychotherapy*. Baltimore, MD: Johns Hopkins University Press.

Lowenthal, D. and Samuels, A. (2014) *Relational Psychotherapy, Psychoanalysis and Counselling: Appraisals and Reappraisals.* Hove: Routledge.

Marks, I.M. and Gelder, M.G. (1966) Common ground between behaviour therapy and psychodynamic methods. *British Journal of Medical Psychology,* 39: 11–23.

Martin, C.G. (1972) *Learning-based Client-centred Therapy.* Monterey, CA: Brooks/ Cole.

McLeod, J. and Wheeler, S. (1995) Person-centred and psychodynamic counselling: A dialogue. *Counselling,* 6: 283–7.

Messer, S.B. (1992) The clinical challenges of assimilative integration. *Journal of Psychotherapy Integration,* 11(2): 21–42.

Moss, D. (ed.) (1999) *Humanistic and Transpersonal Psychology: A Historical and Biographical Sourcebook.* Westport, CT: Greenwood Press.

Nelson-Jones, R. (2001) *Theory and Practice of Counselling and Therapy.* London: Continuum.

Newman, C.F. and Goldfried, M.R. (1996) Developments in psychotherapy integration. In W. Dryden (ed.), *Developments in Psychotherapy: Historical Perspectives* (pp. 238–60). London: SAGE.

Norcross, J.C. (1997) Light and shadow of the integrative process in psychotherapy. Paper presented at Psychotherapy in Perspective. Congress of the European Association for Psychotherapy, June.

Norcross, J.C. and Arkowitz, H. (1992) The evolution and current status of psychotherapy integration. In W. Dryden (ed.), *Integrative and Eclectic Therapy: A Handbook* (pp. 1–39). Buckingham: Open University Press.

Norcross, J.C. and Beutler, L.E. (2014) Integrative psychotherapies. In D. Wedding and R.J. Corsini (eds), *Current Psychotherapies* (10th edn). Belmont, CA: Brooks/Cole.

Norcross, J.C., Karpiak, C.P. and Santaro, S.R. (2005) Clinical psychologists across the years: The division of clinical psychology from 1960 to 2003. *Journal of Clinical Psychology,* 61(12): 1467–83.

Norcross, J.C. and Newman, C.F. (1992) Psychotherapy integration: Setting the context. In J.C. Norcross and M.R. Goldfried (eds), *Handbook of Psychotherapy Integration* (pp. 4–45). New York: Basic Books.

Nuttall, J. (2008) The integration: A personal journey. *European Journal of Psychotherapy & Counselling,* 10(1): 19–38.

Nuttall, J. (2016) Working in partnership with IAPT. In J. Lees (ed.), *The Future of Psychological Therapy: From Managed Care to Transformational Practice.* London: Routledge.

Palmer, S. and Woolfe, R. (2000) Preface. In S. Palmer and R. Woolfe (eds), *Integrative and Eclectic Counselling and Psychotherapy* (pp. xv–xvi). London: SAGE.

Phillips, A. (2014) *Becoming Freud: The Makings of a Psychoanalyst.* New Haven, CT: Yale University Press.

Polkinghorne, D.E. (1992) Postmodern epistemology of practice. In S. Kvale (ed.), *Psychology and Postmodernism* (pp. 146–65). London: SAGE.

Prochaska, J.O. and DiClemente, C.C. (1984) *The Transtheoretical Approach: Crossing the Traditional Boundaries of Therapy*. Homewood, IL: Dow Jones-Irwin.

Prochaska, J.O. and Norcross, J.C. (1999) *Systems of Psychotherapy: A Transtheoretical Analysis*. Pacific Grove, CA: Brooks/Cole.

Rihacek, T., Danelova, E. and Cermak, I. (2012) Psychotherapist development: Integration as a way to autonomy. *Psychotherapy Research*, 22: 556–69.

Rogers, C., Perls, F. and Ellis, A. (1965) *Three Approaches to Psychotherapy: Gloria* [video tape]. Available from: Concord Video, Ipswich, England.

Rosenzweig, S. (1936) Some implicit common factors in diverse methods of psychotherapy. *Journal of Orthopsychiatry*, 6: 412–15.

Roth, A. and Fonagy, P. (1996) *What Works and for Whom? A Critical Review of Psychotherapy Research*. London: Guilford Press.

Ryle, A. (1990) *Cognitive-analytic Therapy: Active Participation in Change – A New Integration in Brief Psychotherapy*. Chichester: Wiley.

Safran, J.D. and Messer, S.B. (1997) Psychotherapy integration: A postmodern critique. *Clinical Psychology: Science and Practice*, 4: 140–52.

Segal, V.S., Williams, J.M.G. and Teasdale, J.D. (2012) *Mindfulness Cognitive Based Therapy for Depression*. New York: Guilford Press.

SEPI. (2017) Mission statement. Available at http://www.sepiweb.org (accessed 16 October 2017).

Shamdasani, S. (2005) Psychotherapy – the invention of a word. *History of Human Sciences*, 18: 1–22.

Sussman, M. (1992) *A Curious Calling: Unconscious Motivations for Practising Psychotherapy*. New York: Aronson.

Thorenson, C.E. (1973) Behavioural humanism. In C.E. Thorenson (ed.), *Behaviour Modification in Education*. Chicago, IL: University of Chicago Press.

UKAPI. (2017a) Welcome to UKAPI. Available at http://www.ukapi.com/ (accessed 17 October 2017).

UKAPI. (2017b) The heart of integrative psychotherapy: Putting theory into practice. Paper presented at UK Association of Psychotherapy Integration Annual Conference, London.

UKCP. (2017) How we are structured. Available at https://www.psychotherapy.org .uk/about-ukcp/how-we-are-structured/ukcp-colleges (accessed 9 October 2017).

Wachtel, P.L. (1977) *Psychoanalysis and Behaviour Therapy: Towards an Integration*. New York: Basic Books.

Wachtel, P.L., Kruk, J. and McKinney, M. (2005) Cyclical psychodynamics and integrative relational psychotherapy. In J. Norcross and M. Goldfried (eds), *Handbook of Psychotherapy Integration* (2nd edn) (pp. 172–95). New York: Oxford University Press.

Wilber, K. (1993) *The Spectrum of Consciousness*. Wheaton, IL: Quest Books.

3 The challenges of becoming an integrative therapist

Maria Luca

Introduction

A review of the literature, in particular more recent publications on integration in psychotherapy (Lapworth and Sills 2010; Faris and van Ooijen 2012; O'Brien and Houston 2013) and older publications (Caley and Bond 2004), has demonstrated a variety of ways of developing frameworks for integration to which you might refer for guidance. One example is Orlinsky and Howard's (1986a; 1987) generic model. We use Clarkson's (1995) five-relationship model for guidance in developing our own models of integration. This has been a popular model in psychology and psychotherapy as it highlights modes of therapeutic relationships common to most integrative models:

1. the working alliance
2. the transferential/countertransferential relationship
3. the reparative/developmentally needed relationship
4. the person-to-person relationship
5. the transpersonal relationship.

This chapter is intended to stimulate thinking on the idea of deconstruction as one of the key principles in personal psychotherapy integration. It is a space where the idea of unique human identities is fluid and developing, where this development is a product of practitioners reflecting openly and candidly on the questions: 'How am I in relation to the world of others?' and 'How do my personality, values and relational map manifest and impact on my relationships with clients?' We hope the chapter will provide food for thought and transport the reader to self-challenging avenues. The personal journey of developing an integrative model of therapy is a challenging and ambitious project. This is partly because it involves letting go of pre-existing beliefs, attitudes and theories and partly due to the necessity of intentionally selecting and bringing together diverse, and often paradoxical, experiences and knowledge in a model that can be applied to practice in a comprehensive way that makes sense to the integrative practitioner and can easily be communicated to others. For example, an existential model may reject the value of transference/countertransference. If an existentially orientated therapist finds the technique of transference/countertransference of value, they could integrate it into their model as opposed to rigidly adhering to this particular model.

This is a potentially rewarding endeavour and one that we might understand as involving *deconstruction*. Caputo (1997) defined deconstruction as like cracking open a nutshell and disturbing its tranquillity, which can be seen as an analogy to the psychotherapy trainee's process of integration where it becomes necessary to 'crack open' one's existing self-identity through self-questioning, reflexive analysis and critique, disturbing the day-to-day unreflective harmony of how we understand ourselves and interact with the world and others in order to gain a deeper, more critical understanding of our self-identity. In my own experience, the relational psychodynamic model resonated with me during my training and I had applied it in my practice. With time, I started to question and critically think about flaws in my initial model. Empathy and a conducive therapeutic relationship were the *sine qua non* of what worked in my practice. I therefore integrated certain qualities and elements of existential and humanistic theories in a revised model I now describe as *integrative*. To achieve this, I had to open myself to self-reflection and honest scrutiny, which meant destabilising my identity as a clinician. Despite the experience of destabilisation in the process of adding elements to a 'pure' model, there is much to be gained from this exercise in integration.

Derrida's (1978) postulation that elements have meaning only in the solidarity of their correlation or opposition is how integration can be. What Derrida implies is that deconstruction does not ever reach an end, an absolute conclusion. Rather, it disrupts the absolutism of dominant, pre-existing beliefs that can shift thinking. Psychotherapy and psychology could benefit from the process of deconstruction in that it challenges 'pure' models of psychotherapy and psychology, ones based on fixed truths that could become dogmas. In the same vein, integration as a process needs to be fluid, open to new knowledge and experiences, thus never-ending.

Types of integration

As discussed in Chapter 1, there are different types of integration in counselling psychology and psychotherapy. Before I embark on personal integration, it is important to say that eclecticism and integration have historically been used interchangeably (Hollanders 2000). However, eclecticism involves a wide range of techniques without a unifying theory, whereas integration attempts to synthesise different concepts, techniques and interventions in a unified theoretical mode (Faris and Ooijen 2012). In this chapter, I will focus on integration as distinct from eclecticism. In all types of integration, the therapist's personal identity, personality and resonance with certain theories and concepts impact on the way their integrative model evolves, is shaped and is practised. According to Norcross (cited by Heinonen et al. 2013: 726), integrative therapists may be more independently minded and motivated to seek an inclusive, comprehensive view of things. To illustrate, Heinonen et al. refer to the existing literature, stating: 'after achieving more professional independence, therapists' theoretical affinities might approximate their "true" personality better than the treatment models they adhered to earlier' (2013: 718).

Identification with particular theoretical orientations, then, corresponds to aspects of therapists' personalities. Research also shows psychotherapists espousing different theoretical approaches differing in mentality (e.g. cognitive styles, beliefs and epistemologies) and personality (Heinonen et al. 2013). The key finding in this study is that:

> therapists at work seem either to 'tone up' the qualities recommended by their theoretical orientations or 'tone down' personal qualities that are viewed as detrimental in those frameworks. Of all the groups observed, integrative-eclectic therapists on average seemed most nearly the same in both contexts.
>
> (2013: 727)

What these findings suggest is that who we are influences our resonance with certain theories and, inevitably, our choice of modality.

Why integration?

Recent research suggests there are common factors in all approaches to therapy and differences in outcomes between approaches are negligible (O'Brien and Houston 2013). According to Wampold, evidence gained primarily from meta-analyses of common factors and therapists' differences regarding 'alliance, empathy, expectations [and] cultural adaptation' (2015: 270) are central to effectiveness. The study also presented four factors related to specificity, including treatment differences, specific ingredients, adherence and competence: 'The evidence supports the conclusion that the common factors are important for producing the benefits of psychotherapy' (2015: 270). There are, however, some noteworthy, technique-related differences in approaches found to influence therapy outcomes if applied to specific clinical presentations. Roth and Fonagy (1996) draw attention to these, inviting practitioners to adopt what research has found to work effectively for certain types of psychological disorders, or advocating evidence-informed practice. As O'Brien and Houston argue, 'each therapy model holds definite and firm views about what is therapeutic' (2013: 30). Single models of therapy have their own sets of values and assumptions and adopt a theoretical framework with a set of skills that differentiate them from other models. Pure adherence to rigid frameworks runs the risk of losing sight of the client as a unique human being whose needs, responses and psychic world makes them who they are. A paper by Marguerite Valentine highlights the dangers in therapists neatly fitting clients into their theories: 'political and institutional dynamics, based on power broking and competition between theoretical and institutional "views of the world", may become enacted out within an analysis, to the detriment of the patient' (2007:174).

In contrast, integration provides a model of elasticity whereby therapists can have a theoretical base, arrived at through reflective practice, that is flexible and characterised by fluidity, making it easier for integrative practitioners to adopt interventions that have been found to be effective, whereas therapists with 'pure' approaches tend not to look beyond their immediate model-specific bag of tools. An integrative framework is not set in stone; it is open, allowing therapist responses to clients to be adapted according to who the client is.

Scenario from practice 3.1

At the age of 41, Peter felt aimless after losing his job, finding himself in serious debt and feeling severely depressed. His employers had dismissed him for displaying a lack of motivation and productivity. Following the end of a brief relationship, Peter felt anger and hostility towards his now ex-girlfriend. Coupled with negative feelings resulting from his unemployment, he became depressed. His bitterness towards his previous employer resulted in him being generally 'against the world' for not providing him with that to which he felt entitled: stable employment and a stable relationship.

Peter was sensitive to criticism and responded to his therapist with anger, opposing everything she said; he became unreceptive and withdrawn if he felt negatively judged. Aware of Peter's sensitivity and lack of readiness to confront his own issues, his therapist refrained from voicing her interpretations, despite linking his negative feelings with a compensatory sense of entitlement. His therapist's language was tinged with sensitivity, until such time when she perceived Peter to be ready to receive, in more candid language, the therapist's understandings. She needed to let go of preconceived ideas, judge the appropriate timing for different types of interventions and reflect on Peter's responses to inform her next steps.

Later in Peter's therapy, he arrived 20 minutes late for his session after his therapist offered an earlier appointment at his request. He started his session by saying that he was depressed the whole morning and that therapy had not delivered what he expected, that is, clarifying whether he wants to meet someone and have children. He added that therapy did help him to take control over his financial difficulties and associated disarray, but that he could have done this on his own. Aware of the fact that the issue of an intimate relationship and children had been explored several times in therapy and each time Peter arrived at the conclusion that he did not want the responsibility of a wife and children, Peter's therapist acknowledged his frustration and tried to help him explore the feelings associated with his ambivalence. Knowing how sensitive to challenge Peter was, his therapist waited for the right time to raise what she felt was a necessary challenge. By adopting an empathic, humanistic attitude, the therapist demonstrated what Peter needed during this phase of the work, waiting until she felt he was more receptive to thinking about his own contribution to situations in his life that caused him pain.

Judging the moments when clients are more receptive to exploration is important, given that integrative therapists are mindful of nurturing the therapeutic relationship and ensuring that alliance ruptures are minimised.

Challenges to integration

If, as mentioned earlier, therapists with an affinity for integrative models are independently minded and more motivated in seeking an inclusive and comprehensive view of the world, then they already have the building blocks for personal integration. The process of arriving at an integrative model requires selecting theories, concepts and tools that resonate with the individual therapist – it is therefore a highly personal quest. It is also important that whatever personal model is developed, it is informed by research on what works for whom (Hubble et al. 1999; Roth and Fonagy 2006), and that it is adaptable for the individual client. Clustering clients into diagnostic criteria may be useful for some clinical purposes, such as having a common language to communicate with other professionals; however, it has the potential to blind us to individual differences and deprive clients of their agency and uniqueness and the choice of who they can be. (The use of diagnosis will be discussed in more depth in Chapter 11.)

Trainee counselling psychologists and psychotherapists in the early stages of their training tend to adopt existing theories they understand, resonate with and feel secure about without much critique. They often fight with passion to preserve their beliefs and theories in an effort to belong to a body of theory they believe makes better sense, is superior to other theories and helps them establish a budding professional identity. In the context of a plethora of theoretical modalities being available (as discussed in Chapter 1), choosing one with which a trainee resonates is one of the biggest challenges trainees face. On the other hand, trainees on integrative courses, while not having the certainty of a one-model approach, are exposed to a variety of approaches from which they can develop their own, *personal* integration. Trainings resting on the idea that no one theory is, in all contexts and with all clients, superior to others and that there are multiple and competing interpretations of the world, expose psychotherapy trainees to a wider variety of theoretical modalities with the aim of stretching them to think outside the box. This ability to think outside the box develops over time and requires exposure to multiple concepts and theoretical ideas, a level of clinical experience, as well as psychological maturity. The latter develops through personal therapy and continuing professional development and is influenced by specific attitudes summarised in Table 3.1.

These conditions are an essential foundation for trainees who may lack the confidence to challenge their beliefs. It helps them to accept that the integrative process will not pose a threat to their budding professional identities but can be an opportunity to think more widely. We see a similar idea put forward by Faris and Ooijen:

> an integration of a number of approaches requires a clear understanding and knowledge of the premises behind each of them individually and a

Table 3.1 Necessary values and conditions for an integrative attitude

Keeping an open mind

Criticality

Recognition that there are multiple truths, all subject to human construction and interpretation

Curiosity

Acknowledgement of the uniqueness and value of the intersubjective relationship

Taking context of therapy into consideration

Taking gender, race, religion, culture, and sexuality into account

> rigorous yet flexible stance, where the trainee is invited to entertain a number of ideas simultaneously holding all as contextually true.
>
> (2012: 18)

We might understand Faris and Ooijen's point by highlighting that to reach a place where integration can be contemplated, trainees need to develop the foundations laid out in Table 3.1 before they embark on the level of – to use Caputo's (1997) deconstruction metaphor – cracking open the theoretical nutshell they have developed, disturbing its tranquillity.

Trainees can become confused when beginning to see that different, mutually paradoxical theories make sense in themselves. They may feel perplexed as to how it can be possible to integrate diverse concepts. This is a challenging but normal part of the process of becoming an integrative therapist and becomes more shaped when trainees develop sufficient knowledge and the confidence to question the credibility of a theory in relation to practice. The following principles of deconstruction are useful in the process of becoming an integrative therapist.

Deconstructing our personal identity

Deconstruction in Caputo's (1997) philosophical writings is to break free from the phenomenon and any dogmatic walls built around it. Psychotherapy and counselling psychology trainings using a purist modality contribute to Caputo's metaphor of being stuck behind a wall, in that trainees adopt theories and concepts without much questioning of their value in practice. Trainees on integrative trainings, in contrast, are exposed to various modalities – a more demanding undertaking – that nonetheless provide the foundations to evolve into more mature thinking. By encouraging therapists to question and scrutinise given theories, it has the potential to help them move beyond dogma by embracing criticality and flexibility; in other words, breaking free from the wall that has been built around them. Caputo uses this as a methodological tool to reject definable, objective and static things, claiming that any attempt to reduce a thing to something permanent is of necessity a failure:

> The very meaning and mission of deconstruction [are] to show that things . . . do not have definable meanings and determinable missions, that they are always more than any mission would impose . . . what is really happening, is always to come. Every time you try to stabilize the meaning of a thing . . . the thing itself, if there is anything at all to it, slips away.
>
> (1997: VP 117/SP 104)

In psychological language, this can be likened to a softening of the individual's defences, which may be clouded in dogma or conceptual walls built during the early foundational phase of becoming an integrative therapist. For example, one trainee was adamant during a class discussion in their second year that *the* superior modality is the humanistic, refusing to consider the value of any other approach. They defended their position vehemently, to the point of wondering out loud whether they should abandon their training. Clearly, they had not reached the stage in their development as a therapist of softening their rigid attitude and defences. Trainees' journey to integration requires:

1. building a conceptual basis, the beginning;
2. testing its viability in practice, the middle; and
3. questioning and strengthening it with concepts, values and interventions from a variety of perspectives, the final, ongoing phase.

This process requires an open mind, fluidity and elasticity in one's attitude (neither contempt for certain theories nor reverence). What strengthens and gives validity to personal integration is evidence-based practice. To achieve this, it is important for therapists to adopt the qualities of a researcher seeking to test the efficacy of their practice in a transparent way. *Transparency* involves honesty with oneself and others and appropriate self-disclosure, both in peer development groups and in personal therapy. Trainee therapists who make good use of clinical supervision are those who are honest and transparent with their supervisors. This is often a challenge, especially in situations where trainees do not have a supervisor they can trust and relate to, but transparency as a principle to be striving towards is fundamental to the development of the integrative therapist.

Commonly, deconstruction as a hermeneutic or method of interpretation is translated as to 'tear down' or 'dismantle' what has been assembled. Early trainees' theoretical absorption and acclimatisation to different ways of being and working as therapists (assembling) need to be processed through reflective questioning (dismantling). Moreover, it is important to identify any cracks, such as ideas and skills that do not seem to make sense once applied, before theoretical and practical integration can be achieved and fluidly reflected upon and revised. This is an ongoing process, which is a core value of personal integration. The following principles can help guide you in your personal act of deconstruction (Table 3.2).

Table 3.2 Principles of deconstruction

Cracking open a nutshell and disturbing its tranquillity. Analogy of deconstructing one's existing self-identity through self-questioning, reflexive analysis and critique

Readiness to dismantle theories we assembled

Developing an independent-minded approach to integration and motivation in seeking an inclusive and comprehensive view of the world

Thinking outside the box

Challenging our beliefs and assumptions

Tolerating confusion in relation to the process of making sense of a diverse and paradoxical body of theory

Softening our resistance and considering the value of theories other than those we resonate with

Questioning the credibility of our theories against practice

Holding an open mind, stretching our concepts to reach fluidity and elasticity

Being earnest in our striving for authentic understanding of our theories and practice

Embracing the not-knowing

As therapists, we are familiar with defensive reactions from clients. Nobody likes to be told they got something wrong. Our understanding of the client matures through engagement and the level of depth we reach in ourselves and in our therapeutic interactions. *Depth* is achieved through engaging in personal development, reaching awareness of our own issues and how they translate into the way we interact with others. It is enhanced through listening to clients' negative feedback to our work without resorting to defensiveness (e.g. not using conceptualisations to place blame on the client but instead acknowledging the activation of our own emotional reactions linked to our personal history). To save ourselves from embarrassment when clients criticise our work, we may attempt to justify our position by dressing it up with theoretical language, re-establishing the 'expert' role. However, this type of relating with a client can lead to an impasse, leaving the client bewildered and unsafe. We advocate that therapists try to embrace a position that is responsive and containing to clients; by noticing their own defensive behaviours without acting upon them, allowing themselves to feel vulnerable by being aware of the potential pitfalls of entering into an unhelpful power dynamic, the therapist becomes more receptive.

Scenario from practice 3.2

Joanna treated her therapist, Mike, as an extension of herself, dismissing his views and understandings, only to later adopt them and claim them as her own. She was adamant that she herself was the expert, refusing to acknowledge that some of the insights she arrived at actually came from her therapist and the work they did together. She seemed to enjoy rubbishing her therapist, although she attended sessions regularly. She came to therapy after a period of severe depression following the break-up of only a brief relationship. Her sense of feeling alone and isolated grew and she became hostile towards her family, pushed friends away and tried to find solace in withdrawing from socialising. The more she felt in need of love and nurturing, the more she pushed people away – to protect herself, she would hide away from those who could offer the support she most needed. She was afraid people would ridicule her if she appeared vulnerable, in the same way she harshly judged herself when vulnerable.

Being dependent on people was Joanna's greatest anxiety. During her first therapy session, she cross-examined Mike, questioning him about his values, qualifications and experience and displayed suspicion of his motives in being a therapist. Mike knew early on that Joanna's difficulty in trusting people would pose an obstacle to her trusting him. However, he held back from sharing his interpretation with Joanna, because in his understanding she might become defensive and withdrawn. He thought it best to wait until Joanna appeared more receptive to his therapeutic input before sharing what he thought might cause a rupture in their therapeutic relationship.

Mike's patience and sensitivity paid off. Joanna became increasingly aware of her need for self-sufficiency and accepted Mike's view that allowing herself to depend on him was equally challenging. Mike also felt that Joanna's relationship with a rejecting father had contributed to her severe anxieties, which were themselves connected with her dependency needs, and he shared this insight during a session. Joanna became furious. She accused him of inappropriately psychoanalysing her, something she detested, exclaiming: 'You are insensitive! Knowing how much I'm struggling to deal with my dependency needs and self-sufficiency, with everything that's been happening with my family recently, how could you bring this up? I do not want to talk about my father. Family is the only thing I have. I lost my friends, I was rejected by my boss, I'm just not ready to think about my childhood traumas.' Mike acknowledged how upset and angry she was with him and accepted that the timing of his interpretation was perhaps inappropriate. Mike also said that he felt she reacts with anger every time he introduces something new to their work and suggested that staying with her feelings and trying to understand her reactions to him might be useful to explore further.

To his surprise, Joanna's tone softened. She considered what Mike had shared, treating what he said as genuine. She apologised for being angry with him, saying that she knew he was trying to help. Mike experienced a strong connection to Joanna during this exchange. By being authentic and acknowledging a premature intervention inviting Joanna to think about her early life, Mike gained her trust and repaired the alliance rupture. During this stage,

Joanna also became more receptive to her therapist's attempts to help her understand how her break-up from a brief relationship evoked a catastrophic depression that was partly residual and linked to her father rejecting her because she was a girl.

Understanding how we feel, act and react to the *not-knowing* and treating what we *do know* with scepticism opens the way to a climate of deconstruction. Human beings feel more secure in the familiar and often treat the unfamiliar with misgivings. Once we identify the kind of 'tribe' to which we wish to belong – usually sitting within the parameters of the four foundational schools (see Chapter 1) or indeed any of the many practices worldwide – we tend to avoid deviating from the tribe's norms and expectations out of fear of being expelled, with the concomitant loss of belonging and having a clear identity. The danger of conforming to a psychotherapy tribe lies in the risk of becoming entrenched and rigid, rather than learning from different psychological perspectives, integrating these insights into a more effective and personal therapeutic approach; pluralist and integrative perspectives embrace the idea of value in different perspectives and denounce the idea of purism. To embrace different perspectives, therapists need to develop a flexible attitude that holds enough strength to survive the pull from their schoolism, while at the same time not being weighed down by the pressure of myriad perspectives. We refer to this type of integration, where our knowledge from exposure to many perspectives does not exert too much pressure on us, as a *distillation* of perspective. In this way, we need to distil our perspectives to a point of choosing the essence, by reducing the detail and dressing up with a simple and accessible understanding of the perspectives; a process that is constant throughout our life as a practitioner.

Letting go of our preconceptions in relation to our clients is accompanied by pressure. For example, clients who pay for a professional service expect the professional to know what they are doing. Indeed, we know from research of the significance of the placebo effect (Hubble et al. 1999) that a key factor in positive therapy outcomes is when clients believe in the expertise and knowledge of their therapist. Therefore, destroying the placebo effect, risking making the client less convinced of your expert role as therapist, could compromise positive outcomes. Inexperienced therapists tend to disown their expertise and the power invested in them by clients, a factor compromising the alliance, trust and safety that clients need by perceiving therapists as having the 'professionalism' to be of help. The pressure to be effective makes it harder to stay in the landscape of not-knowing, of recognising the limitations of our understanding of the client and their circumstances, which opens the way to being creative and drawing on different models of therapeutic care. The way therapy is documented and published is also a major source of pressure for therapists. We read accounts from therapy with clear formulations conceptualising the process and managing challenging situations with such ease; we assume that therapy is a simple task, with the implications of feeling inadequate with our own performance. But we need to start somewhere, and initial formulations of our understandings is the first step before we develop the confidence to test them in collaboration with our clients.

The importance of being earnest

Depth and emotional honesty in therapists are fundamentals in therapeutic work, as well as other affective responses, such as empathy, attunement, and the ability to contain powerful emotions in our clients and in ourselves, such as fear and anxiety. If therapeutic relationships were accompanied by an openness to our passions, they would be the hosts of emotional connection as well as the guardians of relational work, important principles in personal integration. It is therefore necessary that the integrative therapist is sincerely committed to knowing the client, being a companion in their journey through thick and thin (that is, not taking flight when therapy becomes negative or the client becomes difficult) and meticulously wondering curiously about what is going on between them. The dynamic produced by the (client–therapist) dyad has the potential for creative understandings on the relational spectrum in both participants' lives. It is an intersubjective dynamic common to relational approaches and a characteristic to which integrative therapists aspire.

We all function with the influence of social conventions and the values of those close to us. Our 'mottos' in life (beliefs and ideals) are often the silent protagonists that come to a climax in our day-to-day interactions with others and our approach to therapeutic work. Knowing and owning our mottos and their potential influence can help us appreciate the professional landscape within which we operate, challenge it and open our minds further to being informed by practice rather than simply having our practice informed by our preconceptions and personal values. All psychotherapy training programmes require trainees develop self-awareness. As far as personal integration is concerned, such self-awareness results from asking oneself such questions as: What am I feeling in relation to this client? How has this feeling come about? Is my affective response to this client related in any way to my own history and/or traumas? Is my response related to the role and relation my client has forged with me? These questions are useful in developing what Clarkson (1995) described as the person-to-person relationship where people do not perceive each other as consisting of specific, isolated qualities, but engage in a dialogue involving each other's whole being.

The role of the trainer

Trainers of psychological therapies play an important role in helping trainees develop the confidence and open attitude to learning – the self-awareness – that is achieved through deconstruction. As a trainer, I believe that one of my objectives is to facilitate the development of an optimum level of curiosity, contain trainee anxiety, stimulate reflective thinking, create sufficient safety to be able to cultivate growth and allow the challenge of arrested, fixed ideas. Enabling *play* can also make learning fun and lead to interesting discoveries about ourselves. Play, first postulated by Winnicott (1971) as an important developmental process in children, is a process of stimulating interest and enjoyment in children that emerges through interaction with others. Elements of fun including surprise can evoke positive affect, which is fertile ground for motivation and creativity. Intimacy, love and togetherness are the result of parent–child play, which helps the child develop interpersonal skills, emotional negotiation and tolerance of disappointment associated with not winning a game. In short, it is fertile ground for growth, not only in children, but also in adults.

Trainees tend to rely on positive role models during their development, so trainers themselves have a responsibility to think through how they interact in all training situations, which values and attitudes they portray and convey, and the extent to which they practise what they preach. I support Faris and Ooijen's commitment to avoiding the dangers of fixed, reified truths, while being 'irreverent to one's own ideas' (2012: 3). In my experience, trainees nurture the hope that those in positions of authority will respect them, listen to them, constructively challenge them and display an attitude of inviting wider involvement in dialogue. In class discussions, trainee assumptions are likely to surface and must be responded to with sensitivity and care. As Faris and Ooijen remark, 'trainees are not the trainers' clients, but they are not their friends either' (2012: 19), therefore, the power differential must be acknowledged and worked with. As a trainer, I have long experience where trainees relate to me in all sorts of distorted ways. For example, through idealisation (I am the all-knowing, perfect therapist/lecturer) and denigration (I am the hopeless, terrible, even hateful trainer, therefore a bad therapist). Receiving such projections and tolerating them without unhelpful, defensive reactions is important in providing a safe space where trainees can challenge their assumptions and begin to understand the transference relationship, until they resolve it in the service of acquiring a reality-based attitude that people in authority are 'good and bad', or are people, complete with the associated limitations and strengths.

But there is a fine balance between tolerating and allowing trainees to be abusive. The latter has potentially negative consequences for group process in that it can sabotage learning. Therefore, trainers must be aware of class process, open and collaborative, but also be appropriately challenging when creativity is compromised and the process becomes stuck. Trainers need the skill of navigating through the process of learning with an open attitude and the ability to deconstruct their own subjective feelings so that an honest and open dialogue can develop. The following example aims to highlight dynamics found both in therapy and in training.

Scenario from practice 3.3

Antigone, a 36-year-old trainee psychotherapist, originally from Greece, was in her second year of training in psychotherapy. She studied psychology at the University of Athens before embarking on a foundation course in psychodynamic therapy, leading to a diploma in an institute of higher education in her home country. She harboured aspirations to study in the UK with the ambition to benefit from the English education system, which she held in high esteem. Antigone had learned from her father, an academic in Greece, that the UK was the hub of 'Europeanism', representing post-modern and scholarly knowledge taught by academics holding positions through merit and not nepotism.

In the class I taught, Antigone often avoided eye contact with me and, on a number of occasions, she strongly objected, in an aggressive tone, to concepts I presented. Her responses to fellow students' expressed views of theories were more open and validating, even if these belonged to perspectives other than her own. By opposing the lecturer's concepts while being open to peers, it raised the question whether Antigone had issues with authority, what we refer to as *transference* (relating to the lecturer as if she were a parent whose authority she was opposing).

During Antigone's aggressive responses to me, other students remained quiet, neither agreeing nor disagreeing with her ideas. My attempts to encourage her to consider the value of concepts from perspectives different to the one she espoused (regardless of their source, be that student or lecturer) seemed futile. She seemed unreceptive to everything I was saying, blocking me out altogether.

I was beginning to feel under attack and outside class I tried to understand what was going on. I entered into a process of deconstruction where I questioned my own stance, beliefs and personality. I acknowledged that I come across as confident and own my views, which may trigger specific responses in people, including this student. I felt that Antigone's behaviour towards me, aggressively dismissing everything I said, was associated not only with my power or authority as a trainer but also with me as an individual with a certain personality. I thought it more conducive to engage in dialogue with her in class, not individually, given that other students seemed to be intimidated by her. From this vantage point, an open challenge might provide role modelling rather than appeasing. During another attack in class, I said: 'Perhaps you are afraid that I will not value what you believe and stand for and others may value my perspective more than your own; so by dismissing the ideas I present, you are trying to protect the modality you embrace.' She looked at me and said: 'Just because you are a lecturer, it doesn't mean I should agree with you.' It seemed that Antigone was not hearing me, which triggered anger in me. Students began to interject on this occasion, some as peace-keepers, others attempting to make Antigone aware of how she is with trainers generally, and others trying to rescue her. The dynamic of previous paralysis in the group shifted and students found their voices. Antigone approached me during the break to say: 'You and I are the same, that's why we clash.' I felt that Antigone's stance towards me was dismissive and devaluing of my experience, and my anger was directly associated with this.

I acknowledged my anger with her attitude and encouraged her to explore how she relates to authority in her personal therapy. Antigone explained that the competitiveness she displayed towards me in class was not unique to me, so I should not take it personally.

My experience evoked much reflection and deconstruction on my part, including questioning how the need I felt to hold onto my professional authority to enhance the placebo may evoke strong reactions in others.

Conclusion

Deconstruction, in the process of developing as an integrative practitioner, is first and foremost reflection in action and a fluid, open attitude. Most practitioners will be aware that effective healers are therapists who know their own wounds, have found a way to be with them and learned to allow others to help in their journey to personal healing. In short, 'know thyself' is a key requirement in the development of the professional integrative psychotherapist. It is about emotional and personal intelligence, which the psychologist John D. Mayer (2014) described as people having the ability to practise self-understanding, make an accurate evaluation of others and acknowledge their own limitations. As a result, these people can make more accurate guesses on people's likely behaviours. They are aware of how others perceive them and know that revising their perceptions of others is necessary at times. Deconstruction is a quality that helps us engage with the world fluidly and understand who we are in relationship to ourselves and others. In the process we may sometimes encounter our shadow side and experience pain. Wrestling with painful aspects of ourselves can help illuminate our blind spots and prevent us from taking flight into self-deception and, by implication, burying what we dislike about ourselves, which could later become an obstacle to effective therapy.

References

Caley, S. and Bond, T. (2004) *Integrative Counselling Skills in Action* (2nd edn). London: SAGE.

Caputo, J.D. (1997) *Deconstruction in a Nutshell: A Conversation with Jacques Derrida*. New York: Fordham University Press.

Clarkson, P. (1995) *The Therapeutic Relationship in Psychoanalysis, Counselling Psychology and Psychotherapy*. London: Whurr.

Faris, A. and Ooijen, Els van (2012) *Integrative Counselling and Psychotherapy: A Relational Approach*. London: SAGE.

Heinonen, E., Elliot, D. and Orlinsky, D.E. (2013) Psychotherapists' personal identities, theoretical orientations and professional relationships: Elective affinity and role adjustment as modes of congruence. *Psychotherapy Research*, 23(6): 718–31.

Hubble, M.A., Duncan, B.L. and Miller, S.D. (eds) (1999) *The Heart and Soul of Change: What Works in Therapy.* Washington, DC: American Psychological Association.

Lapworth, P. and Sills, C. (2010) *Integration in Counselling and Psychotherapy: Developing a Personal Approach* (2nd edn). London: SAGE.

Mayer, J.D. (2014) Know thyself. *Psychology Today.* Available at: https://www.psychologytoday.com/articles/201402/know-thyself (accessed 21 September 2015).

O'Brien, M. and Houston, G. (2013) *Integrative Therapy* (2nd edn). London: SAGE.

Orlinsky, D.E. and Howard, K.I. (1986) Process and outcome in psychotherapy. In S.L. Garfield and A.E. Bergin (eds), *Handbook of Psychotherapy and Behavior Change* (3rd edn). New York: Wiley.

Orlinsky, D.E. and Howard, K.I. (1987) A generic model of psychotherapy. *Journal of Integrative and Eclectic Psychotherapy,* 6: 6–27.

Roth, A. and Fonagy, P. (eds) (2006) *What Works for Whom? A Critical Review of Psychotherapy Research* (2nd edn). New York: Guilford Press.

Wampold, B.E. (2015) How important are the common factors in psychotherapy? An update. *World Psychiatry,* 14(3): 270–7.

Winnicott, D.W. (1971) *Playing and Reality.* London: Routledge.

4   A framework for personal psychotherapy integration

John Nuttall

Introduction

The quest for a 'grand model' of psychotherapy integration has been elaborated by several leading thinkers in the field (Arkowitz 1989; Mahrer 1989; Goldfried 1995; Lapworth et al. 2001), all of whom have attempted to reify in some way the various procedural pathways individuals or groups might take in determining such a model. However, considering Horton's (2000) assertion that 'personal integration is an individual construction that can be developed to reflect the thinking and practice of the individual therapist' (2000: 326), or the idea that integration is a personal quest through which the therapist critically reflects on a range of approaches and theories to develop an approach that works for them, I should like to outline a framework for the integration quest that adds to the leading conceptualisations by contextualising the development of the integration movement and considering it as a higher-order dialectic process consisting of three developmental modalities.

The three modalities

The first modality, *constructive integration*, constitutes the relatively simple synthesising of the four major schools of therapy and embraces the procedural pathways, as outlined in Chapter 2. The second modality, *complicit integration*, represents *rapprochement* within the profession, where meta-relational processes are identified and acknowledged as present across all the schools. The third modality, *contiguous integration*, involves the synthesis of psychotherapeutic concepts with other explanatory paradigms of group, organisational and societal artefact, and seeks integration with the lived world and the allied disciplines, such as those of neuropsychology, sociology and anthropology.

I have recognised this dialectic process as part of my personal experience of psychotherapy integration, and I believe all three modalities remain active throughout a therapist's clinical and professional life. They are modes or states of an integrating process in and between which the would-be integrationist can weave their integrative attitude and approach to practice (Nuttall 2017).

Modality one: Constructive integration

Constructive integration characterises the early stages of the integration movement, discussed in Chapter 2, and represents the desire to reconcile and synthesise different theoretical elements. These elements were, typically, combined to form new systems of psychotherapy that were distinct in themselves and that could be understood by clients, taught, and presented to service providers and funding institutions as empirically sound. Within this mode, Mahrer (1989) identified and critiqued the pros and cons of six strategic routes to integration, concluding that only two were really workable, which were endorsed by Lapworth, Sills and Fish in their conceptualisation of 'framework' and 'procedural' strategies (2001: 28–33).

The 'framework' approach involves the combination of approaches that share the same basic theory of psychological development. This has generally led to the synthesis of already like-minded approaches such as those that have evolved under such umbrella descriptors as 'psychodynamic therapies' and 'cognitive behavioural therapies', each of which encompasses a broad range of skills and techniques. However, this strategy does not foster integration across all the four foundational traditions outlined in Chapter 2. The strategy of 'procedural' integration refers to the combining of specific skills or practices that have proven efficacious but that might originate from different underlying theoretical ideas. Within this strategy, there is more scope for integration across traditions as practitioners pull together complementary therapeutic skills and techniques appropriate to the individual client and their issues. The most significant approach emerging from this strategy is probably multimodal therapy, developed by Arnold Lazarus (1989).

Notwithstanding these strategies, the three routes to integration elaborated by Arkowitz (1989), as described in Chapter 2, can be seen as providing the most comprehensive description of the integrative quest up to the start of the twenty-first century. His routes, described as 'common factors', 'theoretical integration' and 'technical eclecticism', reflect the quest to look beyond the constraints of single schools in order to build combined systems that aim to improve the effectiveness and delivery of psychotherapy to a broad range of clients. (Later, I review three well-known integrative approaches that exemplify the three routes posited by Arkowitz and that exemplify what I have called the *constructive modality*.) At the macro-professional level, these routes have resulted in the integrative quest resembling more of an end-position build than an ongoing process in flux. The result has been the construction of distinct new approaches, usually by a group of professionals, academics or clinicians. Many such approaches have been accepted as received, with therapists believing them to be validated clinical models supported by empirical research or case history. This mode of integration is arguably driven by the professional and economic imperatives discussed in Chapter 2 and has received further recent impetus in the UK from the Improving Access to Psychological Therapies (IAPT) scheme (Lees 2016). Fear and Woolfe thus point out, 'the increase in debate, courses and societies to promote the interests of integrative approaches has been accompanied by a proliferation of integrative theories' (2000: 337).

Arkowitz's common factors route 'seeks to determine the core ingredients different therapies might share in common, with the eventual goal of developing more efficacious treatments based on these components' (Norcross and Grencavage 1990: 8). This, I believe, incorporates the procedural strategy discussed earlier and is a method that identifies aspects of theory or practice that are common to all the psychotherapy schools that have proven efficacious in therapeutic practice. Jerome Frank (1961) pioneered this approach in his book *Persuasion and Healing*, in which he identified four common elements for therapeutic provision across a broad spectrum of healing paradigms. These are summarised in Frank and Frank (1993) as (1) a 'conducive therapeutic relationship'; (2) a 'culturally-congruent narrative'; (3) a 'dedicated space'; and (4) a 'prescription for action'. Within these elements there are probably lower-order levels of commonality. For example, within the element of the conducive therapeutic relationship, such techniques as clear contracting, attentive listening, positive regard, empathy, paraphrasing and reflecting are therapeutic skills (factors) recognised as common to many Eurocentric approaches. Within a dedicated space, the neutral consulting room and the 50-minute hour seem common practices or boundaries. In other cultures, these elements might be constituted by joint trance states, meditation and physical interventions, such as acupuncture and massage. Some of these are now being integrated into western practice, such as the adoption of mindfulness by the cognitive–behavioural school and trance states by the transpersonal school. Overall, this kind of integration occurs inherently through the exchange of ideas that takes place in training, supervision and peer group discussion. A prominent example of the common factors route is Egan's skilled helper model (1975), which is primarily skills-based and concerns the sequential nature of psychotherapy. This model breaks the therapeutic process into three phases: exploration, understanding and action. Each of these phases engages specific relational skills according to the client's needs. Thus, 'far from being rigid and prescriptive, the model is intended to set out how to be with the client, according to the varying needs of the therapeutic process' (Jenkins 2000: 168). There is a strong correlation between the common factors associated with positive outcomes identified in the meta-analysis research of Asay and Lambert (1999) and the skills and techniques enumerated in the skilled helper model.

The route called 'theoretical integration' refers to a process whereby the theories (such as those of mind, personality development or psychological distress) on which different therapies are based are reconciled or synthesised into a new coherent model. Norcross and Grencavage also make the point that it should be a 'conceptual or theoretical creation beyond a technical blend of methods [and provide] an articulated framework or roadmap' (1990: 1). Although this is conceived as a desirable goal, Jung reminds us to be sceptical of theories when dealing directly with human distress in the consulting room. He admonishes, 'learn your theories as well as you can, but put them aside when you touch the miracle of the living soul' (1928: 361). Yet, integrationists, like Clarkson, acknowledge that as practising clinicians in search of understanding, theories emerge from our direct clinical experience and research studies. She asserts, 'Theories are the stories we tell about the facts, about how we constitute the phenomena' (2000: 311) and are too necessary to abandon.

The use of theory allows us to recognise change or difference in the client and provides a locus of evaluation for our practice (Casement 1995). It also facilitates dissemination of knowledge and experience to others. However, at the individual level, building an integrative approach based on the theoretical integration route necessitates the therapist developing and adhering to a coherent frame of reference for their practice. This principle was asserted by the famous psychoanalyst Wilfred Bion during a period when there was an increase in psychoanalytic theories – even 'as a method of making clear to himself the analyst needs his own book of psychoanalytic theories that he personally frequently uses' (Bion 1962: 39). And clients, too, will bring their own expectations of the therapist's theoretical orientation, which may offer a placebo effect to the therapy (Asay and Lambert 1999). Theories change over time as they get tried and tested, and even the grandees of our profession have modified their ideas over time. Examples of this are Freud's changing views on the drives and structure of the mind, and Ellis's development of rational emotive behaviour therapy (REBT) in 1955 (Ellis and Dryden 1997).

Theoretical integration generally develops from the considered academic learning and theorising of experienced practitioners and academics, and good examples of this are REBT and more recently cognitive analytic therapy (CAT), developed in the 1980s by Anthony Ryle (Ryle 1990). As Lapworth et al. point out, CAT 'is an example of an approach which started as an integration of theories and methods and then solidified into a recognised model with its own name, training courses, and so on' (2001: 8). Transactional analysis (TA) also brings together a variety of theories and skills, and there are now several approaches to TA with differing theoretical emphases. Pioneered by Eric Berne (1961), its integrative nature has been highlighted by various leading figures (Clarkson 1992; Tudor 2002; Erskine 2010). Like CAT, TA is a good example of the approach to integration called 'complementarity', where complementary techniques from different systems are combined into a more effective whole (Evans and Gilbert 2005). TA has a heritage that dates back to French and Alexander (see Chapter 2) and, in arguing that it should be viewed as a relational psychotherapy they assert that 'the plethora of different developments in transactional analysis (of which ours is just one), from the psychoanalytic to the constructivist, is testament to its flexibility and integrative nature' (Hargaden and Sills 2002: 5; parenthetical in original). The core principle introduced by Berne and his followers is that of ego states, called Parent, Adult and Child, that have associated feelings, thoughts and behaviours that manifest in relationships with others in their conscious and unconscious communications, which he called *transactions*. Psychological distress is conceptualised as the development and habitual enactment of ineffective or problematic transactional sequences called rackets, games and scripts. TA aims to understand these transactions and their underlying meaning in order to elucidate them in a way the client will recognise and be able to reformulate for the future. Many authors (Beitman 1994) have attempted to show similarities between approaches in order to build bridges and somehow bring coherence and certainty to the integrative quest. The following chapters aim to demonstrate and help resolve some of the struggles to reconcile the different perspectives of the four foundational schools.

The definitions of integration discussed here evoke a sense of synthesis that seems to exclude any regard for eclectic practice. Indeed, eclecticism is generally seen as maintaining segregation in so far as only parts of different systems or schools are brought together, often in a seemingly ad hoc fashion, in contrast to the kind of integration where an entirely new and coherent approach is created. However, evidence-based technical eclecticism has become generally accepted as one form of integration (Beitman 1990), which can be characterised as using 'prescriptive treatments based on empirical evidence and client need, rather than theoretical and personal predisposition' (Lazarus 1990: 40). In other words, it involves the system-atic use of a variety of techniques in the treatment of an individual regardless of the theoretical basis of those techniques: 'Eclectic practitioners are continually making decisions as to which approach they will apply, with which clients and under which circumstances' (Austen 2000: 127). Eclecticism has acquired negative associations among both integrationists and schoolists alike, but this form of systematic eclecti-cism must be distinguished from the haphazard and incoherent nature of much eclectic practice that stems from poor training or the adherence to outmoded or inappropriate favoured techniques. A number of therapeutic systems have brought some coherence to this integrative route, the best known of which is multimodal therapy (MMT), pioneered by Arnold Lazarus (1989). This is based on a diagnosis of the client's psychological distress across a range of functioning for which he coined the mnemonic BASIC I.D. This represents: Behaviour, Affect, Sensation, Imagery, Cognition, Interpersonal and Drugs/biology. It is a highly manualised system with assessment and progress based on questionnaires. The underlying principle is that different techniques can be used or combined, without integration of the under-pinning theories, and that clinical or research-based evidence should be the only criterion for deciding which therapeutic interventions are effective and for whom. A similar and more recent therapeutic regime has been developed by Cooper and McLeod in their proposition that therapists should adopt a 'pluralistic framework' in their practice. This involves adopting a range of therapeutic approaches suitable for the client's individual needs and engage the therapist's knowledge and experi-ence. They claim an evidence base for the framework and it fits the definition of technical eclecticism as it 'operates as a meta-theory within which it is possible to utilise concepts, strategies and specific interventions from a range of therapeutic orientations' (2007: 135). They argue that it provides a direct means for empirical research to inform practice.

Critics of the mode of constructive integration might consist of single school adherents ('schoolists') at one extreme and pure form integrationists ('purist inte-grationists') at the other. Schoolists might denounce any form of integration as heretical 'eclecticism', while purist integrationists might consider the common fac-tors and technical eclectic routes incoherent 'hybrid' practice. In spite of these immanent contradictions, I believe there are higher-order integrative processes tak-ing place within the profession and the integration movement generally. These lead me to elaborate two further modalities of integration: complicit and contiguous integration.

Modality two: Complicit integration

Complicit integration represents how some integrative models of psychotherapy describe emergent patterns that explain higher-order characteristics of the therapeutic process. In *Figments of Reality*, Stewart and Cohen define such emergence as 'the appearance of recognisable large-scale features in a system whose chains of small-scale causality are far too intricate to describe, let alone follow in detail' (1997: 149). The book breaks new ground in explaining the evolution of humankind's consciousness as an emergent phenomenon evolving over time from the interaction of the environment, language and culture. The authors posit that, in evolution, *simplicity* emerges from *complexity* by an iterative process they call 'complicity' (1997: 74). The term represents the simple joining of parts and meaning from simplicity and complexity, and they propose that 'things are complicit when their interactions change them, so that soon they become different things altogether' (1997: 63). They conceive the human condition as a complicit phenomenon brought about by interaction between culture and the individual, with each influencing the other. The book expresses a somewhat Heraclitian view of the world as a place of interaction and flux, the reality of which the authors contend we might never understand.

In deference to this view, I adopted the word 'complicit' to describe those integrative approaches that demonstrate such emergent and higher-order features (Nuttall 2002a). From this perspective, the grand design of psychotherapy integration might be something that appears, and be described, in quite different ways from the simple combination of its constituent theoretical or practice-based elements. This process might represent the optimum integrative synthesis and herald a *rapprochement* whereby the different schools begin to recognise the same healing processes at work in the others.

Although constructive integration seems to have heralded a proliferation of approaches, Clarkson argued that successive research studies showed that it is the therapeutic relationship *per se* more than specific therapeutic techniques or skills that determine the efficacy of psychotherapy (1995a: 4). This had already prompted several distinguished theoreticians and practitioners to examine what aspects of the therapeutic relationship are integral to the efficacy of therapeutic practice. Carl Rogers probably originated this thinking in his concept of the core conditions (1957), but later thinkers have been more concerned with identifying structural categories that prescribe the range of relational experiences and skills that constitute the therapeutic process. Such ideas have come from many theoretical schools, such as psychoanalysis (Greenson 1965; Kahn 1997), transactional analysis (Barr 1987), gestalt (Hycner 1985) and counselling psychology (Gelso and Carter 1985). Each of these thinkers have, quite independently, identified and described qualities of the therapeutic relationship that appear common and efficacious. However, none of these initiatives developed into integrative models of psychotherapy. This perspective prompted Clarkson (1995a) to reflect on her extensive practice and knowledge of the literature from which she distinguished discourse about five modes of therapeutic relationship, a detailed exposition of which is presented in *The Therapeutic Relationship*. She asserted that there are five modes of relationship potentially present in any therapeutic encounter and advocated, as Hollanders described, an 'integrative approach based essentially on the nature of the therapeutic relationship' (2000: 23) that could form a pan-theoretical approach to psychotherapy (Clarkson 2000). This approach brought a new perspective to psychotherapy integration that is less about directly synthesising ideas from disparate schools and more about understanding the emergent properties within the complexity of psychotherapy proliferation – how the many different approaches might be doing the same thing, only with different emphasis, perspective and nomenclature.

Clarkson's work highlighted the variety of narratives the various schools bring to the therapeutic process. Building on Gelso and Carter (1985), who postulated three relational facets – the working alliance, the transferential and the real relationships – Clarkson added the reparative and transpersonal modalities. Gilbert (1995) later added a sixth modality, which she named the contextual relationship, to include the socio-cultural backdrop of the therapeutic participants. However, this is arguably more about the boundaries of the relationship rather than its intersubjective nature and, in Clarkson's framework, might be considered an aspect of the real relationship. At first sight, this view of integration seems like a common factors approach, but Clarkson argues that these modalities are not necessarily common to all approaches and do not constitute skills or demonstrable techniques. They represent intersubjective attitudinal states upon which different therapeutic schools place different emphasis and within which they employ a range of varying skills and techniques. By taking an overview of all the approaches together, what she identified is a relatively simple pattern of therapeutic relationship consisting of five overlapping relational states, which accommodate a complexity and variety of techniques, methods, interventions and interactive processes that are difficult to fully explicate.

Clarkson's approach provides a principle for integration and a framework for deepening the understanding of any given approach. Clarkson argues that all five modalities are potentially immanent and 'it is important to remember these are not stages but states in psychotherapy, often "overlapping", in and between which a patient construes his or her unique experience' (1995a: xii). She considered the framework to have fractal qualities (Clarkson 2002a: 6; see also Gleick 1988) constituting an attractor that maps the dynamic and seemingly chaotic interaction of all human relationships and, therefore, applies to different scales of relationship from internal object relations, the family, through to organisations and society at large. Clarkson (2002b) has examined how these modes of relationship emerge in existential therapy, and I have contributed to this reflexive process in articles on the framework in Kleinian psychotherapy (Nuttall 2000a), Jungian psychology (Nuttall 2000b), brief dynamic therapy (Nuttall 2002b) and understanding sexual attraction in therapy (Nuttall 2014). Clarkson has also elaborated how her framework helps the understanding of group and organisational behaviour (Clarkson 1995b), which has been extended to leadership and executive coaching (Nuttall 2004; 2012). It is a framework that goes some way towards combining individual and social psychology, and of demonstrating the mode of integration called contiguous integration, discussed next.

Prochaska and Norcross (1999) also identified an emergent pattern of psychotherapy, which they called a 'transtheoretical' model. They described how they have constructed a 'higher-order theory of psychotherapy' (1999: 491) that respects the diversity in the profession, can be evidence-based, allows for extra-therapeutic change, addresses a broad range of human distress and exhorts innovation. In concluding a review of a broad range of systems of psychotherapy, they write, 'we set out to construct a model of psychotherapy and behaviour change that can draw from the entire spectrum of the major theories' (1999). However, I contend that they have not constructed a model of therapy, but *identified* what appears to be a simple emergent process in and among the complex variety of psychotherapy approaches. As they confirm, 'in colloquial terms, we have *identified* the basics of *how* (process), *when* (stages), and *what* (levels) to change' (1999: 505; emphasis added). In developing this change model into therapeutic action, they emphasise the importance of determining the level of change or degree of psychological problem first and describe five interrelated levels from:

1. the simplest problems to do with symptoms/situational issues;
2. maladaptive cognition;
3. interpersonal conflict;
4. family/systems conflict; and
5. deeper intrapersonal conflict.

Whatever the level, therapy aims to guide the client through five *stages of change*, seen in Figure 4.1.

During this journey, any number of interventions or *change processes* can be stimulated by the therapist such as consciousness-raising, catharsis, self-re-evaluation, counterconditioning and contingency management. This process framework allows the many psychotherapeutic approaches to be used as appropriate in accordance with the client's needs. So, psychoanalysis might be best suited to clients with intrapersonal conflict at the precontemplation stage, as this corresponds with 'consciousness-raising' as the appropriate change process. On the other hand, clients

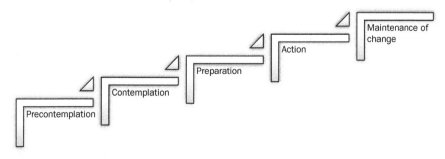

Figure 4.1 Five stages of change

with situational issues requiring action or maintenance of change might find behavioural therapy most suitable because 'contingency management' or 'stimulus control' are the change processes most needed.

Clarkson and Prochaska et al. present models of psychotherapy integration that describe the essential features or components of therapy that result from the inter relationship and synthesis of different theories, skills and techniques, rather than from the simple combination of these elements. Thus, what emerges as an overall pattern from all the different psychotherapies, mediated by training institutions, journal articles, supervision groups and other variables is that psychotherapy is a dynamic process of relational states regardless of the different theories, skills and techniques that are employed or drawn on. Their descriptions do not produce new manualised models of psychotherapy that we can pick off the shelf and practise; they are higher-level descriptions of the therapeutic process that bring us to the core of what we do as psychotherapists. They provide us with a coherence and simplicity that concentrate our endeavours. As Clarkson often said after a theory seminar, 'And remember, it's only one of the many stories; the thing we are more certain about, is that two people sit together and there is relationship' (personal communication).

Modality three: Contiguous integration

Contiguous integration seems driven by an imperative for psychological theories to explain our experience and understanding of society and the world in which we live (Nuttall 2002a). This modality sees psychotherapy not only as a meta-psychology of the individual, but also of the group, organisation and society, and exhorts engagement with the world and other disciplines, such as neuroscience, sociology, anthropology and philosophy. In the quest for integration, such internal–external correspondence or contiguity is useful in testing an approach's robustness and efficacy.

This principle of interrelatedness is traceable to Heraclitus (535–475 BCE) and is exemplified by the simplified Hermetic adage, 'as above, so below' (Marshall 2001: 251) and the Kabbalistic aphorism, 'so, too, does the lower sphere affect the upper' (Hoffman 1996: 167). The principle seems to have been important for individual and social psychologists alike as it provided validation of their theories and gave meaning to their endeavours. Freud probably started such inquiry in the field of psychotherapy in *Totem and Taboo* (1922a [1913]) and later in *Group Psychology and the Analysis of the Ego* (1922b), which followed two similar works by Le Bon (1920) and McDougall (1920). These works represent the origins of how psychotherapy has developed 'an ambition to give therapy to the world' (Samuels 1995). Similarly, Freud's *Project for a Scientific Psychology* (2001 [1895]) was an early attempt to integrate psychoanalysis with the more recognised biological sciences; a synthesis apparent in the work of Bowlby (Mitchell and Black 1995) and, more recently, Schore (2001).

Freud was the first to postulate that unconscious identification was at the core of group cohesion and collusion. He developed the idea that people often emulate the characteristics and attitudes of others they admire or need, usually without conscious awareness, and wrote that 'identification is known ... as the earliest expression of an emotional tie with another person' (1922b: 60). Such identification forms a desired ideal image of the self that, if shared, leads to social cohesion, and he proposed the idea that groups consist of 'a number of individuals who have substituted one and the same object for their ego-ideal and have consequently identified with one another in their ego' (1922b: 60). Further contributions from Klein (1994 [1940]) and the object relations school established that in infancy the processes of introjection and projection help to form an internal phantasy world of selves in relationship with others that correspond to counterparts in the external world. In adulthood, this internal relational world influences and is influenced by real interaction with others and is especially activated in group situations. In asserting the use of object relations theory as a model for group behaviour, Ashbach and Schermer write: 'Thus the system of inner objects and the group system could be seen to work in tandem' (1994: 17), that is, to be in some sense contiguous.

As mentioned earlier, Clarkson considered patterns of relationship to be fractal and to have the same shape at different degrees of scale and that her five-relationship framework applied to varying social scales. Thus, the simplified Hermetic adage 'as above, so below', or as Clarkson wrote, 'as within, so without' (2002b: 100). This inner–outer correspondence was elucidated by Menzies Lyth in her analysis of relational dynamics in healthcare settings in which she demonstrated her assertion that 'psychoanalysts have been interested in society and its institutions since ever there were psychoanalysts' (1986: 284). Following Freud, it was probably the psychiatrist and psychoanalyst Wilfred Bion who developed the psychoanalytic theory that became the mainstream explanatory paradigm for group and organisational behaviour. In a series of papers between 1943 and 1952, he presented a theoretical framework for group dynamics positing that, in stressful situations with others, individuals regress and engage psychological defences Melanie Klein described as typical of the earliest phases of infancy (Bion 1961: 141). Klein's and Bion's object relations theories are now well-accepted explanations of group and organisational behaviour (Jacques 1985 [1955]; Menzies Lyth 1986; Kets de Vries and Associates 1991; Nuttall 2001). In a review of the origins of object relations theory, Scharff and Scharff (1998) demonstrate theoretical links with chaos and fractal theory and with neuroscience. They further assert that 'the relational paradigm first described by Fairbairn, Klein and Winnicott has become the organising set of ideas in modern psychoanalysis, and has influenced literature, philosophy, and organisational development' (1998: 63).

More recent examples of contiguous integration within the psychoanalytic tradition demonstrate this inner–outer correspondence. Fairbairnian object relations theory has helped to explain how the arrival of HIV might have been experienced as 'the return of the repressed bad object' by the gay community (Nuttall 2000c) and how the collective response to this, in terms of social structures and attitudes, resembles the neurotic defences individuals use against intrapsychic situations. More recently, Rizq (2011) elaborates how Klein's theoretical framework offers a way of understanding the organisational dynamics and dilemmas evident in the NHS's IAPT programme. At the political level, Moses (1987) and Elliot (2005) show how psychodynamic processes affect and often hinder the political process of conflict resolution, such as that needed in the Middle East and Northern Ireland. More recently, Layton, Hollander and Gutwil have compiled a book in which a number of leading psychoanalytic practitioners write about their clients' experiences of, and reaction to, social and political events. It falls within the concept of contiguous integration in so far as it 'represents a radical psychoanalytical appreciation of the interpenetration of subjectivity and the socio-political order' (2006: 2).

In the humanistic school, Berne's approach of transactional analysis developed, like Bion's, from experience as an army psychiatrist. His concept of ego states became central to his understanding of organisational dynamics (1963), group treatment (1966) and theory of human interaction (1968). Many management consultancies have used TA, correctly or not, in human resources or customer relations training. This no doubt harmed TA as a serious psychotherapy. Such a view is represented by Prochaska and Norcross who wrote that 'all too often TA sounds like a system of slick Madison Avenue slogans' (1999: 229). However, TA, when combined with Fairbairnian object relations, has been shown to provide a useful explanatory model for work-based relations: 'Fairbairn's theories offer a more lucid insight into the intrapersonal nature of anxiety and ego defences, and transactional analysis is more descriptive of behaviour and interpersonal relations' (Nuttall 2000d: 74), and this synthesis of approaches demonstrates the modalities of both constructive and contiguous integration.

A further example of the contiguity between psychotherapy and other disciplines is provided by the extent to which phenomenology is now incorporated into clinical and, especially, research practice. Elucidation of the highly intersubjective nature of the therapeutic relationship has been deepened by the concepts of perception (Spinelli 2005) and embodiment (Merleau-Ponty 2002 [1962]) that emanate from the phenomenology movement. Examples of how these ideas can be incorporated into integrative therapeutic practice are richly described in several chapters of this book. Taking embodiment as an example, Merleau-Ponty exhorts us to move beyond the concepts of subject and object that can be empirically or intellectually defined and consider ourselves embodied beings coexisting with the world and others. He argued that we perceive and make sense of the world through our physical senses working collectively at a very primordial level. He asserted:

> The body is our general medium for having a world. Sometimes it is restricted to the actions necessary for the conservation of life, and accordingly it posits around us a biological world; at other times, elaborating upon these primary actions and moving from their literal to a figurative meaning, it manifests through them a core of new significance: this is true of motor habits [sic] such as dancing. Sometimes, finally, the meaning aimed at cannot be achieved by the body's natural means; it must then build itself an instrument, and it projects thereby around itself a cultural world.
>
> (2002: 169)

Such a perspective has profound implications for how therapists perceive and relate to their clients, and how they understand themselves as therapists.

In a seminal exposition of how Jungian and post-Jungian psychology should, at least, be considered part of the postmodern critique of contemporary culture, Hauke writes:

> Unlike other cultural theorists, Jung writes from a background of the psychoanalytic treatment of the *individual* in a way that valorises subjective experience as a legitimate approach to concerns of the wider, collective culture and to 'scientific' investigation in general.
>
> (2000: 1)

Jungian psychology is, perhaps, one of the best examples of the principle of contiguous integration in depth psychology. Jung studied the curious way in which symbols and myths of different cultures and individuals parallel each other, even across historical divides. From this, he developed his concept of archetypes and the collective unconscious. Archetypes are universal symbolic forms that attract psychic energy and become active propensities in our lives (Stein 1998: 85). Jung believed that social artefacts, such as alchemy, religions and churches, represent collective identification with one or more archetypes. At the individual level, he recognised how his personal struggles for individuation were expressed in the building of his 'tower' at Bollingen (Jung 1961: 250). At a collective level, in contrast, such an expression of archetypes is illustrated in *On the Nature of the Psyche and Canary Wharf* (Nuttall 2002b). This describes how the call for urban regeneration in London's Isle of Dogs seems to have evoked the archetype of the *coniunctio* in the designers and developers concerned. The result is architectural features that curiously parallel the symbolism of a sixteenth-century alchemical text called the *Rosarium Philosophorum*, which Jung (1946) believed represented the quintessential expression of the archetype of relationship and new birth. As archetypes are experiences embossed upon the minds of humanity throughout history, the Canary Wharf scheme is a contemporary example of the contiguous process, which seems an innate feature of human nature.

Conclusion

These three dimensions of integration, the constructive, complicit and contiguous, emerged from a heuristic self-search inquiry of my own quest for integration (Nuttall 2006). The quest moved from a conceptually naïve position of seeking an ideal system, to one of accepting psychotherapy integration as a continuous process; something necessarily personal and contextual and, therefore, at the profession level, diverse yet inclusive. It represents a developmental process:

1. of reconciling parts (theories, techniques, factors);
2. of then seeing larger-scale features or higher-order patterns;
3. while dialoguing with the world, with other disciplines and social artefact. It is a process redolent of a number of developmental models.

Stern (1998) describes how the infant first integrates a range of experiences as Representations of Interactions that have been Generalised (RIGs), which form the basis of the core self. This is extended by interaction with others for a sense of a subjective self to emerge. A Kleinian metaphor also seems applicable, as there is movement from part-object splitting to depressive position wholeness negotiated by projection and introjection. A Jungian alchemical metaphor also seems applicable as the *prima materia* of the four 'forces', rather like the ancient elements, undergo a *coniunctio* in search of the elusive philosopher's stone, a metonym for the integrative quest. The similarity of the integrative quest I describe with these developmental models suggests this conceptualisation might be meaningful for the profession.

In an insightful review of the issues facing psychotherapy integration, Hollanders enumerated nine dilemmas an integrationist should, at least, consider if not resolve. As one of the issues, Hollanders, somewhat provocatively, asks whether the integrationist is a charlatan or statesperson. He is quite emphatic about his own position on this matter, proposing that the integrationist's job is:

> to develop connectedness with the different parts of the field, to stand between the various schools, to encourage dialogue and debate, and to find ways of helping each to discover and respect the contributions of the other. In short, her role is to serve as a kind of 'statesperson' within the field.
>
> (2000: 44)

This represents an optimistic prospect and there is need for communication and dialogue at a profession-wide level. But this must also encourage the continuous and individual quest for integration that can only take place within the person of the therapist and be mediated within the therapeutic relationship. The individual may take their lead from other, more experienced or learned practitioners whose approaches might be already well developed and recognised in the profession. But, as the 2017 UKAPI conference emphasised, it is still, as Norcross and Arkowitz wrote in their summary analysis of the status of psychotherapy integration in 1992, 'premature to advance any one integrative system . . . I urge students, in the integrative spirit, to take the "best" from each model and to discern converging themes for themselves' (1992: 23). The process is necessarily a personal one and the framework outlined here for the integrative quest is intended to promote the activity of questioning, experimenting, discovering and inventing, and of researching the discipline of psychotherapy in relationship with the world we seek to understand and in which we, and our clients, operate. The quest should be viewed more as an evolving way of being, constantly becoming and unfolding, than something with a determined and definitive end to which the trainee is striving. The upshot of this is that integration happens at the level of the therapist and not necessarily at the level of the profession, school or clinic. It is a personal quest that develops within the context of an individual's skills, knowledge and philosophical outlook and must, therefore, in its professional expression, inevitably embrace conceptual diversity. This view is not an invitation to anarchic relativism or poor eclectic practice. On the contrary, even in their pluralistic and individualistic perspective of what constitutes integrative psychotherapy, Evans and Gilbert assert that 'any model of integration needs to offer a conceptual framework that reflects a consistency between philosophy, theory and practice' (2005: 149). It is an admonition to abandon rivalry and the certitude of ideologies and not to forsake the quintessential element that our experience tells us matters above all: the quality of the therapeutic relationship. Rumi (1991) expresses this beautifully:

Out in the Open Air

There is a kind of food
Not taken in through the mouth:
Bits of knowing that nourish love.
The body and the human personality form a cup,
Every time you meet someone, something is poured in.

When two planets draw near, they affect each other.
A man and a woman come together and a new human being appears.
Iron and stone converge and there are sparks.
Rain soaks the ground and fruits get juicy.
Human beings walk into a ripe orchard and a happiness enters their soul.

From that joy emerges generosity.
From being out in the open air appetites sharpen.
The blush on our faces comes from the sun.
There is a majesty in these connections,
A grandeur that has an invisible quality.
Mohammed's horse, Boraq, Arabian stallions, and even donkeys,
Every creature grazes there, whether they like it or not.

(Re-used with permission from translator, Coleman Barks.
Original poem by Rumi [1991].)

References

Arkowitz, H. (1989) The role of theory in psychotherapy integration. *Journal of Integrative and Eclectic Psychotherapy*, 8(1): 8–16.

Asay, T.P. and Lambert, M.J. (1999) The empirical case for the common factors in therapy. In M.A. Hubble, B.L. Duncan and S.D. Miller (eds), *The Heart and Soul of Change: What Works in Therapy*. Washington, DC: American Psychological Association.

Ashbach, C. and Schermer, V.L. (1994) *Object Relations, the Self, and the Group*. London: Routledge.

Austen, C. (2000) Integrated eclecticism: A therapeutic synthesis. In S. Palmer and S. Woolfe (eds), *Integrative and Eclectic Counselling and Psychotherapy*. London: SAGE.

Barr, J. (1987) The therapeutic relationship model: Perspective on the core of the healing process. *Transactional Analysis Journal*, 17(4): 134–40.

Beitman, B.D. (1990) Why I am an integrationist (not an eclectic). In W. Dryden and J.C. Norcross (eds), *Eclecticism and Integration in Counselling and Psychotherapy*. Loughton: Gale Centre Publications.

Beitman, B.D. (1994) Integration through fundamental similarities and useful differences amongst the schools. In J.C. Norcross and M.R. Goldfried (eds), *Handbook of Psychotherapy Integration* (pp. 94–129). New York: Basic Books.

Berne, E. (1961) *Transactional Analysis in Psychotherapy: A Systematic Individual and Social Psychiatry*. New York: Grove Press.

Berne, E. (1963) *The Structure and Dynamics of Organisations and Groups*. New York: Grove Press.

Berne, E. (1966) *Principles of Group Treatment*. New York: Grove Press.

Bion, W.R. (1961) *Experience in Groups and Other Works*. London: Tavistock.

Bion, W.R. (1968) *Experiences in Groups*. London: Tavistock.

Bion, W.R. (1999 [1962]) *Learning from Experience*. London: Karnac.

Casement, P. (1995) *On Learning from the Patient*. London: Routledge.

Clarkson, P. (1992) *Transactional Analysis Psychotherapy: An Integrated Approach*. London: Routledge.

Clarkson, P. (1995a) *The Therapeutic Relationship in Psychoanalysis, Counselling Psychology and Psychotherapy*. London: Whurr.

Clarkson, P. (1995b) *Changes in Organisations*. London: Whurr.

Clarkson, P. (2000) Eclectic, integrative and integrating psychotherapy in beyond schoolism. In S. Palmer and R. Wolfe (eds), *Integrative and Eclectic Counselling and Psychotherapy* (pp. 302–14). London: SAGE.

Clarkson, P. (2002a) *The Transpersonal Relationship in Psychotherapy*. London: Whurr.

Clarkson, P. (2002b) *On Psychotherapy 2*. London: Whurr.

Cooper, M. and McLeod, J. (2007) A pluralistic framework for counselling and psychotherapy: Implications for research. *Counselling and Psychotherapy Research*, 7(3): 135–43.

Egan, G. (1975) *The Skilled Helper*. Pacific Grove, CA: Brooks/Cole.

Elliot, M. (2005) Cain and Abel: A study of the societal dynamics of ethnic conflict. *Psychotherapy and Politics International*, 3(1): 1–16.

Ellis, A. and Dryden, W. (1997) *The Practice of Rational Emotive Behaviour Therapy* (2nd edn). New York: Springer.

Erskine, R.G. (2010) *Life Scripts: A Transactional Analysis of Unconscious Relational Patterns*. London: Karnac.

Evans, K.R. and Gilbert, M. (2005) *An Introduction to Integrative Psychotherapy*. Basingstoke: Palgrave.

Fear, R. and Woolfe, R. (2000) The personal, the professional and the basis of integrative practice. In S. Palmer and R. Woolfe (eds), *Integrative and Eclectic Counselling and Psychotherapy* (pp. 329–40). London: SAGE.

Frank, J.D. (1961) *Persuasion and Healing*. Baltimore, MD: Johns Hopkins University Press.

Frank, J.D. and Frank, J.B. (1993) *Persuasion and Healing: A Comparative Study of Psychotherapy*. Baltimore, MD: Johns Hopkins University Press.

Freud, S. (1922a [1913]) *Totem and Taboo*. In Standard Edition, vol. 13. London: Hogarth Press.

Freud, S. (1922b [1955]) *Group Psychology and the Analysis of the Ego*. In Standard Edition, vol. 18, pp. 69–144. London: Hogarth Press.

Freud, S. (2001 [1895]) Project for a Scientific Psychology. In *The Standard Edition of the Complete Psychological Works of Sigmund Freud*, vol. I *(1886–1899): Pre-Psycho-Analytic Publications and Unpublished Drafts* (pp. 283–392). London: Vintage.

Gelso, C.J. and Carter, J.A. (1985) The relationship in counselling and psychotherapy: Components, consequences and theoretical antecedents. *The Counseling Psychologist*, 2: 155–243.

Gilbert, M. (1995) *The Integrative Psychotherapy Handbook*. London: Metanoia Institute.

Gleick, J. (1988) *Chaos*. London: Sphere Books.

Goldfried, M.R. (1995) *From Cognitive-behaviour Therapy to Psychotherapy Integration: An Evolving View*. New York: Springer.

Greenson, R.R. (1965) The working alliance and the transference neurosis. *Psychoanalysis Quarterly*, 34: 155–81.

Hargaden, H. and Sills, C. (2002) *Transactional Analysis: A Relational Perspective*. London: Brunner-Routledge.

Hauke, C. (2000) *Jung and the Postmodern*. London: Routledge.

Hinshelwood, R.D. (1990) Editorial. *British Journal of Psychotherapy*, 7(2): 119–20.

Hoffman, E. (1996) An introduction to Kabbalistic psychotherapy. In S. Boorstein (ed.), *Transpersonal Psychotherapy* (pp. 165–80). New York: New York University Press.

Horton, I. (2000) Principles and practice of a personal integration. In S. Palmer and R. Woolfe (eds), *Integrative and Eclectic Counselling and Psychotherapy*. London: SAGE.

Hollanders, H. (2000) Eclecticism/integration: Some key issues and research. In S. Palmer and R. Woolfe (eds), *Integrative and Eclectic Counselling and Psychotherapy*. London: SAGE.

Hycner, R.H. (1985) Dialogical Gestalt therapy: An initial proposal. *Gestalt Journal*, 8(1): 23–49.

Jacques, E. (1985 [1955]) Social systems as a defence against persecutory and depressive anxiety. In M. Klein, P. Heimann and R. Money-Kyrle (eds), *New Directions in Psychoanalysis* (pp. 478–99). London: Maresfield Library.

Jenkins, P. (2000) Gerard Egan's skilled helper model. In S. Palmer and R. Woolfe (eds), *Integrative and Eclectic Counselling and Psychotherapy* (pp. 163–80). London: SAGE.

Jung, C.G. (1928) Analytical psychology and education. In C.F. Baynes (ed.), *Contributions to Analytical Psychology*. London: Trench Trubner & Co.

Jung, C.G. (1995 [1961]) *Memories, Dreams, Reflections*. London: Fontana.

Jung, C.G. (1998 [1946]) *The Psychology of the Transference*. London: Routledge.

Kahn, M. (1997) *Between Therapist and Client: The New Relationship*. New York: W.H. Freeman.

Kets de Vries, M.F.R. and Associates (1991) *Organisations on the Couch.* San Francisco, CA: Jossey-Bass.

Klein, M. (1994 [1940]) Mourning and its relation to manic-depressive states. In *Love, Guilt and Reparation and Other Works 1921–1945.* London: Virago Press Ltd.

Lapworth, P., Sills, C. and Fish, S. (2001) *Integration in Counselling & Psychotherapy: Developing a Personal Approach.* London: SAGE.

Layton, L., Hollander, N.C. and Gutwill, S. (2006) *Psychoanalysis, Class and Politics: Encounters in the Clinical Setting.* Hove: Routledge.

Lazarus, A.A. (1989) *The Practice of Multimodal Therapy: Systematic, Comprehensive and Effective Psychotherapy.* Baltimore, MD: Johns Hopkins University Press.

Lazarus, A.A. (1990) Why I am an eclectic (not an integrationist). In W. Dryden and J.C. Norcross (eds), *Eclecticism and Integration in Counselling and Psychotherapy.* Loughton: Gale Centre Publications.

Le Bon, G. (1920) *The Crowd: A Study of the Group Mind.* London: Fisher Unwin.

Lees, J. (ed.) (2016) *The Future of Psychological Therapies: From Managed Care to Transformational Practice.* London: Routledge.

Mahrer, A.R. (1989) *The Integration of Psychotherapies: A Guide for Practicing Therapists.* New York: Human Sciences Press.

Marshall, P. (2001) *The Philosopher's Stone: A Quest for the Secrets of Alchemy.* London: Pan Books.

McDougall, W. (1920) *The Group Mind.* Cambridge: Cambridge University Press.

Menzies Lyth, I.E.P. (1986) A psychoanalytic perspective on social institutions. In E.B. Spillius (ed.), *Melanie Klein Today*, vol. 2: *Mainly Practice.* London: Routledge.

Merleau-Ponty, M. (2002) *Phenomenology of Perception.* C. Smith (trans). London: Routledge.

Mitchell, S.A. and Black, M.J. (1995) *Freud and Beyond: A History of Modern Psychoanalytic Thought.* New York: Basic Books.

Moses, R. (1987) Projection, identification, and projective identification: Their relation to political process. In J. Sandler (ed.), *Projection, Identification, and Projective Identification.* London: Karnac Books.

Norcross, J. and Arkowitz, H. (1992) The evolution and current status of psychotherapy integration. In W. Dryden (ed.), *Integrative and Eclectic Therapy: A Handbook* (pp. 1–39). Buckingham: Open University Press.

Norcross, J. and Grencavage, L.M. (1990) Eclecticism and integration in psychotherapy: Major themes and obstacles. In W. Dryden and J.C. Norcross (eds), *Eclecticism and Integration in Counselling and Psychotherapy.* Loughton: Gale Centre Publications.

Nuttall, J. (2000a) Modes of therapeutic relationship in Kleinian psychotherapy. *British Journal of Psychotherapy*, 17(1): 17–36.

Nuttall, J. (2000b) The *Rosarium Philosophorum* as a universal relational psychology: Jung and object relations. *Psychodynamic Counselling*, 6(2): 70–100.

Nuttall, J. (2000c) Fairbairnian object relations as an intra-social paradigm: The gay community's response to HIV. *European Journal of Psychotherapy and Counselling*, 3(2): 213–27.

Nuttall, J. (2000d) Intrapersonal and interpersonal relations in management organisations. *Transactional Analysis Journal*, 30(1): 73–82.

Nuttall, J. (2001) Psychodynamics and intersubjectivity in management organisations. *Journal of Change Management: An International Journal*, 1(3): 229–41.

Nuttall, J. (2002a) Imperatives and perspectives of psychotherapy integration. *International Journal of Psychotherapy*, 7(3): 253–67.

Nuttall, J. (2002b) On the nature of the psyche, and Canary Wharf. *Harvest Journal of Jungian Studies*, 48(2): 7–29.

Nuttall, J. (2004) Modes of relationship in management organisations. *Journal of Change Management*, 4(1): 15–30.

Nuttall, J. (2006) Researching psychotherapy integration: A heuristic approach. *Counselling Psychology Quarterly*, 19(4): 429–44.

Nuttall, J. (2012) Relational modalities in executive coaching. In E. de Haan and C. Sills (eds), *Coaching Relationships: The Relational Coaching Field Book*. Faringdon: Libri Publishing.

Nuttall, J. (2014) Sexual attraction in the therapeutic relationship; An integrative perspective. In M. Luca (ed.), *Sexual Attraction in Therapy: Clinical Perspectives Moving beyond the Taboo* (pp. 22–37). Chichester: Wiley.

Nuttall, J. (2017) Out in the open air: The quest for integration. *British Journal of Psychotherapy Integration*. Special Edition 13: 15–29.

Prochaska, J.O. and DiClemente, C.C. (1984) *The Transtheoretical Approach: Crossing the Traditional Boundaries of Therapy*. Homewood, IL: Dow Jones-Irwin.

Prochaska, J.O. and Norcross, J.C. (1999) *Systems of Psychotherapy: A Transtheoretical Analysis*. Pacific Grove, CA: Brooks/Cole.

Rizq, R. (2011) IAPT, anxiety and envy: A psychoanalytic view of NHS primary care mental health services today. *British Journal of Psychotherapy*, 27(1): 37–55.

Rogers, C.R. (1957) The necessary and sufficient conditions of therapeutic personality change. *Journal of Counseling Psychology*, 21: 95–103.

Rumi, J. (1991) *One-handed Basket Weaving*. Barks, C. (trans.) Athens, GA: Maypop.

Ryle, A. (1990) *Cognitive-analytic Therapy: Active Participation in Change – A New Integration in Brief Psychotherapy*. Chichester: Wiley.

Samuels, A. (1995) *The Politician Within: Andrew Samuels in Conversation with David Sherrington*. Godalming: Alternative View (video tape).

Scharff, D.E. and Scharff, J.S. (1998) *Object Relations Therapy*. London: Karnac.

Schore, A. (2001) Mind in the making. *British Journal of Psychotherapy*, 17(3): 299–328.

Spinelli, E. (2005) *The Interpreted World: An Introduction to Phenomenological Psychology*. London: SAGE.

Stewart, I. and Cohen, J. (1997) *Figments of Reality: The Evolution of the Curious Mind*. Cambridge: Cambridge University Press.

Stein, M. (1998) *Jung's Map of the Soul*. Peru, IL: Carus Publishing Company.

Stern, D. (1998) *The Interpersonal World of the Infant*. London: Karnac.

Tudor, K. (ed.) (2002) *Transactional Analysis Approaches to Brief Therapy*. London: SAGE.

5 The therapeutic relationship at the core of integration

Claire Marshall

Introduction

Previous chapters have covered the history of the integrative quest in therapy; a distinction between integrative practice and treatment; an exploration of some of the challenges of integration; as well as an analysis of different types of integration (including technical eclecticism, common factors and theoretical integration). As a counselling psychologist who believes in the importance of evidence-based practice and practice-based evidence, in this chapter, using the therapeutic relationship as a focal point, I will argue that for a robust approach to integration, having a clear conceptual framework is paramount. Furthermore, in order to arrive at this conceptual clarity, it is important for practitioners to interrogate their own ontological and epistemological positions. In this way, I promote *criticality* and *reflexivity* as necessary positions for a lucid integrative practice.

In terms of my own positionality, I currently define myself as a 'phenomenological counselling psychologist'. Hence, I adopt a relativist ontological position and a constructivist epistemology and I contextualise this within an interpretivist theoretical framework. Furthermore, I draw from postmodern ideas. I argue that for true conceptual coherence, one's ontological and epistemological position should be aligned with those underpinning the theories being integrated. That is, in order to integrate consistently, the theories being integrated should be aligned in terms of their ontic and epistemic underpinnings. Because at present there are very few psychological theories that I consider underpinned by the underlying philosophical assumptions implicit in postmodernism, it would be limiting to practise from an epistemologically cohesive integrative postmodern approach.

Establishing definitions

It will be useful for us to have working definitions of the main concepts that feature in this chapter before we point to them in relation to integration and the therapeutic relationship.

Epistemology is a branch of philosophy that is concerned with knowledge. Specifically, it is 'concerned with issues such as the nature, extent, sources and legitimacy of knowledge' (Craig and Craig 2000: 250). It investigates issues like the nature of knowledge (e.g. seeking a definition or conceptualisation); the scope of knowledge (e.g. what we can know and what we cannot know); where knowledge originates (e.g. how we gain knowledge); the role of reliability and whether we can be certain (e.g. to what extent we should remain sceptical); and in what circumstances, and under what conditions, a belief can be justified (Craig and Craig 2000). Some epistemological positions are briefly defined in Table 5.1.

Ontology is about what exists or has being – that is, it is the 'philosophical investigation of existence, or being' (Craig and Craig 2000: 645). This study might be focused upon questions such as: 'What does it mean to "be"?' and 'What does it mean for something to "exist"?' A person's ontology might refer to the things they take to exist, and the ontology of a theory refers to the things that need to exist for the theory to stand (Craig and Craig 2000). Epistemology and ontology are intimately

Table 5.1 Four epistemological positions

Objectivism	Constructivism	Social constructivism	Subjectivism
Knowledge is of objective, external objects, which we can identify or know with certitude and precision. Knowledge claims (and related epistemic issues, like norms and justification) are assessed relative to objectively applicable conditions – conditions that hold in all cases. Knowledge is therefore *discovered* by experiencing 'real' external objects in a way that meets objectively valid conditions.	Knowledge is neither 'simply' subjective nor 'simply' objective, it is *created* through the individual subject's interaction with the world. For example, particular conditions for knowledge are collected together to formulate a construct that tells us what counts as knowledge in the domain of science. Because all knowledge is constructed, it is therefore neither absolute nor generalisable.	Knowledge is *constructed in a social process*; hence, it emerges from the interaction between people and society. Therefore, the focus is on the influence of culture and temporality and the way this shapes perception. Knowledge claims count as knowledge *within that society* given its particular conditions for knowledge. Knowledge has no context transcendent significance.	Knowledge is inseparable from the subject. Knowledge claims (and related epistemic issues, like norms and justification) are assessed, in part, relative to feelings, experience, intuition, cognition (etc.), which vary from subject to subject. Knowledge is therefore *relative* to an individual or group.

Table 5.2 Epistemological implications of ontological positions

Realism and critical realism		Relativism	
Ontological position	Epistemological implication	Ontological position	Epistemological implication
Facts exists outside or independently of the subject. They are objective in this sense.	Our senses can (though do not always successfully) perceive the world exactly as it is. This depends, in part, on our expectations, beliefs and environment.	Facts do not exist outside or independent of the subject (or, what set of facts exist varies and no set of facts is objectively 'right').	We cannot know that facts exist outside or independent of the subject but we have cause to believe they don't exist in such a way (or, what facts exist depend on subjective factors).

tied as 'ontological issues and epistemological issues tend to emerge together . . . to talk of the construction of meaning is to talk of the construction of meaningful reality' (Crotty 2015: 10). Table 5.2 demonstrates ontological notions and their epistemological implications.

Theoretical perspectives

There are various philosophical systems, which we might refer to as 'theoretical perspectives', that seek to describe the *data* of social experiences. Although complex and often lacking in a unified theory, they are briefly defined in Table 5.3.

Phenomenology is a philosophical tradition and an investigative method (encompassing a range of research approaches). Phenomenology is generally the study of the contents of conscious experience, the study of the world (i.e. intentional objects) as it appears to the subject – the study of *phenomena*. The basic idea being that, regardless of what in the world is 'out there' – regardless of ontology – we can study the way intentional objects appear to the subject (i.e. how they are in the 'lived world'), which the subject plays an active role in. This has major implications for epistemology and meaning.

One of the aims of phenomenology is to collapse the dualism inherent in separating subject and object as two discrete entities. The outcome of this investigation calls into question what in recent times we took for granted regarding our experiences and perceptions, in particular with regard to the natural sciences, in what has been described as

> a radical ontological revision of Cartesian Dualism. It has implications for epistemology: the claim that, when the foundations of empirical

knowledge in perception and action are properly characterized, traditional forms of scepticism and standard attempts to justify knowledge are undermined.

(Craig and Craig 2000: 670)

While there are various interpretations of phenomenology (most notably by Brentano, Husserl, Heidegger, Sartre and Merleau-Ponty), all are in agreement that *intentionality* is a defining characteristic of consciousness – in other words, consciousness is *intentional* (i.e. directed towards objects). Another defining facet of phenomenology is the assertion that first comes 'practical knowledge' and thereafter we might be able to describe or declare something about the object towards which we are directed. In other words, 'knowing *that* arises from knowing *how*' (Craig and Craig 2000: 671; emphasis in original). Phenomenologists also claim that there are essential features of the lived world, including embodiment, society, time, discourse, identity and space (Moran 2000; Moran and Mooney 2002; Finlay 2011; Crotty 2015; Kaufer and Chemero 2015). Phenomenology influenced postmodernism in its critique that, with regards to how experience is understood, epistemic assumptions had become over-influenced by

Table 5.3 Theoretical perspectives

Positivism	Post-positivism	Interpretivism	Postmodernism
Reality is a singular entity that exists and can be understood and discovered. There is a universal scientific method that is the same for social science and natural science alike. All truths should be reducible to physical phenomena and any theory must be scientifically, logically or mathematically verifiable. (Often associated with naïve or direct realism.)	Reality exists independent of a subject but it is not possible to fully understand it, hence understanding is imperfect. (Often associated with critical realism.)	There are a multitude of realities and ways of accessing them, hence different perspectives. (Often associated with symbolic interactionism, hermeneutics and phenomenology – an expanded definition follows.)	Emphasises multiplicity, ambiguity, fragmentation and ambivalence. It focuses on deconstructing how the world has become represented – (An expanded definition follows.)

natural science. However, postmodern thinkers critiqued the phenomenologists' claim that there are fundamental characteristics of the lived-world.

Postmodernism is not one unified theory; rather, it encompasses a wide range of sometimes differing perspectives in ongoing debates about what postmodernism is and how it might be defined. For example, one account of postmodernism might be as an aesthetic and philosophical project. Notwithstanding, postmodernism, with its ideological implications, is no longer a highbrow cultural moment, as can be seen in contemporary culture. As the prefix 'post' suggests, it refers to what comes after modernism. *Modernism*, in European history, is a period beginning from around the nineteenth century to the mid-twentieth century. Postmodernism arose after the Second World War (i.e. after 1945). Postmodern thinkers often posit that there are no overarching theories, no absolute homologies that secure the possibility of objectivity or singleness. Thus, concepts such as the future, truth or deities do not hold the same weight as they might do within other frameworks of understanding. In addition, arguably another premise of postmodern thought is that organisations or systems relating to people function much in the same way as language – that is to say, they create and preserve values and meanings (Craig and Craig 2000). One can hear echoes of phenomenology's critique of natural science in postmodernism, where rejections of master narratives are given priority over truth (Craig and Craig 2000).

Fredric Jameson (1992) characterised postmodernism as the weakening of history, the lack of depth and the waning of affect. Jean-François Lyotard (1986) is frequently invoked when defining postmodernism for his rejection of grand narratives and universal truths. Lyotard also argued that regarding the production of culture, postmodernism represents a significant change in tense, identifying this as the 'future anterior' (Lyotard 1986: 81). Postmodernism examines the world through *deconstruction*, often casting things as fabrication, surface or fictional. However, whether the postmodern project is considered primarily a relationship with the future or primarily a relationship with truth, is debatable. (The definition of postmodernism will be expanded further later in this chapter.)

Problematising the philosophical underpinnings of contemporary psychology

We will now explore objectivist and constructivist epistemologies. An objectivist epistemology posits that reality exists independently of consciousness. It is therefore a *realist* position (see Table 5.2), as this 'external' reality can be identified with precision and certitude. This is often contrasted with a constructivist epistemology, which sees the subject as inherently implicated as both subject and object, the knower and the known being inseparable and co-constituting meaning – a more *relativist* position (see Table 5.2). The subject, and their wider social sphere, formulate concepts and models that are deemed 'true' relative to how viable and explanatorily helpful they are for working in the world and understanding the objects of experience. As subjects construct meaning in different ways, there can be multiple (and equally valid) accounts of the world for constructivists.

In its endeavour towards establishing itself as a legitimate discipline, psychology has traditionally aligned itself with natural science. Positivism (see Table 5.3), immensely influential in the natural sciences, asserts that the same universal scientific method can be used in both the natural and human sciences; that reality exists external to the subject; that inquiry should be based on scientific observations; and that there is a focus on causality. Positivism is often closely linked with an objectivist epistemology.

Human science, by differentiating between what is observable (including behaviour and speech) and what is not observable (including private emotions or sensations) and demarcating lines of causality, polarises experience and behaviour. The result is that subject and object are demarcated as separate parts and psychology has aligned itself with this assumption – it, too, espouses the dualistic, dichotomous relationship between subject and object. Valle, King and Halling describe this in the following way:

> Behaviour, therefore, came to represent the objective ('object-like') aspect of people, whereas experience came to represent the subjective ('subject-like') aspect. This brand of philosophical dualism (the famous Cartesian split between observable, accessible body and the unobservable, inaccessible mind) is still foundational to most theory and practice in psychology . . . Psychology, formed by individuals embedded in this very same natural sciences world was, therefore, fashioned as a natural scientific psychology.
>
> (1989: 3–4)

In contemporary psychology, the prevalent symptom-based approach, which emphasises the measurement of observable phenomena and encourages the practitioner to interpret this within a framework of illness, disease or dysfunction is one example of dichotomising the behaviour–experience polarity. This polarisation is evident in, for example, the invocation of the four 'Ds' (Deviance [from a statistical norm], Distress, Dysfunction and Danger) when conceptualising and providing therapeutic intervention based on psychiatric labelling (Davis 2009). When adopting this approach to understanding experience, criteria are set in order for a phenomenon to be considered legitimate. The psychologist defines, or rather consults, pre-determined criteria, for example as set out in the DSM-V (American Psychological Association 2013), for what behaviour they will consider as evidence of a given phenomenon. In this way, the phenomenon is confused with the criteria set to define the phenomenon (e.g. sadness *is* the amount of times someone cries). It is in this way that mainstream psychology, based on the natural scientific method, limits itself to engaging with only one aspect of the behaviour–experience polarity (namely, behaviour) (Valle et al. 1989). Furthermore, the evidence base for consistency and validity for concepts and diagnosis is poor in the symptom-based model, yet this model remains prevalent in mainstream psychology and therapists working within most public and private services (Lemma 2008; White 2015).

While many psychologists and psychotherapists may not strictly align themselves with a somatogenic model, it has permeated contemporary culture to such an extent that even if the practitioner does not ascribe to this, their clients might. For example, while clients may not know the criteria for a given label, they might present symptoms as if they were the totality of their experience (i.e. without considering what these 'symptoms' might mean). In this way, clients often narrate their experience through a paradigm of, for example, 'depression' or 'trauma'.

I suggest that symptom labelling is often based on social norms, rather than a rigorous analysis or phenomenological inquiry. Furthermore, based on defining causal explanations when conceptualising models of illness or health, the implicit question inherent in these approaches when working with a client's presentation is: 'Is it a deviation?' A deviation from what (e.g. adaptive and realistic beliefs; an individual not acting out unconscious impulses and unable to be purposeful in the present; a fully functioning person moving towards growth and fulfilment, etc.) depends on the therapeutic approach, which will be explored later in the chapter. A framework that polarises behaviour and experience and that prioritises behaviour over experience is limiting. It does not sufficiently acknowledge the socio-cultural 'situatedness' of experience, nor does it provide sufficient conditions for a holistic appreciation of human psychology. Finally, phenomena are confused with the criteria being used to define them. It is on this basis that I will argue traditional, mainstream psychology is underpinned by positivism and closely linked with an objectivist epistemology.

Most mainstream psychological theories make truth claims (for example, by positing a model of illness), which can be discovered (through the application of the method espoused by that therapeutic approach). Where at times 'truth' in psychology has been assessed through a construct, whereby assumptions are legitimised as true based upon their explanatory value, falsifiability or consistency with other theories or ideas, for the most part this has not been the case. In the prevailing *Zeitgeist*, ontological questions are answered by theories, which represent discrete entities with distinguishable properties. Epistemological questions are answered by truth claims, distinguishing subjectivity and objectivity, abstraction and primacy to reason, as the necessary faculty for reaching truth. In this paradigm, knowledge production concerns itself with the discovery of an external reality that can be identified through deconstructing the elements, with a focus on causal relationships. This objectivist epistemology is often implicit within therapeutic approaches, yet has a self-sustaining, cyclical effect whereby dominant philosophical frameworks dictate economic distribution and therefore influence the focus of future knowledge production. Dominant paradigms take for granted their position and invest in research, contributing ideas to an ever-growing normalisation of the status quo. Arguably, psychology's acclaim in recent years, including its expansion and increased popularity as a discipline, is at least in part due to its identification with the natural sciences. The Anglo-American push towards schooling on subjects traditionally associated with natural science (science, technology, engineering and mathematics) has meant the financial backing of practitioners aligning themselves with natural science. This impacts upon the trajectory of psychology research, and psychologists' research output has a direct impact on knowledge production. Consequently, human experience is oversimplified (and often reduced to cognitive processes) as Burr describes:

> The rising popularity of psychology has for various reasons wished to be regarded as a science and has therefore aligned itself with the natural sciences rather than other social sciences such as sociology and cultural studies ... One of the consequences of such trends is that in the last UK Research Excellence Framework (REF) exercise, the research outputs of psychologists were assessed within a combined unit of Psychology, Psychiatry and Neuroscience, and this alignment seems likely to strengthen the pull of reductionism within the discipline.
>
> (2015: 8)

A kind of psychological *determinism* has traditionally permeated the discipline. In a bid to establish its legitimacy, psychology has aligned, and continues to align, itself with natural science and positivistic assumptions. This has resulted in a dichotomising of experience and behaviour (with priority given to *behaviour* to the detriment of an appreciation of *experience*) and truth claims being made based on an external, objective world. Where does this leave the therapeutic relationship, if its possibilities have already been prescriptively reduced?

The socio-economic context of therapeutic relationships

Current therapeutic discourses share meta-philosophical commonalities, which are influenced by political and economic narratives. In a climate underpinned by an objectivist epistemology, giving precedence to establishing *truth out there* over *truth as being relative to subjective and intersubjective experience* has influenced psychology's need to legitimise and sustain itself, both conceptually and economically, through aligning itself with the natural sciences. This, arguably, has led to a culture of privatisation and commodification premised on outcomes, actions and achievements. Regulatory bodies in the United Kingdom are by definition embedded within this system and, thus, the self-sustaining nature of the dominant narratives is reinforced. This informs the socio-economic context of the therapeutic relationship. One consequence has been that the prevailing paradigm is seemingly ill-fitted to understand or engage with human experience.

Interpretive phenomenology can be traced back to Martin Heidegger (1889–1976). One of Heidegger's central projects was to deconstruct the metaphysical assumptions of the Western philosophical tradition. Heidegger argued that philosophy had neglected a fundamental question: 'What does it mean to be?' Specifically, 'being' is a translation from the German '*dasein*', which could also be translated as 'to exist' or 'to be present'. Heidegger argued that being had to be understood in terms of *temporality* – specifically, in the present tense. Aho (2009) wrote that, in a metaphysical context, a study of substance (or being) is the study of the underlying, permanent essence of the things that are (exist or have being) that make them what is or makes those things things, so to speak – the study of *substrata*. Equivalently, it is the study of *that thing*, supposing *it is*, that grounds the existence of *what is* at the most fundamental level. We might imagine substance as a kind of foundation under the things we experience – the trees we observe, the books we read. The basic point of substance is to underpin the property changes that happen to things (the leaves falling from the tree, the pages of the book turning yellow) and to enable us to ground the existence of properties and the existence of things through time (the tree surviving the seasons, the book ageing with use). Aho explains that: '"substance", referring to the basic, underlying "what-ness" [is] that [which] is unchangeable and essential to all beings as being' (2009: 8).

Over the course of Western history, the metaphysical question of 'substance' has reoccurred and different theorists posit various analyses. Heidegger criticised this, arguing metaphysics had dominated our world-view, rather than being treated as one possible world-view. Furthermore, in doing so, he argued it not only limits our appreciation of experience, it reduces humans to agents of production that are reduced to a source of capital. In other words, if a substance-orientated world-view is the dominant discourse, then 'beings reveal themselves only in terms of substance, and this orientation culminates in the technological age, where our relationship with the world has become purely instrumental, where beings show up exclusively as resources at our disposal' (Aho 2009: 8).

In *Being and Time* (1962), Heidegger posited that, in traditional metaphysics, substances are treated as the most essential entities; they are identified, quantified and categorised by their assets. Phenomena are deconstructed, calculated and reduced to dichotomies (Heidegger 2002). Often these substances are considered in terms of their usefulness, leading to objectification, as worth is attached to output, or assets, rather than the qualities held by the substances themselves. Arguably, if we take Heidegger's critique of a substance-orientated world-view and apply it to the contemporary neo-liberal capitalist context – the unequal distribution of global wealth, economic materialism, the culture of privatisation and commodification – it is a conceptual framework that reveals people as being degraded to object status. If we apply Heidegger's critique to psychology in the contemporary context, we could argue that the deterministic focus on self-actualisation diminishes the individual to an isolated entity – evident in the way we technologise and pathologise. This reductionist compartmentalisation creates a distancing from one another. How we experience and understand the world is implicit within the way we come to be in the world. As a result, we can experience the relationship with ourselves as disjointed, inaccessible and alienated. Therapists in their consulting rooms draw on approaches affiliated with the paradigms that give rise to these conditions. Interrogating the philosophical basis for psychological and psychotherapeutic attitudes therefore becomes a question of *ethics*.

Mainstream psychology and psychotherapy have been criticised for being essentialist, often reducing entities to simple, vital parts, compromising an appreciation of the whole context. Furthermore, they arguably treat the complexity of the human condition too simply, often reducing the totality of human experience to social explanations or, more frequently, to biological ones (Burr 2015). A further criticism identifies therapy's privileging of the individual as an exclusive, autonomous subject over the collective and/or contextual milieu. Rather than focusing on process, the autonomous subject is described in terms of structures, such as personality characteristics, memory functions or economics (Burr 2015). Finally, a focus on the intrapsychic rather than contextual factors can often lead to a confusion between symptom and cause. A formulation that describes a client's internal psychological processes in terms of a given modality and its associated linguistic resources (e.g. unconscious impulses, acting out, transference and defences) without a holistic treatment of their context (e.g. social resources and economic, cultural, physical elements – to name but a few) might lead the practitioner to interpret the client's response as problematic, rather than appreciating the problematic situation that gave rise to this response. What we might learn from this is how psychologists and psychotherapists can work with clients in a way that gives primacy to human experience by adopting a position that sensitively engages with the client and their context as a whole, being careful not to prioritise an aspect of experience at the cost of ignoring others. I posit that it is only through an appreciation of our clients as whole human beings that we can create the conditions for a meaningful therapeutic relationship.

Theoretical conceptualisations of the self and implications for the therapeutic relationship

There is an intimate link between how we conceive the therapeutic relationship and how we view the notion of the self, as understandings of the self have implications for the relationship between self and other.

René Descartes argued that the mind is independent of the physical world – it is the self and it is a thinking thing, something that reasons, imagines and senses. Inherent in this position is the dualist idea that there is an intrinsic divide between mind and body, two distinct substances, which Descartes defined as broadly opposites. Focusing on the self, Descartes proposed that the mind is the seat of consciousness (a source of intellect, drives and identity), something that is independent of the physical world and is characterised by its capacity to think, 'though that' operates in an interactionist framework (i.e. the body affects the mind and vice versa). Stolorow and Atwood (1992) write that this view promoted physical reality as an external, single entity. Descartes also claimed that incontrovertible knowledge is only achievable in the *metaphysical* substance, or the self, not the *physical* substance. In seeking to ground our knowledge in something that could not be doubted, he identified such a ground as the fact that he exists as a thinking thing. Such a claim, however, is not reducible to physical phenomena and it arguably cannot be scientifically, logically or mathematically verified – it is a conclusion one reaches purely by thinking about how the world, including thought, appears to the subject.

Mainstream psychology in the West is dominated by a conceptualisation of the subject as unitary and fairly fixed over time. It is often posited that the self exists at the 'core' of the individual, and as the originator of its actions. Psychology aims at learning about the self in order to ascertain information on characteristics, attributes, social faculties, etc. This *thing* has permeated mainstream thought and people often speak of self-work, self-growth, an ideal self or transcending the self – as if there were something fixed and consolidated that resided 'within' an individual (Spinelli 2005).

The conceptualisation of the self from a phenomenological perspective is based on the premise of *relatedness*; the 'self' broadly correlates with subjectivity and is mutually constituted through being in the world where *a priori* structures make possible particular modes of being. For phenomenological psychologists, the 'self' does not exist inside an individual nor is it the source of consciousness, rather – according to Husserl – it is the *result* of conscious experience. The 'self' might be thought of as a transient, relationally dependent state that is co-constituted with the environment (Spinelli 2005).

Consider again Cartesian conceptualisations and, similarly, Western mainstream psychology in general, which both position the self as a separate substance (i.e. mind has a different essence, one that cannot be reduced to the essence of body, the other substance), but as one that is causally related to body in a binary fashion, body affecting mind and vice versa. In this configuration, the delineation and polarisation of inner and outer (i.e. self and world) separate me from my world and, in another dichotomy, separate mind from body. If I have the capability of independently generating identity, hopes, intellect, etc., then irrespective of my context (family, friends, culture, history, resources, etc.), I alone could be held accountable. My environment is separate to 'my' 'self' and therefore does not necessarily have to be incorporated into any understandings of 'my' 'self'. In the same vein, regarding the relationship between self and other, the implication is that the other must only engage with my mind (not body or environment) if they are to engage with 'my' 'self'. Furthermore, the other is a distinct entity whose interaction with 'my' 'self' is limited and mediated by my own doubting, affirming or judging capacities. In other words, because my mind or self is in some sense separate from the physical world and the source of consciousness, in many ways I exist in isolation.

From a *social constructivist* perspective, some theorists maintain that the social sciences do not merely passively describe but rather *impact upon* the phenomenon under study (Gergen 1973). Applied within clinical work, the therapist is a subjective agent and therefore any interventions we make are weighted with assumptions (MacNamee and Gergen 1992). Our construction of the world, or the set of assumptions we bring to bear in the therapeutic relationship, is limited by discourse – an account either of a phenomenon or of a client's presenting problems is therefore not representational of objective truth, rather of the 'narrating systems' or assumptions available to us. Thus, making sense of experience is an act in which the subject has an influential, dynamic role. Within this conceptualisation, 'self' is not possessed by an individual ('my-self') or even by a group ('our-selves') and can be likened to movements that are spatially located and expressed through, for example, walking or music (MacNamee and Gergen 1992). This might be likened to the concept of a 'songline', which is an Australian Aboriginal musical map that traces a direction within a terrain. It is thought that an individual is born into a 'songline' and only knows a part of it, learning the other parts by walking around regularly and opening up the opportunity to meet others who might share their knowledge of that part. The sharing of this knowledge occurs within a space that is temporally located connecting the exchange with their forebears:

> An exchange of songlines would be tied to the spirits of different ancestors – animals or plants or landmarks – who sprang forth in the 'dreamtime' before people existed. A person might share an ancestor with people who lived in an entirely different part of the territory.
>
> (MacNamee and Gergen 1992: 10)

From this social constructivist perspective, the self is brought into being through an *embodied act* apprehending connecting currents, which are historically situated. It follows that the therapy might create dialogic terrains by not being too prescriptive about meaning, encouraging multiple narratives and formats that these narratives might take (e.g. symbols) so that the client might 'wander around' their terrain, connecting to useful resources.

While generally psychoanalysis might be aligned to modernist values, *Lacanian psychoanalysis* is arguably postmodern. For Lacan, the subject is always *subject to* something. Drawing on de Saussure's semiotics (Berger 2013), Lacan distinguished between signifier (sound or image) and signified (concept) and argued rather than being mutually constituted, the signifier produces the signified (Lacan 2001). Furthermore, non-linguistic entities can constitute signifiers (including relationships). Lacan suggested that humans are subject to language, in that there is no subject without language and the subject is only an effect of the signifier. The subject is constituted by (or rather is *subject to*) language; the subject is a consequence of the signifier expressed through language. This language serves to conceal desire and the precarious relationship we have with others. Lacan argued the self is constituted in the other (a concept). Psychic life for Lacan is about impossibility and loss, therefore Lacanian analysis aims to deconstruct illusions of self to allow the fragmented and de-centred identity to re-emerge (Lacan 1998).

In the *phenomenological conceptualisation of self*, 'self' is characterised by *impermanence*. Here, 'self' and subjectivity are mutually constituted. The implication for the relationship between 'self' and other is complex as it is dependent on things as they appear to us. Phenomenological therapists attempt to enter the client's lived experience and understand it on its own terms. This is done on a macro level, through acknowledging paradigms used to frame experience, which include ideas around 'mental health and illness', as well as on a micro level, through acknowledging the therapist's own assumptions. The way in which we come to understand 'self' and how it *relates-to, comes-into-being-through* or is *subject-to* others is intimately tied to how we construct the notion of the 'self' and vice versa. For this reason, phenomenologically speaking, it is problematic to refer to a 'self' at all.

Psychological conceptualisations of the self and implications for the therapeutic relationship

Mainstream psychological perspectives regarding how notions of self-formation and self–other relations translate into therapy differ. A brief summation of the main psychological paradigmatic differences will now follow. It should be noted that within each of these approaches there exists a plethora of significantly different vantage points.

The cognitive–behavioural paradigm

Cognitive–behavioural conceptualisations of the self suggest it is developed through the formation of beliefs and schemas about oneself, others and the world and therefore give pre-eminence to addressing these. The therapeutic relationship is not given primacy in and of itself; instead, the focus is on explicit supportive exercises, diagnosis, prescription and experimentation, which are reviewed by both client and psychotherapist or psychologist. Empathy and a non-judgemental stance are seen as important enablers in facilitating a specific outcome. Within this paradigm, the relationship is not treated as therapeutic, as the focus is on the *result* of therapy or improvement (O'Brien and Houston 2013). Here, the therapist's 'role' in cognitive–behavioural therapy (CBT) might be characterised as the 'pragmatic instructor' (Cromby et al. 2013: 174).

The psychoanalytical paradigm

In psychoanalysis, the core of the self is seen as an internalised dynamic constellation of the early family group. The therapeutic relationship in psychoanalysis is therefore central to the work. Freud (1926) conceptualised one facet of this relationship as *transference*. When emotions, behaviours and the like relating to childhood experiences are redirected and relocated onto a substitute, namely, the therapist, this is said to be transference. Transference is a projection; however, it only occurs within the therapeutic relationship – that is, between client and therapist. The client may feel, for example, ambivalence, attraction, repulsion or other relational feelings from the therapist who has been *put in the place of* an important figure from their childhood past – usually the mother or father. This redirection of feelings onto a third person is an 'unconscious' process. One of the intentions of psychoanalysis is to make the unconscious conscious. Therefore, the aim of psychoanalytical counselling and therapy is to foster a transferential relationship whereby the therapist can bring elements of the unconscious into consciousness, for example, through offering a transference interpretation. *Countertransference*, on the other hand, is the therapist's own response to the client's transference – the unconscious conflicts that have not yet been resolved that may be triggered in the interplay with the client. If these unconscious conflicts remain so, this can have an adverse effect on the work but with regular therapy the analyst can address them. Alternatively, countertransference can help the therapist have an immediate experience of what the client is experiencing (O'Brien and Houston 2013).

It is important to articulate that inherent in this conceptualisation is the assumption of two subjects, client and therapist, as two distinct entities. Also crucial to this understanding is the therapist's capacity to distinguish between their own feelings and those of the client. This stands in direct opposition to a phenomenological conceptualisation of the self as co-constituted and co-created *in-relation-to* another. The therapist's role in psychoanalysis might be characterised as the 'calm parent' (Cromby et al. 2013: 174).

The person-centred paradigm

From a humanistic, specifically person-centred perspective, the self is developed through interactions with others, principally through positive regard. Furthermore, the self is seen as possessing a self-actualising tendency, which with the right conditions, moves towards fulfilment and peak experiences. Rogers spent his career developing how the therapist can convey love to a client. It has been suggested that:

> by 'love' Rogers meant that which the Greeks name 'agape'. Greek philosophy distinguished between two kinds of love, Eros and agape. Eros is characterised by the desire for something that will fulfil the lover. It includes the wish to possess the beloved object or person. Agape, on the other hand, is characterised by the desire to fulfil the beloved. It demands nothing in return and wants only the growth and fulfilment of the loved one. Agape is a strengthening love, a love that, by definition, does not burden or oblige the loved one.
> (Kahn 1991, cited in O'Brien and Houston 2013: 141–2)

Rogers asserted that a therapist can communicate this love to the client through three facilitative conditions: empathy, congruence and unconditional positive regard. From this perspective, then, the focus is not on addressing schemas or working with transference as it is in cognitive–behavioural conceptualisations or psychoanalysis, as aforementioned; instead, the focus is on embodying and convening certain qualities. The humanistic therapist might be characterised as the 'honest friend' (Cromby et al. 2013: 174).

The existential-phenomenological paradigm

Within many strands of existentialism, the traditional notion of the 'self' is called into question and the concept of a fixed *model* of personality (as an entity or substance) is critiqued, in favour of a constant *state-of-becoming* through relational processes. Perspectives on existential therapy differ; however, it has been suggested that by adopting a specific attitude, which includes acknowledging one's own presuppositions, working with immediacy in a specific way and focusing on description, the intersubjective nature of the encounter is given primacy. In other words, the existential therapist intends to bracket their own assumptions, prioritise the present as it is being experienced by the client in relationship with the therapist, and prioritise description (as opposed to interpretation). It is through this endeavour that an attempt is made by the therapist to adopt a stance towards the therapeutic relationship that is sensitive to and works with relational dynamics. Rather than being a passive observer or a neutral entity, the therapist uses their subjectivity in the work as,

> the existential psychotherapist is implicated via the inquiry in a way that the encounter between therapist and client, while undeniably focused upon the client, is, nonetheless, mutually revelatory. For both client and therapist, the encounter permits a conscious reflection of 'this is what and how it is to be who I am being in this relation'.
>
> (Spinelli 2006: 313)

The relationship that brings our experience into being from the perspective of an existential therapist is co-constructed. The client's relational matrix and co-constituted meaning-making systems are present in the way therapist and client come together. Because the 'self' is not a static, fixed entity, the therapeutic relationship is a given and not something that needs to be *discovered*. However, through the therapist's attempt to enter the client's lived experience, they can attend to the way the client finds themselves in the world and the meaning they have created therein. The existential therapist might be characterised as a fellow wonderer.

Attachment theory

Attachment theory is often integrated into other modalities, however, more recently it has been treated as a stand-alone paradigm. Evidence demonstrates that humans are social beings and the kind of relationships our caregivers provide has a substantial impact on how we understand the world and how we find ourselves responding to it. Attachment theorists argue that interpersonal experiences, primarily in childhood, affect expectations and beliefs about self, others and relationships. Moreover, the quality of the child's relationship with their primary caregiver/s has a direct impact on the type of attachment style that child will have as an adult. Bowlby (1969) argued children's attachment to their primary caregiver(s) directly impacts on their social skills, cognitive growth and emotional development. Specifically, this attachment was said to be influenced by the caregiver's presence or absence, proximity (in terms of intimacy) and attunement to the infant's needs. Where behaviour theorists had claimed the infant's proximity seeking was purely physical (e.g. wanting to be fed), Bowlby's theory emphasises the psychological and interpersonal aspects of

Figure 5.1 Attachment styles

relationships. This, he argued, is fundamental to survival and can be seen within an evolutionary context (Bowlby 1969).

Three major attachment styles were identified: secure, insecure–ambivalent and insecure–avoidant (Ainsworth et al. 1978) (Figure 5.1). The securely attached infant has caregivers who are attuned (sensitive, consistent and containing) and develops into an adult with a strong sense of self, comfortable with intimacy and able to compromise as a response to conflict. The infant with caregivers who are sometimes sensitive and sometimes neglectful, not always responding to the child's needs, develop into an adult with an insecure–ambivalent attachment style: they are self-critical, insecure, approval-seeking, fear-rejecting, exhibit desire-excessive intimacy and, in relation to conflict, are demanding and dominating. They are entangled with their past attachment figures, often still angry with them. The infant with caregivers who are distant and disengaged, discourage crying and encourage independence develop an attachment style characterised as insecure–avoidant. They believe their needs will not be met, avoid intimacy and are uncomfortable exploring difficult thoughts and feelings. They develop a position that leans towards emotional self-reliance and separateness.

Neurobiological evidence suggests attachment processes are linked with the capacity for mentalisation or reflexivity (i.e. the ability to imagine mental states of self and others) (Fonagy et al. 2002). While primacy was given to cognition, contemporary attachment theorists argue this is not the whole story. Although an emphasis on attachment and reflective capacity is still relevant, the nature and function of the attachment relationship are more far-reaching than originally thought. It is argued that attachment theory would be more adequately described as *regulation theory*. Evidence suggests there are implications for the way regulation takes place at a physical and experiential level: 'affective bodily-based processes, interactive regulation, early experience-dependent brain maturation, stress, and nonconscious relational transactions' (Schore and Schore 2007: 9). In fact, early attachment experiences not only affect one's capacity to regulate and mentalise – the quality of relationship we have with our main caregivers impacts on our genes and the way in which our brains develop (Fonagy and Target 2005). There is also significant evidence to suggest our brains are social beings – neuroplasticity of the brain demonstrates that the way we interact with the environment has a direct impact on neural networks and therefore our meaning-making strategies and regulatory systems. Thus, from an attachment perspective, the self is not static and is constantly being affected, to varying degrees, by the environment.

If the 'self' is fluid, influenced by the environment and particularly the experiences of close and important relationships, the implications for therapy are far-reaching. From this perspective, the ways we learn to relate with others and regulate our own emotions are types of adjustments or ways of coping. By providing a different kind of relationship in therapy, a client's expectations, biases and usual ways of being can be challenged. It has been argued that this kind of modification, while slow, is possible. Cozolino posits that if we are to assume that the function of attachment schemas is to operate as strategies to assist us in responding to the relationships in our surroundings, therapy's goal is to provide a setting whereby the client can feel 'safe' (which includes the absence of stress signals sent to the amygdala). Cozolino also claims that it takes an average of five years for someone who is insecurely attached to become securely attached, if they experience 'safety' with a securely attached person. He also posits that secure attachment is less susceptible to adjustment (in comparison with insecure attachment). Self-reflection, he argues, is key to instigating this change: 'thus, the powerful shaping of early childhood can be modified through personal relationships, psychotherapy, and/or experiences that increase self-awareness' (2016: 108–9).

Being aware of attachment styles, both our own and those of the client, can support our formulation and conceptualisation of the therapeutic relationship. Moreover, providing a secure attachment may be useful for the client to gain a different relational experience. Within the context of this relationship, according to attachment theorists, the emphasis should be on specific affective conditions and responses, namely, those ordinarily associated with primary states. These can be understood as 'dysregulated right brain "primitive affects" – such as shame, disgust, elation, excitement, terror, rage, and hopeless despair' (Schore 2003: 280). The way in which such affects are triggered and regulated is as much a conceptual as an embodied response and therefore, when faced with navigating relational dynamics, one's experience is very much shaped by these. Cozolino (2016) asserts that an individual may want to be intimate in a relationship with someone, but their stress response is triggered by their association with difficult past relationships. This stress response is not only emotional – it is physical.

Exploring a client's fear and other primitive affects is, then, an important part of the work. Attuning to the client's regulation and dysregulation cycles has implications not only for their meaning-making structures but also for the neurobiology that impacts upon, and is informed by, sensory experiences. Primed by early life experiences, our clients may expect, or perhaps more aptly *fear*, that we will be criticising, blaming, judging, smothering, ignoring, rejecting, or shaming. Through not re-enacting this and subverting such expectations, as well as through offering the opportunity to learn how to downregulate anxiety and develop self-reflective capacities (including how behaviour might create situations that enforce these fears), our clients might have different relational experiences – ones where they are not constantly surviving adult relationships in much the same way they may have survived early primary attachments. Furthermore, the therapist should be aware of those 'strategies of emotional regulation for avoiding, minimizing, or converting affects that are too difficult to handle' (Schore 2003: 280). Through carefully attending to such aversions, the therapist may be able to better understand how much the client can bear and what they feel most overwhelmed by. Contemporary attachment approaches emphasise that a client's response to the therapist does not function in isolation or from a single direction (Schore 2011) but rather is a 'bidirectional process' whereby both therapist and client are emotionally engaged (Schore 2003). Thus, it is significant that the therapist acknowledges themselves as an active agent within the therapeutic relationship.

Based on this, attachment theorists make explicit how the interpersonal capacity of the therapist can come into being within the therapy in a meaningful and useful way. This is largely through the therapeutic alliance, multi-level communication, addressing suppositions and understanding the client's feelings; in other words:

> central to clinical expertise is interpersonal skill, which is manifested in forming a therapeutic relationship, encoding and decoding verbal and nonverbal responses, creating realistic but positive expectations, and responding empathically to the patient's explicit and implicit experiences and concerns.
>
> (APA Presidential Task Force on Evidence-based Practice 2006: 277)

Here, the 'self' is not a static, fixed concept but rather comes into being through a complex matrix of environmental, physiological and meaning-making systems. From an attachment theorist's vantage point, the therapist's way of being, their relational style and their capacity for self-reflection are at the heart of therapy. Thus, from an attachment perspective, the therapist might be characterised as the attuned other.

The therapeutic relationship at the core of integration

Each therapeutic paradigm posits its own conceptualisation of the self and therefore the self-in-relation. Implicit within these notions are ontological and epistemological assumptions. It is often argued within integrative discourses that across paradigms, the therapeutic relationship is the common factor and therefore a point of convergence. From this standpoint, if one were to compare the different paradigms and the various strands therein, there would be a juncture at which they all meet: the relationship. The fact that therapist and client are in-relation-to one another enables the therapy to come to fruition, for without that relationship the venture would not exist. In this sense, the relationship is very much at the core of integration, just as it is at the core of the therapeutic endeavour, to a greater or lesser extent, in each psychological approach. Yet how the therapy comes to fruition, or rather the conditions under which it operates, is a different matter to the philosophical assumptions therein.

Epistemology of the therapeutic relationship

From an *objectivist epistemology*, reality exists outside of consciousness and therefore the relationship is a conduit through which consciousness or the subject aims to arrive at a given point with certitude. The relationship here might be characterised by action. Arguably, it is also prone to dichotomies, which might be limiting for the therapy. In CBT, for example, if self is formed through schemas and these schemas have traceable relationships that can be characterised through truth claims, which are formulated in binary associations or continuums of diametrically opposed properties, it follows that the therapist navigates on the basis of these properties and therefore the primary relationship is beholden to this.

A *constructivist epistemology* denotes that knowledge cannot be separated from its context, whether historical, cultural or social. To adopt such a stance in therapy means therapists do not syphon off aspects of clients at the expense of understanding the complex myriad ways experience can materialise. This involves an appreciation of the *gestalt*. Driver, Crawford and Stewart assert that our senses are only one aspect of being and all of these other facets must also be acknowledged in the therapy – both in our clients and in the relationship with clients:

> Our senses, as the medieval tapestries depict, are part of our being but if we take the concept 'being of being' to its broadest meaning it is clear that it must be the sum of many parts; parts which include our physical, emotional, affective and relational selves and our states of mind as well as our realities and limitations. Within the therapeutic relationship we, as therapists, need to aim to understand the broader warp and weft of the internal world of the other as well as the intricacies of the individual's pattern of relating.
>
> (2013: 5)

Role of the therapeutic relationship

For the Heideggerian existential therapist, the relationship is *a priori*. It is the way that the therapist and client come into being. From a postmodern perspective, as a different example, the therapist might accept that the relationship is chaotic, not necessarily respond in the way the client wants and not aim for a specific endpoint, for instance, in terms of an overarching theory of health, wellness or optimal way of being. This approach would set itself apart from a person-centric or ego-centric vantage point. (Loewenthal 2016).

Arguably, in practice, the relationship is a common factor across various models of therapeutic integration in so far as it establishes the format of the therapy and defines the necessary components of the practice – namely, that there is both a client and a therapist and they engage in some kind of relationship and refer to this as 'therapy'. However, the way in which the premise of that relationship is constituted depends on the philosophical underpinnings of the theorist, or the specific branch of their approach, rather than the therapeutic modality as a whole. Having said that, it is interesting to note that 'when bonafied therapies are compared with each other, they are usually found to be about equivalent in efficacy' (Cooper 2008: 59). If efficacy is the barometer we want to use to view the therapeutic endeavour and questions of how this is measured are temporarily suspended, then, seemingly, the approaches are equivalent. However, if we are to engage with the issue of measurement, one criticism is that within approaches the underlying philosophies can differ and so too can the way the therapist understands these, making it hard to measure efficacy by comparing paradigms. For example, we might create a standardised measurement to test for success in existential therapy, but some existential therapists contest the notion of measuring efficacy through standardised measurements. As different existential therapists interpret the therapy differently and therefore their practice varies (deciding which theories they might draw on for the interventions they might make), it makes it difficult to make any generalised claims about existential therapy as a paradigm, say, for example, in comparison with CBT.

Conclusion

This chapter has referred to the relationship between therapist and client. However, it is worth noting the array of variations within this – there may be more than one client, for example (e.g. in family or couples therapy). This chapter has explored the dyadic relationship between therapist and client. However, it is worth noting the array of variations within this (e.g. family or couples' therapy). Within any of the different relational configuration between therapist and client/s in the room (if indeed a room is where the therapy is taking place), interpersonal dynamics are key (Lapworth and Sills 2010).

This chapter has focused on the theoretical implications and underpinnings of the therapeutic relationship at the core of integration rather than its application to the clinical setting. It has summarised how the self is conceptualised within the major therapeutic paradigms, including contemporary neurobiological and psychological research, and the implications this might have for the therapeutic relationship. How the therapist conceptualises the relationship and the aim of their engagement or positioning within it are framed within a theoretical standpoint. I would argue that to place the therapeutic relationship at the core of integration, the therapist must do so with an understanding of the philosophical underpinnings of that paradigm so that they are clear about their position in terms of how it constitutes ways of relating with clients and the interventions that follow.

References

Aho, K.A. (2009) *Heidegger's Neglect of the Body*. New York: SUNY Press.

Ainsworth, M., Blehar, M., Waters, E. and Wall, S. (1978) *Patterns of Attachment: A Psychological Study of the Strange Situation*. Hillsdale, NJ: Erlbaum.

APA Presidential Task Force on Evidence-Based Practice (2006) Evidence-based practice in psychology. *American Psychologist*, 61: 271–85.

American Psychological Association (2013) *Diagnostic and Statistical Manual for Mental Disorders* (5th edn). Arlington, VA: American Psychological Publishing.

Berger, A. (2013) Semiotics and society. *Society*, 51(1): 22–6.

Bowlby, J. (1969) *Attachment and Loss*. Vol. 1: *Attachment*. New York: Basic Books.

Burr, V. (2015) *Social Constructionism* (3rd edn). Hove: Routledge.

Cooper, M. (2008) *Essential Research Findings in Counselling and Psychotherapy: The Facts Are Friendly*. London: SAGE.

Cozolino, L. (2016) *Why Therapy Works: Using Our Minds to Change Our Brains*. London: W.W. Norton.

Craig, E. and Craig, E. (2000) *Concise Routledge Encyclopedia of Philosophy*. London: Routledge.

Cromby, J., Harper, D. and Reavey, P. (2013) *Psychology, Mental Health and Distress*. Basingstoke: Palgrave Macmillan.

Crotty, M. (2015) *The Foundations of Social Research*. London: SAGE.

Davis, T. (2009) Conceptualizing psychiatric disorders using 'four D's' of diagnosis. *The Internet Journal of Psychiatry*, 1(1).

Driver, C., Crawford, S. and Stewart, J. (2013) *Being and Relating in Psychotherapy: Ontology and Therapeutic Practice*. New York: Palgrave Macmillan.

Finlay, L. (2011) *Phenomenology for Therapists: Researching the Lived World*. Oxford: Wiley-Blackwell.

Fonagy, P., Gergely, G., Jurist, E.L. and Target, M. (2002) *Affect Regulation, Mentalization and the Development of the Self*. New York: Other Press.

Fonagy, P. and Target, M. (2005) Bridging the transmission gap: An end to an important mystery of attachment research? *Attachment & Human Development*, 7: 333–43.

Freud, S. (1959 [1926]) Inhibitions, symptoms and anxiety. In J. Strachey (ed., trans.), *The Standard Edition of the Complete Psychological Works of Sigmund Freud*, vol. 20 (pp. 77–175). London: Hogarth Press.

Gergen, K.J. (1973) Social psychology as history. *Journal of Personality and Social Psychology*, 2(2): 309–20.

Heidegger, M. (1962) *Being and Time*. New York: HarperOne.

Heidegger, M. (2002) *The Essence of Truth: On Plato's Cave Allegory and Theaetetus*. London: Bloomsbury.

Jameson, F. (1992) *Postmodernism: Or, the Cultural Logic of Late Capitalism*. Durham, NC: Duke University Press.

Kaufer, S. and Chemero, A. (2015) *Phenomenology: An Introduction*. Cambridge: Polity Press.

Lacan, J. (1998) *The Seminars of Jacques Lacan: The Four Fundamental Concepts of Psychoanalysis (Book XI)*. London: W.W. Norton.

Lacan, J. (2001) *Ecrits*. A. Sheridan, trans. London: Routledge.

Lapworth, P. and Sills, C. (2010) *Integration in Counselling and Psychotherapy: Developing a Personal Approach* (2nd edn). London: SAGE.

Lemma, A. (2008) *Introduction to Psychopathology*. London: SAGE.

Loewenthal, D. (2016) *Existential Psychotherapy and Counselling after Postmodernism: The Selected Works of Del Loewenthal*. London: Routledge.

Lyotard, J-F. (1986) *The Postmodern Condition: A Report on Knowledge*. Manchester: Manchester University Press.

MacNamee, S. and Gergen, K. (1992) *Therapy as Social Construction*. London: SAGE.

Moran, D. (2000) *Introduction to Phenomenology*. London: Routledge.

Moran, D. and Mooney, T. (eds) (2002) *The Phenomenology Reader*. London: Routledge.

O'Brien, M. and Houston, G. (2013) *Integrative Therapy* (2nd edn). London: SAGE.

Schore, A.N. (2003) *Affect Regulation and the Repair of the Self*. New York: W.W. Norton.

Schore, A.N. (2011) *The Science of the Art of Psychotherapy*. London: W.W. Norton.

Schore, J.R. and Schore, A.N. (2007) Modern attachment theory: The central role of affect regulation in development and treatment. *Clinical Social Work Journal*, 36(1): 9–20.

Spinelli, E. (2005) *The Interpreted World: An Introduction to Phenomenological Psychology*. London: SAGE.

Spinelli, E. (2006) Existential psychotherapy: An introductory overview. *Análes Psicológica*, 24(3): 311–21.

Stolorow, R.D. and Atwood, G.E. (1992) *Contexts of Being: The Intersubjective Foundations of Psychological Life*. New York: Routledge.

Valle, R.S., King, M. and Halling, S. (1989) An introduction to existential–phenomenological thought in psychology. In R.S. Valle and S. Halling (eds) *Existential–Phenomenological Perspectives in Psychology: Exploring the Breadth of Human Experience*. London: Plenum Press.

White, A. (2015) *Going Mad to Stay Sane*. London: Gerald Duckworth & Co.

6   Postmodern integration

Claire Marshall

Introduction

Chapter 5 discussed the therapeutic relationship by drawing on its philosophical underpinnings and relational implications. This chapter will explore postmodernism within a historical context, followed by the implications for the present day. There will be an analysis of postmodernism, subjectivity and clinical work.

It is perhaps noteworthy to add my own views on postmodern integration within therapy. I align myself with the value base of counselling psychology, which emphasises a clear understanding of its philosophical underpinnings. In order to do this justice, I believe it is necessary to draw upon the discipline of philosophy to promote this clarity of understanding. I am also of the view that counselling psychology, rather than espousing any particular claims rigidly, should adopt a critical, reflexive and philosophically informed position. Finally, I take the view that in order to be coherent when integrating psychological theory, the theories being integrated should be aligned in terms of their ontological and epistemological assumptions. If one modality proposes truth is constructed and another implies it can be discovered, these will be fundamentally different and, I argue, incompatible – from conceptualisation to practice. As we will explore in this chapter, there are few psychological approaches that share the same ontological and epistemological underpinnings inherent in postmodernism, making a coherent postmodern integrative approach in psychology problematic. In the absence of a coherent integrative approach, the chapter will explore what it might mean to draw upon postmodern theory to inform one's work.

A brief history of knowledge: postmodernism in context

Historical pattern finding is a way to contextualise contemporary discourse. Science is a paradigm wholly taken for granted in its current form, yet previously the types of knowledge and indeed the people who contributed to this knowledge were eclectic. Fara posits that:

Now that science dominates the world, it is hard to believe that only two hundred years ago, the word 'scientist' had not even been invented. Over the past few millennia, many people – Babylonians and Chinese, farmers and navigators, colonizers and slaves, miners and monks, Muslims and Christians, astrophysicists and biochemists – have contributed towards building up our current understanding of the cosmos. Like human societies, knowledge is never definitively fixed, but is constantly changing as old categories dissolve and new ones coalesce.

(2010: 430)

What we should take from Fara's analysis is that an examination of history suggests there is no homogeneous, 'deterministic' order, rather a chaotic semblance of many intervening, heterogeneous factors. Furthermore, it tells us that throughout the course of history, well-being or contentment has not featured. As Harari wrote:

The dynamics of history are not directed towards enhancing human well-being. There is no basis for thinking that the most successful cultures in history are necessarily the best ones for *Homo sapiens*. Like evolution, history disregards the happiness of individual organisms.

(2011: 271)

That we might call into question the authority of truth, in particular scientific truth, or see history as only one way of organising events, thus also calling into question our spatial-temporal markers, are characteristically postmodern lenses. (This will be explored further later in the chapter.) Now, we will trace history (in order of ascension) so that postmodernism can be seen in context.

Prehistory and ancient civilisations

Prehistory loosely refers to the time before written accounts were discovered. It is divided into three eras: the Stone Age, the Bronze Age and the Iron Age. These were characterised by advances in knowledge of farming, mining, building and cooking. Religion was the primary authority in the pursuit of knowledge and centred upon metaphysics and morality, the objectives being to assist humans to reconcile and evolve (van Doren 1991). The earliest recorded monarchs and first heroes celebrated were a mixture of humans and 'gods' (Bauer 2007). In ancient China, for example, emphasis was placed on self-development, thought to be achieved through social interactions, according to Confucius's theory (van Doren 1991). An alternate system of belief proposed by Lao-Tzu promoted aligning oneself with nature through a comprehension of the 'tao' or 'way', which might be understood as an underlying unity to all things and the unlimited potential energy of the cosmos (Guignon 1999). An alternative system of belief is that of Buddhism, which promoted the concept of a non-enduring self and suffering as our underlying state

(Kohn 1991). Each moment was here seen as an utterly new existence, influenced by all other moments, and suffering was said to cease with our kinship to earthly matter. A further example might come from ancient India, where the Vedas promoted a cyclical view of the cosmos in which life, death and rebirth were continuous. An individual's actions were considered in light of a mechanism of cosmic justice and suffering was perceived as a spiritually necessary part of life. Wisdom was thought to be attained through the recognition that everything is suffering. There was an understanding that everything, including oneself, is part of a much larger absolute. A final example might be the ancient Egyptians, who were polytheistic: they thought various deities controlled nature with many complex rituals, believing offerings preserved the divine order. They conceded that change in and of itself, or for the sake of change, was unwarranted (van Doren 1991). These ancient societies established elaborate understandings of experience that situated humans within a much larger universal context. In doing so, the subject's relative insignificance was highlighted.

The ancient Greeks

The ancient Greeks are credited with inventing the organisation of knowledge, consolidating and dividing it into discrete schools. The first recognised Greek philosophers, in the sixth century BCE, began what is referred to as 'Western philosophy'. Homer's (2017) great epic, the *Iliad*, suggested there is no single order determining the outcome of an event or providing an overarching reason as explanation. Thales of Miletus (c. 624–546 BCE) predicted the first sun eclipse and proposed that water is the first principle of nature, in the sense that all things are products of water and return to being water. Pythagoras (c. 570–495 BCE) proposed numbers could be treated as objects: because there are irrational numbers, he concluded there must be an equivalent irrational force in nature. Democritus (c. 460–370 BCE) argued there are only atoms, aggregates of atoms and the void. For Democritus, in this type of radical materialism, there is no divinely ordained order although things may appear orderly in an atomist mereological framework.

Perhaps the best-known figure in this tradition is Socrates (c. 470–399 BCE), who met everyday people in the marketplace and engaged them in dialogue. He was known for engaging people with critical thinking via a question and answer method known as the *elenchus*, especially on matters of ethics. Plato (c. 428–347 BCE) revered Socrates. Plato can be read as proposing that the fundamental nature of the cosmos is, in some sense, the universal essence of particular objects. Finally, Aristotle (c. 384–322 BCE), Plato's pupil, distinguished between 'form' (purposeful shape) and 'matter' (the stuff out of which composite substances – the objects we experience – are made), arguing matter is potentiality that is actualised by taking on various forms to create composite substances. Neither form nor matter exist independently. Aristotle argued that matter is intelligible to humans through its formal essential aspect only (van Doren 1991).

The Middle Ages/the Dark Ages/the Age of Faith

From the fifth to the fifteenth centuries AD, drawing upon Greek or Western philosophy, the Romans developed the practical application of knowledge, increasing its accessibility to wider audiences. Emperors were worshipped beside gods and there was much interest in entertainment and little in scientific advancements. Circa AD 410, the invading barbarian army began attacks on Roman settlements and the fall of the Roman Empire began. The economic and social unity that had previously stood was forced to fragment and existence consisted of surviving in a state of poverty and anarchy.

The Roman Empire had been pagan, worshipping deities with rituals focusing on nature and agriculture. However, the Emperor Constantine enforced a new religion: Christianity. When Rome was destroyed and bleak, its people looked for someone or something to hold responsible and pointed the finger at Christians for having cast out pagan gods, destroying their places of worship. The Christians retorted; Augustine of Hippo (354–430) argued the destruction of Rome was a prerequisite to the creation of an environment more congruent with the will of God – a 'city of God'. This environment, a metaphorical place without the distraction of earthly luxuries, was where the Christian deity could be devotedly experienced should one have faith and where the truth of the Christian faith would be revealed (van Doren 1991). Augustine described a transcendent order. His Neoplatonic interpretation emphasised a reality beyond this earthly realm. The underlying assumption of this vantage point was that knowledge, or an awareness of certain and reliable truths, is informed by God and obtainable through reason and faith rather than merely sense experience (Clark 2000). This era was one filled with adversity, as people struggled for basic needs such as food and security against looters and bandits. As society was chaotic and fragmented, the populace adopted a narrative, perhaps in the hope that it would restore some order, and hence became engrossed with the in-vogue institution: religion. Christian architecture, such as Gothic cathedrals, was fashioned and great literary works were written, including by Chaucer (2005) and Dante (2012). Jewish, Arabic and Latin scholars translated the great works by the ancient Greeks, which had previously been in Arabic, into Latin (only later was the original Greek found).

The Renaissance

During the European Renaissance that followed, America was 'discovered', the oceans were understood as being interrelated and, while there was world trade prior to the Renaissance, especially around the Mediterranean and Asia, shipbuilding in the Renaissance acted as a major catalyst at this time, and thus world trade was given a new lease of life. Art also played a key role in this period. Up until then, paintings had been created to capture the world from God's view. During the Renaissance, art developed to instead portray scenes of everyday life from the perspective of humans. There was a general leaning away from highbrow ponderings of theosophical dilemmas towards more generalised, accessible accomplishments by people who were not necessarily experts.

The Enlightenment/the Age of Reason

Aristocratic leaders of the clergy had governed the lower classes in a top-down relationship, which was challenged in the era that followed – namely, the seventeenth and eighteenth centuries. Rather than citizens being ruled by elite representatives of religious paradigms, science proposed an alternative: that reason has the legitimacy and authority of objective truth (Porter 2001). There were many great contributions to this revolutionary paradigm. Francis Bacon, first Viscount St Alban (1561–1626) conceded that scientific experiments should be conducted to amass information, make cautious and modest observations, and thus draw broader conclusions (Fara 2009). Bacon also argued, before proceeding with his suggested inductive method (which he referred to as the 'new instrument'), that it was essential to create the necessary conditions for the researcher by a sort of *cleansing-through-becoming-aware-of* what he termed 'idols of the mind'. An idol represents something or someone who is revered with blind devotion and is often without substance.

Thomas Hobbes (1588–1679) argued society is constructed similarly to how the individual functions, in that both are in pursuit of rational, strategic self-interest. Conversely, in the same period but later, Jean-Jacques Rousseau (1712–1778) posited that individuals in the state of nature do not always act in their own self-interest, to the detriment of others, but have an intrinsic *pitié* or empathic pity for others (Rousseau 1973).

René Descartes (1596–1650) put forward the much-cited aphorism, *I think, therefore I am* (Descartes 2007). Descartes proposed a methodology for grounding epistemology; he sought to remove everything that could be doubted so that we might arrive at something that cannot be doubted and then to rebuild on that secure epistemic footing – including phenomena in the epistemic mix. He did this so that we could then consider phenomena (as well as the truths of religion and metaphysics) in a more epistemically respectable light. As a natural philosopher and a metaphysician, he had a vested interest in us not viewing phenomena as susceptible to extreme scepticism. Descartes claimed that the essence of material things (or 'body') is spatially extended matter; the essence of the self is as a thinking thing; and the essence of the world, in the sense of where all things come from, is God.

Another key figure of the Enlightenment era was Isaac Newton (1643–1727), who combined two types of ancient order: the Platonic notion of an order to social reality and Democritus' atomism. By combining these two positions, Newton argued atoms in the void are indelible through mathematics (Newton 2016). He posited that space is infinite and objective ('absolute space'), an emanative effect of God, mechanistic, and subject to empirical observation and experiment.

Also in this era, Immanuel Kant (1724–1804) proposed that by removing the hierarchical institution of the church, the minds of people would be liberated for free, independent thought (Kant 2009).

Modernism

Modernism refers to a period in the late nineteenth and early twentieth century. While as with any era there are differing positions often grouped together to represent one school of thought, it could be argued that the modernist project was exploratory and explanatory. Modernist assumptions have been articulated in the following way: 'the desire to explore the world (including humanity) . . . on the foundation of rationality alone . . . to move beyond . . . dependency on myths and stories to explain the world' (Grenz 1996: 44).

Theorists associated with this era affirmed human beings' power to create, improve and reshape the environment with the aid of scientific knowledge and technology. The Industrial Revolution took hold, provoking optimism in technology as a productive force. Commerce began to thrive and reading materials were bought by the general literate public. A revolt developed against what was viewed as the explanatory, closed-system, linear, dichotomous ideals of the previous eras. Modernists were subversive, questioning traditional values such as sexuality and religion but nonetheless they still generally based their principles of knowledge acquisition on hierarchical schemas arrived at through methodological, disciplined inquiry governed by rationality and logic. However, this movement contributed to the rewriting of traditionally accepted perceptions of how humans are situated in the world. A call for the re-examination of every aspect of existence served a specific aim: to identify barriers in the way of progress. In direct opposition to many of the ancient societies, new was always seen as superior. Charles Darwin (1809–1882) proposed the theory of natural selection to explain the progression of human evolution from animal species. Karl Marx (1818–1883) called into question the dividing class and socioeconomic structures that organised humanity, proposing communism to replace capitalism.

Postmodernism

What followed was a movement away from scientific rationality, towards deconstruction and critique. Postmodernism, as the name suggests, developed from modernism. It is difficult to pinpoint where the postmodern 'era' began and ended, or even identify it as a predominant movement, bearing in mind that in the twenty-first century dominant discourses in science (including psychology) in the West are still largely aligned with modernist values and assumptions. As is the case with all the historical periods from ancient civilisations to recent times, theorists are often in disagreement about particular details but united through the assumptions underpinning their positions. Postmodernism is no exception. Postmodern theory spans across disciplines – art, architecture, fashion, philosophy, critical theory, psychology – while sharing a common core.

Some postmodern thinkers might argue that when considering the question of what it means to be human, it is important to acknowledge our experience as situated within the myths, language and normative values of our given context. Postmodernists seek to deconstruct concepts claiming to offer total explanations of human experience, arguing against such reductionism, and are generally curious about regional (rather than global) narratives and local societies and symbolic myths as they speak to a community's assumptions and principles. Postmodernism often seeks to critique or delegitimise the truth claims of master narratives, arguing that they perpetuate 'myths' that support particular relationships in society. As Grenz argued: 'These myths sustain social relations within the society and form the basis of its claim to legitimacy . . . Not only have master narratives lost their credibility, but the idea of a grand narrative itself is no longer credible' (1996: 44).

Furthermore, one of the 'grand narratives' often criticised by postmodern theorists is that of *science*. This is because of a fundamental conflict inherent within science: on the one hand, it draws on narrative in an act of knowledge production but, on the other, narrative accounts and stories are the resource that science can use to establish itself as an authority:

> According to the postmodern appraisal, science cannot achieve its goal of expelling myth from the realm of knowledge. In fact, science must inevitably turn to the very endeavour it seeks to explode – narrative – in order to legitimize its own enterprise.
>
> (Grenz 1996: 44–7)

This tendency has implications for the kinds of knowledge postmodern thinkers are concerned with as, rather than 'grand narratives', *local* narratives are of more interest. Such local narratives provide the possibility for individual and social identities to be shaped: 'their major concerns revolve around the process of fabricating stories that can define personal identity and give purpose and shape social existence' (Grenz 1996: 44).

From antiquity to modernity, there have been radical shifts influenced by a multitude of factors: sociological, technological and geo-political. From a postmodern position, our perspective on humans is not static but in a flux that can be characterised by a cataclysmic acceleration (McHale 2015). In the postmodern turn, we responded with inertia to the potency, catastrophe and destruction of the modernist era. From a postmodern perspective, the notion of temporality is challenged and our experience of continually recommencing in the present moment might be experienced as destabilising. Traditionally held conceptions are called into question, through an unravelling, shedding and dismembering of ideological discourses within grand narratives. Within a postmodern account, we have seen the disintegration of cultural normative values that once were tied by reoccurring, predictable routines. The postmodern era is therefore characterised by the 'dissolution of traditional forms of life, forms of life characterized by repetition, the cyclical reproduction of customs, habits and cherished assumptions across the generations' (McGuigan 1999: 97).

Postmodern thinkers are generally suspicious of global social narratives, unpack power relationships, and treat truth or untruth as one of many inaccurate binary dichotomies. Epistemologically, postmodernity is linked with a crisis of representation. Meaning-making is critiqued as being self-referential in that it begins to legitimate itself in an eternal present without past: 'our contemporary social system has lost its capacity to know its own past, has begun to live in "a perpetual present" without depth, definition, or secure identity' (Jameson 1988, cited in Connor 1997: 44).

There is a self-reflective chaos in postmodernism, inviting an engagement with a world that cannot be fathomed through representational truth-claims but rather experienced through a continual self-referential moment-to-moment, here-and-now, questioning and re-questioning. This continual questioning arguably leads to superficiality and indeterminacy. It is necessary to examine and critique the assumptions underlying representations that come into being within societies, as from a postmodern perspective, culture arises from discourse (Harari 2011).

In summary, continental postmodern theorists are antithetical to determinate, omnipotent tendencies, believing humans are *subject to*. The postmodernist deconstructs tacit value systems and recognises contextual issues, including the givens of existence, such as death. Postmodern theory also deconstructs through a lens of paradox and ambiguity, viewing the world as fluid and uncertain. Postmodernists question the utopian representation of progress (including technology and consumer societies) by appreciating both advantages and difficulties. Arguably, this process of deconstruction and appreciation of multiplicity is useful in that it extracts that which seeks to interfere with truth, laying it bare. As Bauman states:

> despite its appearances to the contrary it is not a 'destructive destruction' but a *constructive* one . . . the demolition uncovers *the truth of the truth*, truth as residing in the being itself and not in the violent acts performed upon it.
>
> (1992: ix)

Deconstructing the contemporary condition: global, local, technological and socio-political narratives

Postmodern theorists assert that new structures (including in literature, political discourse and thought in general) are necessary to compensate for what modernist theories lacked (Best and Kellner 1991). Arguably, in postmodern consumerist culture, the emphasis is often on the buying experience over the product itself, an obsession with the latest fads in food and dining, an indeterminacy between high and low art, and architecture aimed to subvert the homogenisation of difference. Abstraction, the questioning of experts, the promotion of popular culture, technological discoveries and the economic crisis have perhaps lent to the erosion of hierarchical structures, the feeling of insecurity and an atmosphere of risk (Smart 1993). The postmodern era also has seen rapid technological advances that are far-reaching and that, concurrently, destabilise what it means to be human. Rather than these technological advances, including in electronics, genetic engineering and atomic energy, being celebrated, some postmodern theorists argue there is a general uneasiness, suspicion and pessimism around technology – its potential threat is anxiety-provoking (Ezrahi et al. 1994). Perhaps this pessimism and suspicion are born from the ever-closing gap between the human and the technological space; from a robot in Saudi Arabia being given citizenship (Juma et al. 2018), to social media's intimate relationship with self- and identity-formation. It has been argued that:

> Electronic and digital technologies, with their immense information-processing, communicative and representational properties are not only significant ... from the point of view of political economy. They have come to mediate identity as well, producing metaphors of deconstruction and reconstruction of the self in the organism/machine interface.
>
> (Turkle 1997, cited in McGuigan 1999: 80)

In the postmodern era, political systems and ideologies have morphed and the power and authority held by governing bodies no longer imply the same meaning or weight. Questions prevailed, challenging previously held rigid constructs, including moral and physical truths. Visible in the dissonance between propositions made by government or media rhetoric and perceptions of the public, the individual is able to affect the community in new ways and is therefore, arguably, more self-determining. Through technology, communities on social media have the power to undermine the state by circulating information, exposing issues at speed. However, this self-determination does not necessarily lead to a sense of power. Growing population numbers and seemingly vast amounts of choices within a constricted capitalist framework render a sense of ineffectual individualistic impotence: 'Post modernity means ... a shopping mall overflowing with goods whose major use is the joy of purchasing them; and existence that feels like a life-long confinement to the shopping mall' (Bauman 1992: vii). The subject navigates through the contemporary context, which accentuates conformity within a framework of vast choice. Creativity might be stifled as the subject continually seeks to navigate the desires of the other – desires that are framed within the currency of economic institutions. Malpas argued:

> Capitalism marks the new globalized horizon of contemporary culture: there is no longer anywhere outside it where one can stand, no straightforward alternative to it that one can champion, and yet its effects must be resisted as they are potentially devastating – politically, socially, culturally and ecologically.
>
> (2005: 107–9)

Indeed, within the postmodern era: 'our lives continue to be lived ... in the shadows of the patched-up remains of medieval institutions (e.g. bank, church, state, university)'

(Smart 1997: 30). In the shadow of these remains, money lies at the epicentre and as science and technology embed deeper into the very fabric of society – personal and psychic spaces, myths and rituals, the practicalities of everyday life – all are imbued with this paradigmatic shift. It has been argued that the boundaries of technology carry risk as well as potential benefits and by appreciating the risks they carry, we are better able to critique technology and science. As Smart articulated:

> Dismantling or breaking up of the great peace or order which in turn creates a power vacuum and precipitates economic crisis . . . the collapse of the automobile industry, the proliferation of important goods, the growing foreign ownership of flagship industries and cooperations; the reality of fear and crime, violence, drugs and signs of increasing deprivation . . . We are living in a society that faces problems (as well as benefits) of technological development, for example 'gridlocks and malfunctions . . . production of poisonous and carcinogenic foods . . . and useless objects . . . deforestation . . . pollution of water, atmosphere, and vegetation, the extinction of animal species, and so on'.
>
> (1997: 30–1)

The postmodern condition is (or was) a state of continual renegotiation with an unstable and ever-changing environment that in turn feeds into and is shaped by human existence. The certitudes of past eras no longer hold true, and in their place stand suspicion and possibility.

Navigating the dialectics of objectivity and subjectivity: a postmodern (de)construction of self

Sigmund Freud asserted that the mind is characterised by an elemental configuration, which is open to the subject of study, understanding and alteration. His proposed method was talking therapy, based on an intricate conceptualisation of the nature of development, systems of personality and meaning processing. He argued there is an unconscious, which serves as a repository for human desires (Freud 1996). Freud also proposed a theory for human development that detailed a series of stages concerning sexual urges that, if not properly resolved, would cause difficulties later in life. However, through a process of analysis, a patient suffering from distress can be led back into childhood experiences, where the self was formed, leading to the resolution of these conflicts (Freud 2005). The implications of Freud's theories are numerous. According to Freud, humans are inherently incestuous, murderous and in a continual state of conflict of varying degrees. Freud's proposal that instinctual, pleasure-seeking drives are responsible for behaviour was ground-breaking (Bentall 2004). Freud studied medicine and later practised as a neurologist. His structural theories on human nature use the logic applied in mathematics, physics, chemistry and biology to understand human experience (Bateman and Holmes 1995). The implication is that objectivity is obtainable through adopting a vantage point negating our subjectivity. I would argue that Freud was a scientific materialist, believing the highest value is the intellect and rational thought. Freud had arguably proposed the existence of a stable, unitary self, evident in, for example, his single most enduring theory – that of the Id, Ego and Superego (see Watson 2014, for an alternative view). Modernist theorists, who stand at the cusp of postmodernism, including some feminist and postcolonial writers, call into question this notion of a unified subject. Authors placing the individual within a cultural-political context, including Hélène Cixous, propose that gender, which they view as an intrinsic part of the subject, is offered through binary, dichotomous categories. These, Cixous argues, elicit male domination; ergo, the experience of females is narrated through a frame of subordination. As an alternative, Cixous (1975) advocates a bisexual conceptualisation of identity that favours transformation and diffusion.

Critical theorists call into question the propensity to place certain countries and continents at the heart of what is posited as *legitimate* discourse. It has been argued that this serves a function, namely, if marginalised groups (including those organised around 'race' categories) are positioned in opposition to those who have manoeuvred into a central space, the very articulation of their identity is often filtered through this central space. The identification and articulation of self–other constructions of 'marginalised' groups by 'mainstream' members of society serve to sustain grand narratives. Arguably, 'existential dependence upon the forms of the Other characterises racial stereotyping as a fetishistic projection of those things which are disavowed by the colonial self' (Connor 1997: 265). Through defining the 'Other', the status quo is sustained – including gendered and racialised constructions of the subject. Moreover, all that cannot be 'owned' is displaced onto the Other. Dichotomous and binary definitions of legitimacy, mainstream and marginalisation used to create identities reinforce the very power structures they critique (Connor 1997).

Some postmodern theorists critique metanarratives, including feminism and anti-colonialism, instead focusing on smaller, multiple narratives (Kottiswari 2008). Within this reconceptualisation, the very notion of identity itself is critiqued for being imbued with the assumptions of the paradigm from which it arose. As Skeggs argued:

> Identity is just one way of thinking personhood, a way that is particularly Western and particularly useful for global capitalism, with a long history through concepts of interest (Adam Smith, 1776/1970), rationality, individuality, self, character, and personality. Identity is one modern variant of speaking personhood that replies upon assumptions about and desires for coherence and completeness. Identity is simultaneously a category, a social position, and an affect.

> (2008: 11)

In *The Metamorphosis*, Franz Kafka, often associated with postmodernism, portrayed what can be understood as the main character's transformative journey from human into insect. His physical appearance seems to become an obstacle preventing him from relating with his family and disrupts the routine of work and financial provision – highlighting the perils of diminishing relationships to revenue and resources. Kafka called into question the notion of linear time as well as engaging with the notion of absurdity. His work renders usual human limitations obsolete and thus offers a framework for a much more fluid notion of personhood (Kafka 2016).

Jean Baudrillard examined the value of objects in terms of exchange and problematised the notion of usefulness and need. He argued that need is maintained via ideology and can only be understood through studying humankind (Baudrillard 1994). Arguably, 'human beings do not search for happiness: they do not search to realise equality; consumption does not homogenise – it differentiates through the sign system. Life-style and values – not economic need – [are] the basis of social life' (Lechte 2008: 234). Objects are consumed not because they are needed but because they are symbolic – of status, for example. The allure of seduction and capture makes subjects unite in extremes, conglomerating into masses. The notion of the self, from this vantage point, is not a vessel for forces striving for ideals such as betterment and progress where the implication is humans are inherently fair and happiness-seeking. Rather, the 'self' is *subject to* a composite of transactional relationships that move the symbolic into the material.

Many postmodern theorists agree with, indeed have placed at the centre of their speculations regarding the notion of, 'the "death" of the subject itself – the end of bourgeois monad or ego or individual' (Jameson 1991: 15). What this means is that within the postmodern era, people are engaged in a constant self-reflexivity and a self-awareness that are constantly recreating and therefore contributing to the rapidly changing narratives around personhood.

> In trying to understand our contemporary selves in the moment of the present, there are no safely-detached observation-posts, not in 'science', 'religion', or even 'history'. We are in and of the moment that we are attempting to analyse, in and of the structures we employ to analyse it.
>
> (Connor 1997: 5)

Throughout the ages from ancient history onwards, humans were seen within a universal context – a matrix of divine forces. The Enlightenment and modernist eras saw this expansive context shrink: the human subject became the central component, able to dominate nature through rationality and capable of influencing the environment though reasoning and deductive logic. In the postmodern context, no longer is the subject at the focus of their world – instead, de-centred, inextricably embedded within an eco-socio-political-cultural environment and dependent on certain conditions to come into being.

Postmodernists argue against the 'transcendental subject, able to exercise choice and embody intentions free from any constraints imposed by their interpretative context' (Connor 1997: 65). Instead, the self from a postmodern vantage point is always in-relation-to and inextricably-linked-with the narratives, rituals, values and practices embedded in the chaotic symbolic (dis)order that emerges in perpetual states of becoming and deconstructing, of being and non-being, of order and chaos that are experienced not as binary dichotomies but as multiple possibilities in the unfolding present moment.

Towards a postmodern understanding of therapeutic integration

Much of psychological theory is located within an objectivist epistemology, born from the modernist era or developed from theories thereafter. The very terms by which the notions of the psyche, self and, thus, intersubjectivity are delineated imply predictability and certitude. This mode of understanding phenomena reduces each whole to the sum of its parts. From a postmodern perspective, importance is given to paradox, disorder, randomness, volatility, vagueness, ambiguity and cataclysm (Lyotard 1984). The de-centred notion of the self, central to the postmodern endeavour, posits that there are many variables that come into play, 'clouding' our direct access to experience. For the postmodernist, we do not have direct access to ourselves or our states of mind – our self-understanding is mediated by concepts and other factors, rejecting the notion of 'an integrated personality in favour of an emphasis upon the destructured, dehumanised subject' (Featherstone 1988: 202). Rather than the subject being seen as the immutable, unchangeable, unified grounds of identity, the subject is seen as fractured and the notion of an essential subjectivity is called into question (including the foundation upon which a theory can be grounded). It is in this way that the concept of identity is immutable (Smart 1993). Here, the subject is constantly co-created within a dialectical involvement of historical, cultural, environmental and socio-political circumstances within the life-span. Life is seen as change encompassing past and present while also acknowledging awareness, meaning and intention. Postmodernists might therefore view the 'self' as being in a *constant state of creating*.

Three forms of a postmodern approach to integration

I argue that a postmodern approach to therapeutic integration can take three forms.

In *the first form*, one can adopt postmodern philosophies and critiques as a way of informing the work, work that might take any form, hence celebrating plurality and giving precedence to different ways of understanding. In this format, there can be any number of integrative configurations. Theoretical integration; pluralism; eclectic integration; assimilative integration; and common factors as a basis for integration, are all equally relevant as they represent different perspectives on how one might draw on psychological theory to conceptualise and engage with the therapeutic endeavour. For example, the practitioner might adopt a framework of eclectic integration, drawing upon Lyotard's concept of time to shed light on a client's narrative but use techniques from Dynamic Developmental Psychotherapy (DDP) and attachment theory. In this form, primacy is not given to one way of perceiving but rather multiple, varying (and potentially epistemologically conflicting) psychological modalities can be brought together. In this approach, the postmodern trend of prioritising numerous perspectives is used to inform the rationale behind this multiplicity.

In *the second form*, the underlying values and assumptions of postmodernism and the therapeutic approaches being integrated are aligned. From this approach, the epistemological and ontological underpinnings of the paradigms are given more credence. In doing this, the therapist ensures that there is cohesion between the implicit assumptions the approaches represent and the ideologies of postmodernism. This approach to postmodern integration requires the therapist to be clear about the assumptions being made regarding the nature of truth and being, not just in terms of postmodernism but also of the psychological approaches. In this way, a more profound engagement with postmodernism and its philosophical underpinnings is required. From the perspective of this form of postmodern integration, it might be argued that it is necessary to promote epistemological and ontological cohesion in this way, to integrate theories based on assumptions that are diametrically opposed to postmodernism poses significant issues. I would argue that the underlying assumptions and central tenets upon which the major psychological paradigms are based (mainstream psychodynamic theory, humanistic theory and CBT) are incompatible with postmodern epistemological assumptions and, if merged, result in epistemological incoherence. Rather, a particular reading of Lacanian psychoanalysis might be integrated with postmodern concepts for an integrated therapeutic approach.

In *the third form*, integration would not appear as a structural modality or therapeutic paradigm that conceptualises the psyche, human development, a model of health or diseases, or recommended interventions. Instead, an attitude, stance or set of values might inform the work. This approach might take some of the key facets of postmodern thinking, as outlined thus far, and apply them to therapy. For example, the therapist may endeavour to deconstruct meta-narratives of not only the psychotherapeutic paradigms but also the local sociological context within which they are operating, so that they can approach the work with radical openness.

The American composer John Cage's piece entitled *4'33*, often associated with postmodernism, is made up of three movements. The score indicates to the musician not to play a single note throughout the duration of the performance and therefore the piece is comprised of the noises that happen to take place in the environment when the listeners attend to the piece. It 'aimed to liberate the materiality of sound from the objectifying, organizing, spatializing powers of the eye and ear' (Connor 1997: 169). The rationale informing this is to promote: '"exhaustion" or "silence", "against interpretation", concerning itself with the signifier, with "participation" and with "process"' (1997: 119). One possibility for this third form of postmodern integration might look like John Cage's score – empty. No longer is the client asked to adopt the grand narratives of the therapist – unconscious desire, projections, transference, neurosis, lack, false self, actualising tendencies, sedimentation, pathology, etc. Arguably,

> once we have spelled out and committed ourselves to a new story, it often acquires the status of an insight, and yesterday's tale seems like a self-deception. The theme of 'foundationlessness' insists that there is no story that ever captures the whole truth.
>
> (Burr and Butt 2000: 197)

This kind of postmodern integrative attitude would favour the arbitrary – the give and take between tensions, between entities – a kind of randomness, unpredictability, linkage at all possible points. If the therapist were to come across a value system and attach meaning to what was occurring within the therapy, they would also hold in mind that it is not absolute. Furthermore, this would be embedded within an appreciation that therapist and client are brought into being within an eco-socio-spiritual-cultural-economic-embodied milieu of symbolic patterning.

Basic assumptions within a postmodern psychology

In order to adopt a postmodern approach to integration, we must not only understand postmodernism in a general sense and then have decided our position regarding how it will feature in our integrative practice (i.e. what form we will adopt), we must also understand some basic assumptions of how a postmodern psychology might reveal itself within that integrative practice.

Within traditional psychoanalysis, there is a tacit assumption that unseen truths about the subject are only accessible through a process specified by the paradigm itself (i.e. bringing the unconscious into consciousness). It is in this way that actions represent workings below the surface that are connected to feelings. The task of therapy might be to let these processes rise to the surface. However, using space as an organising principle in this way is deceiving:

> A postmodern approach to psychology sees depth as merely a spatial metaphor applied to the person. The attribution of causality to deeper layers is seen as misleading.
>
> (Burr and Butt 2000: 197)

Rather than what Deleuze and Guattari (1983) might refer to as a root-like organising principle with which to engage, the therapist might adopt a 'rhizomic' mode of being, which would allow for non-hierarchical relationships with multiple entry and exit points. This could give rise to connecting with process so that something else can emerge but, equally, alternatives would be similarly valid because reality is a collective endeavour, which is given precedence over individual psychic space while being fluid. The metaphor of writing might be employed here whereby meaning is intricate and co-authored and the relationships we have with other authors and with our own story is intimately connected. Berger and Luckmann described it in the following way:

> Reality is a kind of collective fiction – a novel that we are all writing together – constructed and sustained by processes of socialization, institutionalization, and everyday social interaction, and especially through the medium of language. Socially constructed reality is complex, a jostling assemblage of 'sub universes of meaning', reflecting the world-views of different social classes, religious sects, occupations, and so on. Individuals experience a multiplicity of private and peripheral

realities – dreams, play, fiction – but these alternative realities are all subordinated to the shared social reality of everyday life, which is experienced as 'paramount'.

(1991, cited in McHale 2015: 24)

The implication for a postmodern approach to integrating is to allow this matrix to be holistically appreciated. This framework would provide a focus on relationships, particularly the changeability of relationships (Gergen 2011), understood through this 'rhizomic' mode of being, with multiple entry and exit points in a shared lived experience. Within the current neoliberal culture, postmodern integration not only has a place for diversity, it begins from the perspective that this is the preferred reference point from which any trajectory could occur when engaging with the therapeutic endeavour. In practice, then, the therapist would seek to deconstruct, to collude with grand narratives in order to sensitively engage with all that a human might be. This is to say that:

> The task of the postmodern therapist then, is not to deliver explanations of law-like generalisations on universal truths or prescribe meanings applicable to social order. Rather, the task is to explore the systematic unpredictability of humanity, to acknowledge 'volatility and reality-generating capacity of (human) agency'.
>
> (Smart 1993: 78)

This jostling assemblage would also apply when engaging with the notion of the subject. Subjectivity could no longer be seen in the same way; indeed, identity should be provided with the proper space in therapy so that all possibilities could emerge for the client and not be subjected to acts of measurement or any other imposing agenda the therapist might have. This could also be understood in the following way:

> The identity of the agent is neither given nor authoritatively confirmed. It has to be constructed, yet no design for the construction can be taken as prescribed or foolproof . . . It lacks a benchmark against which its progress could be measured . . . It is now the incessant (and non-linear) activity of self-constitution that makes the identity of the agent.
>
> (Bauman 1992: 193)

The therapeutic task calls for an essential openness in the continuous present as client and therapist come together to deconstruct, reconstruct, feel, process, think, speak, act, make silence, be and become.

Conclusion

Postmodernism spans across disciplines and is recognised within social, economic, cultural, political, technological, aesthetic, philosophical and psychological fields.

Within the latter, the proliferation of therapeutic approaches speaks of a transformation in the way counselling psychologists and psychotherapists work. Arguably, integration in psychological therapies is inevitable in the postmodern era. Postmodernism sits within a wider historical context and an appreciation of the (d)evolution of therapeutic conceptualisation of the human condition, while associated interventions embody the values inherent within the postmodern endeavour. Postmodern integration is interested in stories that can narrate personhood and speak to the notion of the de-centred subject. Postmodernism adopts a position of criticality towards any theory that espouses authoritarian claims about the complete, sum total of experience, as Deleuze and Guattari posit:

> We live today in the age of partial objects, bricks that have been shattered to bits, and leftovers . . . We no longer believe in a primordial totality that once existed, or in a final totality that awaits us at some future date.
>
> (2004: 45)

A postmodern approach to integration would, at the very least, be attuned to this and other postmodern concepts.

This chapter has put forward three forms of a postmodern approach to integration. The first, any number of integrative configurations are possible; within the second form, there is epistemological and ontological coherence between postmodernism and the theories being integrated; and the third form is characterised by a lack of structural paradigm or therapeutic model. Within the first two forms, the therapist can utilise their inherent values as an organising principle to formulate integration of pre-existing psychotherapeutic paradigms; whereas in the third form, it is a mode by which therapists engage with the work. Within the latter, opportunities would arise for moments where the therapist or client experiences the loss of self in undifferentiated time, where the words uttered by the therapist may be no truer than those uttered by, say, a witchdoctor. Through this deterioration of authority, opportunities arise for an exploration of the emerging holistic, relational, contextual, sensing, moment-to-moment process.

References

Bateman, J. and Holmes, A. (1995) *An Introduction to Psychoanalysis: Contemporary Theory and Practice*. London: Routledge.

Baudrillard, J. (1994) *Simulacra and Simulation*. S. Faria Glaser, trans. Ann Arbor, MI: University of Michigan Press.

Bauer, S.W. (2007) *The History of the Ancient World: From the Earliest Accounts to the Fall of Rome*. London: W.W. Norton.

Bauman, Z. (1992) *Intimations of Postmodernity*. London: Routledge.

Bental, R. (2004) *Madness Explained: Psychosis and Human Nature*. London: Penguin.

Best, S. and Kellner, D. (1991) *Postmodern Theory: Critical Interrogations*. London: The Macmillan Press.

Burr, V. and Butt, T. (2000) Psychological distress and postmodern thought (Part IV: Toward new Approaches: Epistemology, Research, Politics). In D. Fee (ed.), *Pathology and the Postmodern: Mental Illness as Discourse and Experience.* London: SAGE.

Cixous, H. (1975) 'Sorties: out and out: attacks/ ways out/ forays', in *Cixous and Clément, 1975. La Jeune Née.* B. Wing, trans. London: I.B. Tauris and Co.

Chaucer, G. (2005) *The Canterbury Tales.* J. Mann, trans. London: Penguin Classics.

Clark, M.T. (2000) *An Aquinas Reader: Selections from the Writings of Thomas Aquinas.* New York: Fordham University Press.

Connor, S. (1997) *Postmodern Culture: An Introduction to Theories of the Contemporary* (2nd edn). Oxford: Blackwell Publishing.

Cooper, M. (2007) *Existential Therapies.* London: SAGE.

Dalal, F. (2012) *Thought Paralysis: The Virtues of Discrimination.* London: Karnac.

Dante, A. (2012) *The Divine Comedy: Inferno, Purgatorio, Paradiso.* R. Kirkpatrick trans. London: Penguin Classics.

Descartes, R. (2003) *Discourse on Method and Meditations.* New York: Dover Publications.

Descartes, R. (2007) *Meditations on First Philosophy.* New York: BN Publishing.

Deleuze, G. and Guattari, F. (1983) *Anti-Oedipus: Schizophrenia and Capitalism.* Minneapolis, MN: University of Minnesota Press.

Ezrahi, Y., Mendelsohn, E. and Segal, H.P. (eds) (1994) *Technology, Pessimism, and Postmodernism.* Amherst, MA: University of Massachusetts Press.

Fara, P. (2009) *Science: A Four Thousand Year History.* Oxford: Oxford University Press.

Featherstone, M. (1988) In pursuit of the postmodern: An introduction. *Theory, Culture & Society*, 5: 195–295.

Gergen, K.J. (2000) *The Saturated Self: Dilemmas of Identity in Contemporary Life.* New York: Basic Books.

Gergen, K.J. (2011) *Relational Beings: Beyond Self and Community.* Oxford: Oxford University Press.

Grenz, S. (1996) *A Primer on Postmodernism.* Cambridge: Eerdmans Publishing.

Guignon, C. (ed.) (1999) *The Good Life.* Cambridge: Hackett.

Harari, Y.N. (2011) *Sapiens: A Brief History of Humankind.* London: Vintage.

Homer (2017) *The Iliad.* Stockholm: Wisehouse Classics.

Jameson, F. (1988) Postmodernism and consumer society. In S. Connor, *Postmodernist Culture* (2nd edn). Oxford: Blackwell.

Jameson, F. (1991) *Postmodernism: Or, the Cultural Logic of Late Capitalism.* London: Verso Books.

Juma, J., Murwa, V. and Rabah, K. (2018) Technologies: the good, the bad & the ugly … a camouflaged innovation? *Mara International Journal of Computer Science & Information Security*, 1(1): 28–34.

Kafka, F. (2016) *The Metamorphosis.* S. Bernofsky, trans. New York: W.W. Norton.

Kant, I. (2009) *Answering the Question, What Is Enlightenment?* London: Penguin.

Kohn, L. (1991) *Early Chinese Mysticism: Philosophy and Soteriology in the Taoist Tradition*. Princeton, NJ: Princeton University Press.

Kottiswari, W.S. (2008) *Postmodern Feminist Writers*. Delhi: Sarup & Sons.

Lyotard, J-F. (1984) *The Postmodern Condition: A Report on Knowledge*. G. Bennington and B. Massumi, trans. Minneapolis, MN: University of Minnesota Press.

Lechte, J. (2008) *Fifty Key Contemporary Thinkers: From Structuralism to Post-Modernity*. London: Routledge.

Malpas, S. (2005) *The Postmodern: The New Critical Idiom*. London: Routledge.

McGuigan, J. (1999) *Modernity and Postmodern Culture*. Buckingham: Open University Press.

McHale, B. (2015) *The Cambridge Introduction to Postmodernism*. Cambridge: Cambridge University Press.

Newton, I. (2016) *The Principia: Mathematical Principles of Natural Philosophy*. B. Cohen, A. Whitman, and J. Budenz, trans. Berkeley, CA: University of California Press.

Smart, B. (1993) *Postmodernity*. London: Routledge.

Van Doren, C. (1991) *A History of Knowledge*. New York: Ballantine Books.

Watson, A. (2014) *Who Am I? The Self/Subject According to Psychoanalytic Theory*. London: SAGE Open 4(3). Available at: https://dash.harvard.edu/bitstream/handle/1/12328212/watson_who_am_i.pdf?sequence=1 (accessed 17 January 2019).

7   An example of phenomenological integration

Claire Marshall

Introduction

Chapter 6 discussed postmodern integration by first contextualising postmodernism and then positing three forms of a postmodern integrative approach. This chapter will explore what a postmodern integrative approach might look like in practice. True integration, if we, as practitioners, are to engage with the richness of human experience, integrates across disciplines including but not isolated to anthropology, pedagogy, andragogy, neuroscience, psychology, psychiatry, geopolitics, philosophy and sociology.

Preamble: doing, being and receiving

I would argue that there are multiple, sometimes conflicting ways to conceptualise and engage with reality. Rather than being able to identify an objective truth with precision and certitude, we are limited to human-fashioned perspectives that can be understood through engaging in similar meaning-making processes. Furthermore, we are not naïve observers – we influence our experience. We also interpret and understand the world from our subjective vantage point.

I align myself with a constructivist epistemology. I believe that both subject and object contribute to the construction of models or frameworks that act as the standards for truth. I would speculate that two or more opposing and conflicting truths (i.e. p is true and not true) can be equally valid and there is no single illustrative system or view of reality that can account for all phenomena. Sources that I draw on in my practice that might be read as aligning with this position include but are not restricted to Heideggerian phenomenology (Heidegger 1962; 1982) and critical psychology (Hook et al. 2004; Fox et al. 2009).

Where phenomenologists from the Heideggerian tradition are purely interpretative, narrating experience through a perspective that assumes the intersubjective is at the heart of the endeavour, transcendental phenomenologists, such as Jung (1995), make claims about intangible concepts, such as projections and unconscious archetypes. From a hermeneutic perspective, abstract interpretations (e.g. archetypes) by themselves are unobservable. Yet, arguably there is overlap between these phenomenological positions and it may be more useful to conceive of them as being on a continuum. There are experiential territories that can never be expressed through words. That which goes beyond what language could convey reveals itself through symbols, feelings, sensations or visceral experiences. Therapy is not only doing and being, it is also arriving at a language for each client and finding a way to attune to and work with that-which-goes-beyond language. Humans are meaning-making creatures, existing through and within narratives. While linguistically exploring this is pertinent, it is only one aspect of our experiential milieu. There is a rage, a sorrow, a grief, an unravelling, a joy, a rapture that cannot be spoken, only felt. States of experiences reaching beyond linguistic artefacts into the realm of affect and beyond transcend paradigmatic cognitive understanding. It is only in the vicissitudes of psyche and the physical realm that the clinician can engage with unfolding processes in a truly organic way. This mode of being might extend to the experience of time itself. Indeed, there are different verbs describing time, depending on the language – variations on past, present and future tenses. Our worlds are in a continuous moment-to-moment process of becoming, within past and future. In this ontological reality, life can be experienced in the continuous present tense.

Phenomenologically speaking, from a Heideggerian perspective, being-in-the-world, where self and world are one entity, relationships are not 'out there' to be discovered but are instead inherent in the nature of our existence. For Heidegger, our existence is akin to a clearing in the forest (Finlay 2011) – only visible in an opening, away from the trees' shadows. We understand through language that interpretations are inevitable. In therapy, it is imperative that we strive toward a commitment to openness and interpret tentatively. This is so that, rather than assuming causality, the practitioner adopts a position that can more readily attune to the 'clearing in the forest'. As Deleuze and Guattari posit: 'It would be an error to believe that content determines expression by causal action' (2004: 99). For Merleau-Ponty (2002), we are engaged in a process of constituting and being constituted by the world in a whole-body dialogue. Todres (2008) advocates for an embodied and relational consideration, which involves being affected, going beyond ourselves to attend to that which is past the construction, a holistic venture allowing for the quality and character of things to be experienced. In such a mode of being, mood takes precedence over cognition. Indeed, there are implicit ways of engaging that can give rise to new ways of meeting within a relational dynamic. It is this mode of knowing and communicating that is responsible for much therapeutic change. Hart (1999) distinguishes between two forms of empathy: the first is when the therapist appreciates the client's experience but remains outside of it, so to speak; the second occurs when the boundary between self and other is less fixed and the therapist is able to imaginatively connect to the client's experience.

When integrating, having a meta structure through which to formulate is essential, in order not to practise anecdotally. Complexities of human experiences do not easily lend themselves to words or language and therefore, if universalities exist, they cannot be known in any definitive way. I understand the model of the psyche as being co-constituted, always in-relation-to and intersubjectively negotiated. I am of the assumption that affect, or perhaps more accurately a *sensory experiencing*, is pre-cognitive and pre-verbal. I would argue that truth is subjective – truth is a paradigm. As human subjects, we find ways of negotiating relatedness – from the local global community, to nation states, to cultures within societies, people reacting, societies grouping to form sub-cultures, ostracised members of society and the multitude of variants of social and interpersonal relationships. Transformation is relational and not dependent on one subject, something also explicitly recognised by community psychologists and systemic therapists.

Within my practice, my model of relating seeks to co-construct meaning and process experience in a way that includes but goes beyond descriptive, language actions that are culturally-historically-socially-politically embedded but, most importantly, intend to connect with a sensing-becoming-mode-of-being. From this vantage point, when considering the notion of what a feeling is and how it might come into being, rather than cognition preceding affect (i.e. thoughts trigger how we feel), affect precedes cognition. 'Symptoms' do not need to be combated, rather they have meaning and are indicators of phenomena, which should be the focus of the therapeutic work.

A case example from my practice: Working from a relational, phenomenological vantage point

The following account has its basis in actual sessions but combines several issues from various clients. Care has been taken to ensure anonymity by concealing or omitting certain aspects of the presentation and assembling it with aspects of multiple clients, to preserve confidentiality in line with ethical sensitivities and best practice guidelines.

'Gail's' account, Part 1

Gail walked into the room, carefully taking off her coat, folding it tidily beside her and placing her bag on the floor. I sat down across from her in a large armchair. I observed Gail – she sat on the sofa, perched at the edge, her head propped up with one hand. She didn't stay in this position for long, propping herself up, half-sitting and half-lying in quick, jolting movements. Sitting up, slouching back, and sitting up, her feet intermittently swinging off the sofa. She stood up suddenly, walked to the bookshelf, picked off a book from the centre, seemingly at random, and started flicking through. It didn't appear as if she was reading it but rather the act of engaging with the book in this way gave the impression that this was more important. She sighed and put it back on the shelf, this time at the end of the row of books. She walked back around and sat on the sofa, on the floor, legs outstretched in front of her, knees moving nervously up and down. She looked at me for the first time that day.

'How are you?' I asked. 'I'm fine. I hope you're OK,' she said, almost absent-mindedly. 'I've been sleeping OK and studying lots this week,' she said. A half-smile flickered momentarily across her lips. Based on the smile and on our previous encounters, I wondered if she was seeking my approval – either because she said she had been studying or because she said she had slept. Whenever we are with clients, we are faced with a multitude of decisions and responses, many of which are not formulated cognitively but rather come to fruition on an embodied-response level. I believe that how we feel about our client, what they are talking about and who we are in relation to them, are woven into the fabric of this co-creation (Gergen 2011). In Gail's smile, I wondered if she was relating to me as an authority who might grant her validation, based on acting in a particular way. She had placed the book in a different place to where she took it from, which might be a subtle disruption to this stance. I also noticed she had not spoken about her feelings. Bearing in mind it was only my hypothesis, I responded with what I hoped was an inquisitive, gentle look. She averted her eyes and began running the tassels of the cushion through her fingers, crossing and uncrossing her legs periodically in swift, sharp movements again. It seemed as if her breathing was light and quick. She looked up and almost whispered 'I don't know what to say.'

Gail had arrived in therapy wanting to 'get back to [her] normal self'. She was a high achiever at school, involved with sports clubs, had learnt several languages, maintained many friendships and attended numerous social events. Now midway through her university degree, she was struggling with what she had articulated as stress. She recounted periods when she felt nauseous and had even vomited or fainted. This, at times, was accompanied by a lack of focus and a difficulty in expressing herself, where ordinarily she was very articulate. Gail described this as 'zoning out and losing words'. After significant health checks by professionals, they had found no medical condition present. Gail was shaken by the apparent randomness of her 'illness' and was afraid that if there was no organic cause that could be pinpointed, it might be her 'just going mad'. During the initial assessment, when I had asked if there were triggers, she had said it was 'completely random' but she was extremely worried that it would happen again, and she would be at the mercy of her sickness, out of control. She had spent much time detailing the negative impact this would have on the various projects she was undertaking and study commitments she had made.

Gail's mother was a director of a recruitment company and her father was in advertising. Her father was often absent with work commitments. He was also emotionally unavailable, often seeming cold and distant, placing a great deal of emphasis on Gail's schooling. Her mother travelled a lot with her work but when she was at home she was chaotic, placing importance on Gail's diet and education. At times she was overbearing in her involvement with Gail and often unable to empathise. Gail had described how she was financially dependent on her parents. Both her parents had struggled economically in the past and had worked hard to build lucrative careers that afforded opportunities for Gail and her three younger siblings, all a year apart. They often told their children to 'be grateful' and, if Gail or her siblings expressed difficulty or distress, they were each told to 'keep your chin up' and reminded how tough life was for others 'less fortunate'. In this way, her parents would frequently provide their children with ultimatums that involved suppressing their emotions or risk damaging their relationship.

Gail had described a series of intimate relationships with men who, although on first appearances seemed exuberant, passionate and exciting, ended up being cold, independent and aloof. She strove to please them and capture their affections by going to great lengths to learn their likes and dislikes in music, food, drink and art. Armed with this knowledge, she would play their favourite music, cook their preferred meals, provide their favoured drink or surprise them with gifts of desired artworks. She also recounted how important it was for her to capture their experiences through photographs and post it on social media, often spending so much time preparing the presentation of the photo that it would take her away from being able to enjoy the actual experience.

Analysis

Gail and I had tentatively formulated together. We acknowledged the core phenomenon as a fear of abandonment. Perhaps because her parents were unable to contain anxiety, Gail had quickly learnt, especially as the oldest sibling, that to preserve the relationship with them, as well as not to unsettle the family dynamic and thus preserve the status quo, she could not rely on her parents to contain her distress. Ergo, she could not contemplate trusting others and – now inwardly directed – she did not trust herself. She had overcompensated, becoming a 'super-performer', attempting to manage relationships through asserting control. Gail had dichotomised society, fearing she would be substandard or mediocre, polarising her self-worth whereby she was either part of an elite or feeling worthless. If she 'failed' in some way, she became overwhelmed by guilt and disgust. When she felt out of control, her anxiety provoked nausea and difficulty in articulating herself – a stress response with dissociative traits. Growing up, she was often made to feel guilty or wrong and felt much anger around this, which I had tentatively formulated was anger invested in others. Gail was perhaps controlling the possibility of disappointment, while mitigating the needs of others. Although attempting to create the perfect relationship with her romantic partners, their taciturn and standoffish stance may have been part of this dynamic. She may have taken pleasure in their defiance.

I formulated early on how this relational constellation might play out in our relationship. I wondered if Gail might worry she would overwhelm me, careful with how much she shared and how much of her true self she would show. She might even try to contain me. I also wondered if the anger, guilt and disgust would be enacted by trying to create the perfect relationship between us, knowing that the boundaries of the therapeutic frame would inevitably give her something to push against and that she might take pleasure if I became steadfast in this. I thought that ultimately, although this would validate her position, it might lead to reinforcing her narrative that people are not to be trusted and leave her feeling alone. If the work were to be of value, this would need to be offered in a way that she might hear and I would need to be open to other possibilities, other ways of understanding her experience.

We had contracted that the work would be open-ended. I tentatively formulated that the first 'phase' of the therapy should focus on understanding the nature of our therapeutic relationship. When a sufficient amount of trust had been established, talking about what happened might allow us to begin deconstructing and processing the phenomenon. In practice, this may include linking the manifestation of anxiety with what it might represent, in terms of affect. Thereafter, therapy could provide a forum for Gail to voice how she feels in relation to this, which may be that she is disappointed with life. Overcoming distressing incidences may also involve a commitment. This is to say that, rather than guilt negotiation or pole relocation, which would maintain an either/or stance, instead it might be useful for Gail to try to make a commitment decision in clarifying why she wants a relationship. This could enable her to ask for her needs to be met, rather than coercing the other.

Concurrently, it would also be important to address Gail's fears. She was terrified that it could happen again, therefore it would be necessary to work with her on projecting forward and thinking through helpful ways of negotiating it (from a bio-medical perspective, this is sometimes referred to as 'devising a relapse plan'). Furthermore, connecting with and then trusting her sense of emotions, articulating these and thereafter acting on her needs might assist her in finding other ways of circumnavigating her anxiety. Finally, it could be useful to explore how she might feel about fostering a sense of independence. Based on the tentative hypothesis that Gail might be dissociating because she could not understand or regulate her emotions, it might be useful to explore with Gail what it is she finds so disturbing about listening to her emotions. Through these discussions, the work might support her in integrating them. These phases assume that some awareness requires dialogue, some understanding requires language and some motivation requires the consideration of secondary gains and then capacity to respond. While I proceeded by loosely holding these assumptions, I was also mindful that there might be a completely different way of conceptualising and engaging with Gail's experience.

'Gail's' account, Part 2

'I – just – don't – know,' Gail pronounced again, sitting on the edge of the sofa. She began meticulously plucking the fluff from the cushion in even, intentional gestures, collecting it into a ball. We had been working together for several sessions. I wondered whether there had been sufficient trust established to explore the relationship between how her affect manifested and the underlying phenomenon. It was my bias that, through engaging in this dialogue, we might foster awareness. 'What would it be like to connect with the feeling, rather than trying to understand through thinking?' I offered. Immediately, I thought I could have suggested this in a more tentative, open-ended way, not through wanting to align myself more closely, theoretically, to a phenomenological approach, but more because I was aware at this stage Gail might find it difficult to assert herself concerning anything that might be counter to what I said. In wanting to preserve our relationship, at least how she might think it should be, she might not want to disagree with me. Gail stopped picking at the fluff and looked up and slightly to the left. I wondered if she was accessing a memory or feeling so, rather than reformulating my question, I waited to give her the space to calibrate and process. She resumed eye contact and absentmindedly brushed the pillow – 'it feels like, like I . . . I just don't want to go into all of that feeling stuff.' I noted that, counter to my worries, she had asserted herself and while that might be worth validating or exploring, it seemed more pressing to stay with the reluctance of engaging with her emotions.

Analysis

One of the tensions and wonders of therapy is that moment-to-moment we are presented with a multitude of different possibilities and, despite intending to 'horizontalise' (i.e. not give priority to any one presenting phenomenon), there is an inevitable influence that occurs as we are both subjective agents in the co-construction of the therapeutic endeavour. It is often, but not always, the case that when clients place precautionary statements in the path of exploration, this is precisely the issue they are avoiding and, therefore, the thing that is most helpful to explore in the work. It is not always the case, of course, but frequently clients who have constructed coping mechanisms that involve keeping their feelings at bay are the ones who protest the most when they are invited to connect with them. With Gail, however, I was mindful that she tended to become quickly overwhelmed by her feelings. While I did not want to collude with the tacit assumption that feelings are overwhelming, I also needed to be mindful of her capacity to tolerate them. This has been described in the following way: 'the therapist may take on more and more of an advocacy role for the patient. By so doing, she implies that the patient is not capable of acting for herself' (Herman 1997: 142). In order not to collude with the fear and imply she was not capable of acting for herself, nor overwhelm her by being insensitive to her vulnerability, I instead hoped to offer her the opportunity to explore her reservations. 'You don't want to go into the feeling stuff?' I repeated, this time as a question. 'No, there's no point.' I was struck by her assumption that discussing feelings had to have *a point* – the implication potentially being that feelings should only be allowed if they are useful, purposeful and serve some kind of productive conclusion. This relationship with emotions stands diametrically opposed to the notion that feelings are meaningful indicators of our responses to the world and part of our inherent way of living as human beings. In her family constellation, Gail had learnt it is easier to contain the other. She carried this burden, rather than being dependent, which within her family context would have invariably led to disappointment, rejection or suffering, as her distress would not have been responded to.

It has been said that 'intuitive acts are things like perception, memory, sensation and imagination' (Adams 2001: 68). We bring intuition into being through tools that access the symbolic. This symbolic realm is manifest within the concrete but, in essence, exists in liminal spaces within our relational lived experiences. It might be that our symbolic experience of the world is primordial and translating this into language comes later. The body is also implicated in this translation as it interacts with the environment. Gendlin posits that:

> It is not the body of perception that is structured by language. Nor is the body's interaction structured by culture and language alone. Rather, it is the body of interactional living in its environment . . . The human symbolising kind of experience is not necessary for differentiated communication . . . You sense behind you not just the space, not just space-filling visible things. You sense behind you the people to whom you could turn and speak.
>
> (2003: 102–3)

Similarly, I would argue that the way we engage surpasses a utilitarian position whereby entities can be assessed on their functionality. The way we intuitively see, remember, sense or imagine and find ourselves in the world as embodied proximity-seeking beings lends itself to an entirely different conceptualisation of experience. This is not the dominant discourse adopted in European and American contemporary societies. As I hear Gail state to me that there is 'no point' in discussing her feelings, feelings that are causing her distress and feelings that, as they go ignored, may find ever more complex ways to manifest in her behaviour and the various ways she 'acts them out', I lament that this is something not only she has had to adopt to be able to cope within her particular family constellation, but it is also endemic within the wider system of local socio-cultural and political norms she is embedded within.

'What is it like – needing feelings to have a point?' I asked. A definitive aspect of phenomenology is its focus on 'understanding rather than explanation' (Spinelli 2005: 109). Therefore, the phenomenological psychologist does not ask 'why?' but rather 'what?' or 'how?' I take the position that 'symptoms' (an unhelpful term that mars experience with pathology but is common vernacular nonetheless) have meaning and, rather than treating the 'symptom', it is necessary to engage with the underlying phenomenon. Thus, the base question around such a presentation centres on the following notion – not 'how can we take feelings away?' merely because they are painful, but 'how can we understand them?' or even 'how can we process them experientially?' If we are to adopt the 'symptom reduction' approach, the underlying phenomenon may manifest in a different form. Gail manages affect through external entities, which is why it cannot be held in mind. How this might unfold in therapy, despite my formulation, is yet to be seen.

'Gail's' account, Part 3

Gail distractedly released the pillow and it half fell to the floor, wedged between her leg and the sofa. She looked at me directly, her brow beginning to furrow, and her breath deepening. I noticed my chest felt tight, my heart beat faster and my breath felt constricted. I also sensed a tightening in my stomach. I wondered if these were partly her sensations I was attuning to and I then wondered if this was because she felt emotionally exposed. I was mindful of wanting to convey empathy but at the same time not to appear overly emotional so that she might want to take care of me – in principle, my intention was to navigate collaboratively and tentatively how much I did and did not ask of her. Her hands began to shake and she began to cry small, constrained sobs that she held inwards, hardly making a sound. There was a box of tissues on the table to her right, but she reached into her bag and pulled out her own packet, carefully pulling one out and dabbing her eyes. 'I'm sorry,' she apologised. 'It's OK. It's painful,' I said.

The work then began articulating patterns – her tendency to suppress her emotions with manifestations in her body. She also began noticing patterns that previously had gone unseen. That her sickness came when she was most stressed and anxious, was perhaps the most poignant of revelations. We explored what motivated her to be in a relationship and some of the tensions, paradoxes, frustrations and secondary gains that came from engaging with men who left her feeling alone. The question then became not so much 'can she trust anyone again?' but 'does she dare trust anyone again?', given how terrifying it was to engage with someone who might be more available and therefore more able to contain her, thus evoking in her a vulnerability and fear of being dropped, neglected, rejected or abandoned. Feelings surfaced that had long been kept at bay – disgust and anger that had been invested in the other in a bid to control the possibility of disappointment (through mitigating the other's needs), as well as acknowledging the disappointment of being let down by her parents.

Analysis

Gail had invested heavily in keeping her feelings at bay. Diametrically opposed to her stance is a moment-to-moment head-on confrontation with these feelings as they arise. It may have been that by providing a consistent frame, validating her distress, creating spaces where she could be heard, intending towards a relationally attuned stance, engaging in a dialogical process and not reacting when Gail acted out, would be the grounds for the therapeutic work. Perhaps this would interfere with her template – a template that posited nothing is reliable, nothing is stable, and relationships are to be survived through withholding and controlling. However, these are all assumptions. As much as I try (and attempting this remains valuable), I can never truly enter into Gail's world, never completely grasp what it means to experience her disappointments, sorrow, fear, revulsion, shyness, anxiety, hope and relief. At the end of the work, we may have had more of an understanding than at the beginning but, more importantly than that, the way Gail experientially found herself in the world, the way she responded to given situations and her general mode of being had shifted to a place *she* was more comfortable inhabiting.

Conclusion

My approach to integration here is first and foremost *relational*. I drew on the work of Merleau-Ponty and Heideggerian phenomenology, which informed my formulation and interventions. Tailoring the work to each individual client, couple or group is of great importance if inter-relationality is to be given precedence and the client's own process is to be respected. This calls for a constant tentative revisiting of the formulation, which is core to informing how the work is tailored with the individual client.

Language and culture are closed systems. When two people come together in therapy, it is often useful to transcend the constraints of words and create our own 'language'. If the work is truly dialectical, the therapist finds a different way of communicating with each person. Indeed, this communication goes beyond words, so that both client and therapist would have a lived sense as corporeal beings and the ineffable that has passed between them.

References

Adams, M. (2001) Practising phenomenology – some reflections and considerations. *Existential Analysis*, 12(1): 65–84.

Deleuze, G. and Guattari, F. (2004) *A Thousand Plateaus*. B. Massumi (trans.) London: Continuum.

Finlay, L. (2011) *Phenomenology for Therapists: Researching the Lived World*. Oxford: Wiley-Blackwell.

Fox, D., Prilleltensky, I. and Austin, S. (eds) (2009) *Critical Psychology: An Introduction* (2nd edn). London: SAGE.

Gendlin, E. (2003) Beyond postmodernism. In R. Frie (ed.) *Understanding Experience: Psychotherapy and Postmodernism*. London: Routledge.

Heidegger, M. (1962) *Being and Time*. New York: HarperOne.

Herman, J. (1997) *Trauma and Recovery: The Aftermath of Violence – from Domestic Abuse to Political Terror*. New York: Basic Books.

Hook, D., Collins, A., Mkhize, N., Kiguwa, P., Parker, I. and Burman, E. (2004) *Critical Psychology*. Lansdowne: UCT Press.

Jung, C.G. (1995) *Memories, Dreams, Reflections*. London: Fontana.

Merleau-Ponty, M. (2002) *Phenomenology of Perception: An Introduction*. London: Routledge.

Spinelli, E. (2005) *The Interpreted World: An Introduction to Phenomenological Psychology*. London: SAGE.

8 The relational therapist

Maria Luca

Introduction

This chapter will explore three phases of reflection that could support integrative therapists to make sense of their clinical experience and interactions with clients in the clinical context. The concepts of the pre-reflective, reflective, meta-reflective and mentalised attitudes will be used as the relational conceptual landscape for exploring clinical experience. This landscape will be discussed as a transformational space where the integrative practitioner can engage with the understandings they reach, to reflect and develop a greater depth of knowledge. As thoughts develop in the field of awareness through a shared, engaged action, participants cognitively register the connection emerging between them. This involves two subjectivities coming together willing to engage with each other in shared reflection that evokes not only the cognitive dimension but also the emotional dimension. Understanding emerging through this level of interaction can therefore be considered as embodied experiencing. It contains the reflected negation of the old pre-reflective order. Without interest or desire on the part of therapist and client in any given activity, the goal of achieving reflective awareness and meaningful knowledge in therapeutic contexts would be hindered.

The relational therapist

Psychotherapy consists of the interaction between two people, their histories (including traumas), world-views, personalities, values and expectations, to name but a few of the factors that mediate the therapy interaction (Hill 2005). Who the therapist is as a person, their attachment style, personality, ability to contain difficult emotions (both their own and the client's), how they manage conflict and negative or idealised transferences, and fundamentally their level of psychological maturity will impact on the intersubjective space and on the effectiveness of therapy.

The therapeutic relationship and the alliance are fundamental to successful therapy and would inform personal integration. Historically, therapy was viewed differently. For example, Skinner 'viewed successful therapy as a learning process in which the "teacher or trainer's" interventions (techniques), rather than the relationship between the participants, [was] the significant factor' (Skinner 1985, cited in Hubble et al. 2000: 135). Rogers (1951; 1957) first introduced the alliance as central to therapeutic success. Unlike Skinner's notion of therapy being a learning process, Rogers emphasised the therapeutic relationship as characterised by engaged client–therapist subjectivities, where the alliance develops and helps the therapeutic process to achieve positive outcomes. He advocated for a therapy of empathy, congruence, acceptance and unconditional positive regard, the core conditions known to facilitate rapport between client and therapist. Rogers knew early on in his work that warmth, listening and non-judgemental therapist attitudes enabled clients to develop trust, important for the alliance. The idea of a collaborative relationship was found much earlier than the 1950s, in Freud's (1913) early writings where he stressed the significance of 'an unobjectionable positive transference' from the patient. However, Freud placed the emphasis on the analysand's capacity to develop a positive transference and not on the analyst, who should attempt to remain neutral. Subsequently, researchers (Frank and Frank 1991; Lambert and Bergin 1994; Lambert and Barley 2001) embarked on a quest to identify factors common to all therapies that account for positive outcomes in different types of treatments (Hubble et al. 2000).

Therapist factors found to impinge on the development of a therapeutic alliance include certain personality attributes such as rigidity, coldness, hostility, uncertainty, defensiveness and unresponsiveness (Ackerman and Hilsenroth 2001) and unsuccessful management of their countertransference (Benjamin and Critchfield 2010). The relational therapist possesses attributes of honesty, respect, trustworthiness, flexibility, competence, confidence, expertness, warmth, empathy, openness (Ackerman and Hilsenroth 2001) and appropriate use of verbal and non-verbal communication (Bedi et al. 2005). The ability of therapists to form alliances with their clients, as well as flexibility, interpersonal perception, warmth and acceptance, have been proposed as crucial to positive therapeutic outcomes. Therapists' ability to create trust in their clients at the outset and understanding clients have also been found to positively influence outcomes irrespective of treatment modality (Wampold 2011). (Therapists adopting the personal integration approach would also be free to adopt existing qualities from the literature to form part of their integrative model.)

Therapists who possess good interpersonal and communication skills, with the capacity and willingness to relate, including addressing therapist–client conflict, tend to be more effective in resolving alliance ruptures (Safran et al. 2014). In contrast, therapists who adhere religiously to their preferred model of working tend to rely more on this, which leads to poor alliance rupture resolution and poor therapy outcomes (Castonguay et al. 1996; 2006). Real effects of therapy are associated with therapist and patient characteristics, interpersonal values, personality, gender, social skills and attachment levels (Castonguay and Beutler 2006; Duncan and Miller, in Norcross and Beutler 2006; Ogunfowora and Drapeau 2008; Petronzi and Masciale 2015).

Research (Schürmann and Mühlmeyer-Mentzel 2016) on what clients find helpful and what leads to positive change in therapy confirms that a client–therapist relationship characterised by accepting and caring support, as well as activating client resources, leads to positivity in the therapy relationship. They also provide self-soothing factors that impact on treatment compliance and increase emotional stability with the outcome of empowerment. The relational, integrative therapist adopts these qualities and adapts them to the individual client needs.

A portrait of a personal integration model

We have just explored what it means to be a relational therapist because at the core of my own continuous journey of personal integration is the therapeutic relationship. Also important is an attitude of fluidity and flexibility consisting of keeping an open mind, questioning one's psychological formulations, revising these according to evolved understandings and modifying treatment goals and choice of interventions to ensure they are congruent with what research has found to be effective, as well as one's own experience with an individual client. The therapeutic relationship consists of elements important to creating a foundation of trust and safety from which the therapeutic relationship springs. As discussed in Chapter 3, Clarkson's (1995) model consists of the following elements and these inform my model:

- the working alliance;
- the transferential/countertransferential relationship;
- the reparative/developmentally needed relationship;
- the person-to-person relationship;
- the transpersonal relationship.

(A more detailed portrait of my model is presented in Chapter 9.) The words of Maslow (1966) capture the drawback of the single-school approach and the importance of taking an integrative approach in therapy: 'if you only have a hammer, you treat everything like a nail' (cited in Norcross 1990: 21). Research shows that no single school is more efficacious than others (Hubble et al. 2000). Models of psychotherapy are, in my view, constructions of reality; they are narratives and stories we construct using our subjective lenses in relation to another. Being prepared to abandon one's beliefs and opinions contributes to feeling vulnerable. However, it is an important attitude in that it reinforces the fluidity and openness of the relational integrative model I explore here.

Finally, I should like to sum up the notion of a relational therapist with the idea that being married to our modality/theoretical approach (an absolutist, dogmatic attitude) could stifle the possibility of a creative, authentic and effective relational therapy. Fixing our models is like fixing an irreducible reality. Jean-Paul Sartre's advice to his pupil was a reminder of being free to choose: 'You are free, therefore choose – that is to say, invent. No rule of general morality can show you what you ought to do: no signs are vouchsafed in this world' (1973: 38).

Applied to the therapeutic encounter, a relational therapist acknowledges their own and their clients' subjectivities as coming together in the therapeutic encounter, producing a unique dynamic for that encounter. An important component of therapy, particularly relational therapy, is the capability for *reflexivity*. This will be the subject of exploration that follows.

Pre-reflective and reflective experience

Within the intersubjective domain of therapy, abstract understanding of clinical process and the therapy relationship itself is insufficient to produce the necessary relational depth that activates healing and facilitates change; this level of insight only comes as therapeutic understanding develops through a felt connection with clients and reflection on the therapeutic process, unlike cognitively focused approaches that give primacy to theory. Direct face-to-face therapeutic experience, clinical supervision, as well as personal therapy, when combined, are fundamental drivers for understanding our clients. The experiential domain where the therapeutic relationship lies easily lends itself to developing individualised constructions of client understanding. The process integrates the core practitioner perspective adding selected concepts and practices from other perspectives that make sense to the individual practitioner and, most importantly, are shown to be illuminating in practice. Effective therapists can reflect on and think about their thinking. But, as Wampold (2011) identified, the effective therapist also reflects on their own reaction to the client (i.e. countertransference). Relational depth is therefore achieved through a process consisting of three domains of experiencing: the pre-reflective, reflective and meta-reflective or mentalised dimensions (Figure 8.1).

The pre-reflective dimension

According to Legrand, 'Pre-reflective self-consciousness *sensu stricto* [or strictly speaking] is an awareness of oneself as subject' (2007: 586). Practitioner knowledge of theory is initially housed in the pre-reflective domain of consciousness. Pre-reflective consciousness is a feature of self-experience. It is (1) how the subject

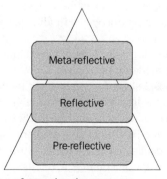

Figure 8.1 Three domains of experiencing

experiences (or is conscious of) themselves; (2) a form of self-recognition, like when standing in front of the mirror and the subject recognises their image as the self; and (3) a form of first-person perspective. It is the experience of a 'me' in relationship with '*myself*'. Legrand postulates that,

> any experience is pre-reflectively experienced as intrinsically subjective in the sense that it is experienced from the perspective of the experiencing subject (Zahavi 2005). The latter is a first-person perspective; it is tied to a self in the sense of being tied to the point of view of the experiencing, perceiving, acting subject.
>
> (2007: 584)

For example, my experience of the concept of reflection is the quality I place on the concept from my perspective, which is situated in my own subjectivity; it is my perception of the concept and my understanding and use of it, which are located in my primary form of self-consciousness. Pre-reflective consciousness is a recognition of self, a form of self-relatedness. It is, in other words, 'the ability to attribute one's action to oneself' (Zahavi 2005: 593). The pre-reflective level is characterised by what could be defined as raw, unprocessed experience of being-in-the-world. This is what is often referred to as the concrete level of experience whereby consciousness is far from being translucent, as Kaufmann (1992) argues. (A *translucent* consciousness is aware of itself and its contents.)

The reflective dimension

Reflection is a concept found as early as the seventeenth century in the empiricism of John Locke (1632–1704) in his *An Essay Concerning Human Understanding* (see Aaron 1937). Part of this essay attempted to develop a theory of mind from an empirical perspective. Locke was interested in the psychological realm of experience, with how the mind comes to know the world, contrasting reflection, or inner sense (the mind's reflective experience of its own experience of things), with sensation, or outer sense (the mind's experience of things).

The reflective dimension operates outside the recognition of self and awareness of one's consciousness. It is a shift from the relationship with self in the pre-reflective dimension, to an experiential relationship with another subject (a client) captured in the term 'intersubjectivity' (Stolorow and Atwood 1997). Stolorow and Atwood suggest that the psychotherapy situation is an intersubjective system of reciprocal mutual influence and the concept of neutrality is an illusion. They regard interpretations as suggestions and believe transference is contaminated by therapist and client subjectivities, unlike the classical Freudians. To replace the Freudian attitude of neutrality, they used the term 'empathic-introspective inquiry', which captures the reflective dimension of therapy. Buber's (1970; 1992) writings are central to our understanding of intersubjectivity; '[Buber] conceived of relationship between self and other as mutual and reciprocal and central to the emergence of the self into being. The emphasis here is on the primacy of dialogue and relationship' (Bradfield 2012: 266).

It is within this intersubjective domain of relating that the reflective dimension is at play. This is not in a me–self recognition (pre-reflective), but in an I–Thou reflective awareness. Reflective awareness within a relationship is the channel of intersubjectivity that is co-created in the relationship between therapist and client. The relational aspect in therapy refers to two individuals being aware of and engaging with each other. Intrinsic to this relating is the consciousness of each person reflecting on itself in relation to another. Thus, the I–Thou experience goes beyond pure awareness of another and into thinking about oneself and one's being in relation to another.

Bradfield (2012) refers to the relationship between qualitative researcher, participant and research context to describe a dynamic that evolves between them. This is analogous to the therapist–client and therapy context relationship. He argues that '[the] phenomenological concept of *verstehen* . . . denotes a felt subjective engagement with the lived experience of another, in which one subjectivity witnesses the depth of experience of another' (2012: 264).

However, hearing of my client's experience in itself is not sufficient for understanding it. My *involvement* with the client's experience supports a more engaged understanding and reflection plays a central role in this understanding. What mediates the hearing and understanding, the *involvement*, with the client's experience can therefore be understood as *embodied* intersubjectivity. The Rogerian concept of 'empathy' captures this type of engagement eloquently. Rogers' (1957) conception of empathic understanding requires the therapist to feel at home in the client's universe (familiar and sensitive). It is about allowing the client's world to touch (sometimes infect) the therapist and for the therapist to experience it as if it were their own without losing the 'as if' quality.

For example, in my therapy relationship with one client, I felt a sickly sensation in my stomach that arose out of my engagement with his feeling nauseous. The client expressed this through bodily movements and gestures representing an inner feeling that had no analogues in words and cognitive understanding for him or for me. At this stage, it is bodily empathy. Moments later he said: 'I think she [his mother] sexually abused me.' With his uttering these words, my perceptual and cognitive fields were activated and produced a mental representation that led to understanding my response to his nausea. I spontaneously reflected on this interaction with my client, processing my felt response, his bodily behaviour and my mental sense of the experience. The process of engagement between client and therapist involves a meeting of their respective subjectivities. It is through an open, engaged intersubjective negotiation that insights emerge and are shared, tested, revised and reach peek shared understandings. The reflective domain is therefore analogous to Buber's I–Thou experience, where the contents of the therapist's subjectivity relate to the client's subjectivity and are experienced in the here and now interaction between the two subjects, either through focusing on what has been said (language) now and before, what's been felt (emotions), what's been bodily sensed (bodily experience), and what's been intuited (beyond direct experiencing). This sentiment is echoed by Polkinghorne who states: 'Understanding experience merely as a mental projection onto the world (the idealistic fallacy) or as a reflection of the world (the realistic fallacy) misses the necessity of the person–world relationship in the constituting of experience' (Polkinghorne 1989, cited in Bradfield 2012: 271).

The philosopher Walter Kaufmann's (1992) 'foggy mind' also captured the reflective level involving a transparent mind. It referred to a process of drawing out pre-reflective knowledge (which requires intentionality) and scrutinising its contents – these are then transformed into a new order. To achieve this transformation, the therapist is required to have the capacity to move away temporarily from the raw knowledge into meta-reflection and this would rest on the individual's ability to exercise their agency not just cognitively but also affectively. This idea refers to the directing of attention to the contents of experience, the phenomenology of experience, and thinking about and experiencing these contents at different levels. Agency requires deliberation and intentionality, qualities found in individuals focusing on particular aspects of living in the world. Without interest in and desire for both being sources of affective vitality in humans, the goal of achieving reflective awareness would be hindered.

The development of relational, intersubjective negotiation is not without risk of a rupture in the therapeutic alliance. However, research into alliance ruptures shows that if therapists and clients actively engage and try to deal with ruptures, it leads to more successful outcomes (Lansford 1986; Safran and Muran 2000; Stiles et al. 2004). Empathic introspective inquiry is synonymous with the reflective function. This I describe as a *circling of consciousness*, a process whereby the therapist's consciousness critically reflects on its own contents, testing them against the client's reactions, perceptions and understanding so that the therapist's understanding can be re-shaped. In brief, the process involves *thinking about thinking*. Research has found that 'self-practice/self-reflection can be particularly helpful for increasing empathy for clients, highlighting the difficulties they may encounter' (Gale and Schröder 2014: 373). Empathy is about deep understanding that has the potential to enhance the therapeutic alliance, hence sowing the seeds for more challenging work, especially around traumatic client experiences.

The meta-reflective dimension

The meta-reflective dimension concerns the capacity of practitioners to reflect on the therapeutic aspects after they have happened. Schön's (1987) reflection-on-action is a close cousin of meta-reflective practice that transforms experience into knowledge. This type of reflection can highlight assumptions, beliefs, expectations and biases and, by recognising them, identify any influence they may have on the therapy relationship. This dimension is predominantly performed by more novice practitioners. It occurs after the event when we think about a therapy session, what emerged, how we reacted, whether what happened influenced the outcome and what could be done differently to maximise positive outcomes. It is a dimension involving a translucent consciousness, a term used by Kaufmann (1992) to denote clarity of mind as opposed to his idea of a foggy mind.

Theriault and Gazzola (2005) found that 74.3 per cent of psychologists reported feeling distress in the previous three years and 90 per cent of psychotherapists reported emotional problems directly linked to their professional work. Their study found that despite several years of experience, many therapists feel incompetent in their work (Theriault and Gazzola 2005: 11). Supervision, one of the professional requirements of registering bodies, provides opportunities for therapists not only to reflect on and understand the therapy relationship, but also to process their personal anxieties and stress as a result of their role. Safety and the development of a working alliance between supervisor and supervisee maximise the opportunity for reflection and provide the foundations for creative work. However, little is known about whether therapists receive sufficient support from supervision, which Theriault and Gazzola's study found to be important in the management of their professional practice. Supervision is a space where practitioners can be encouraged to meta-reflect.

Psychodynamic theory emphasises the importance of forging links between the affective and mental representation of experience. 'Mentalised affectivity' is about the process of the different levels of experience reaching mental representation, which influences the development of a coherent understanding of the self (Fonagy et al. 2002). Semerari et al. (2003) make the same point with the concept of 'meta-cognitive functions'. In certain phenomena, such as somatisation, there appear to be aspects of client experience that somehow cannot be reflected upon and therefore remain as unreflective consciousness. The failure of meta-reflection becomes an intersubjective problem and impacts on both therapist and client. These would include meta-reflective blocks to the development of a dialogical, reflective therapeutic relationship. Therapy provides the space where mentalisation could be developed for both client and therapist. This could be achieved in a variety of ways for therapists, including supervision, case discussions and self-reflection. Clients develop meta-reflection through the process of therapeutic engagement where therapists invite them to enter the reflective phases, depending also on therapists' ability to meta-reflect.

Mentalisation and meta-reflection

The impact of interaction on learning and development was Vygotsky's (1896–1934) key theoretical formulation (Gallagher 1999), in which he argued that social interaction provides the scaffolding for a child's development of thought and behaviour. The key principles of this theory were that children construct knowledge, that knowledge is developed in a social context and that language plays a central role in mental development. The early psychology of Piaget and Inhelder (1948) also suggested that a combination of hands-on touching and integration of different viewpoints is instrumental in children's development of spatial ability and mental models of spatial objects. This psychology recognises the importance of experience in child development, especially experience placed within a social and cultural context and that is gained through interaction with others.

Developments in contemporary cognitive science have generated more detailed understanding of the relationship between social interaction and mental development, not only in children but in adults too. The concept of 'metacognition' (Semerari et al. 2003) proposes that the individual recognises both their thoughts and emotions while simultaneously comprehending the mind of another person. Meta-reflection could be seen to be the mediating factor, the vehicle through which metacognition can be developed.

Mentalisation refers to a process mainly developed through attachments. The concept has come to be synonymous with reflection, albeit in a more elaborated sense. The concept of the 'reflective function' was described by Fonagy et al. (1998) as follows: 'we have operationalized the ability to apply a mentalistic interpreta-tional strategy as reflective function, as the plausible interpretation of one's own and others' behaviour in terms of underlying mental states' (Fonagy et al., in Pfafflin and Adshead 2003: 30). The authors explicitly state that they link the reflective func-tion to Bogdan's interpersonal interpretative function (IIF) and to Bion's (1962) basic model of thinking (Bateman and Fonagy 2004).

Mentalisation also refers to the symbolisation of secondary representation, a level assigned to the representation of states of mind, formed in childhood out of parental mirroring. From this perspective, mentalisation is an experiential concept, developed through the interaction between child and carer (Falkenstrom 2003). Unlike the Cartesian doctrine of first-person authority, which assigns reflection to intentional states of mind and makes mental agency innate, Fonagy et al. claim, through the concept of mentalisation, to have given the notion of self as a mental agent an interpersonal or constructed capacity. They argue that it is through the primary object relationships that we discover affects. In their words:

> Affect regulation, the capacity to modulate affect states, is closely related to mentalisation in that it plays a fundamental role in the unfolding of a sense of self and agency. In our account, affect regulation is a prelude to mentalisation; yet, we also believe that once mentalisation has occurred, the nature of affect regulation is transformed.
>
> (2002: 4–5)

This relationship between affect regulation and mentalisation describes the process of affectively experiencing and knowing one's inner world. If this is achieved, then it is automatically transformed into a deeper level of knowing, described as 'mentali-sation'. The concepts of 'mentalisation' and 'meta-reflection', with roots in social behaviour, can be seen as contemporary attempts to link 'mind' and 'body'.

Studies of borderline patients conducted by Bateman and Fonagy (2004) found that non-reflective internal working models come to dominate the behaviour of individuals with borderline personality disorder, especially in emotionally charged intimate relationships. The authors postulate that patients who lack the ability for reflective learning experienced problematic early attachments that led to a developmental deficiency. From this vantage point, mentalisation aids the unfolding of agency in clients and the therapy relationship is the vessel through which this process takes place. As Stolorow explains: 'The essence of psychoanalytic cure lies in the establishment of new, alternative principles for organizing experience, so that the patient's experiential repertoire becomes enlarged, enriched, more flexible, and more complex' (Stolorow and Atwood 1996: 2).

Conclusion

A relationship between therapist and client involves relating through dialogue where their respective subjectivities meet. Therefore, 'the intersubjective dialogue between patient and analyst can produce powerful therapeutic reactions in liberating the patient's affectivity and in strengthening the patient's capacities for affect tolerance, integration and articulation' (Stolorow and Atwood 1996: 2).

The intersubjective position moves away from the notion of the objective therapist observer that can be neutral in relation to the client. We consider a therapist's subjectivity not as an obstacle to understanding the client's internal world, but as a tool thereto. Susie Orbach, in *The Impossibility of Sex*, suggests that:

> Today's analyses consist not of the earth-shattering realization, insight or interpretation, but of the slow building up of conditions in which it is possible for the patient to understand herself afresh and to construct a meaningful relationship with the therapist in which she feels more fully accepted and understood.
>
> (1999: 4)

These words, in my view, capture the Rogerian *Humanism* reincarnated! Relational psychotherapy is a postmodern perspective that postulates a humane therapeutic approach. The distant, neutral observer of Freud's times aimed at evoking the transference, is an attitude of the past. In my experience, irrespective of neutrality or relationality in the therapist, the transference will be present. Research has helped psychotherapy recognise the importance of relationality and connectedness, qualities that do not necessarily exclude the use of transference and countertransference interpretations. Integration is described as

> [a] personal journey, as a way of being that is constantly becoming and unfolding in relation with the therapist's training, experience and interaction with peers and clients. The result is indefinable and unnameable, and perhaps represents the soul of integrative psychotherapy.
>
> (Nuttall 2008: 19)

Every therapist is on a journey of development and growth. The therapist's integration model also evolves, develops and matures with time and clinical experience. 'Practice makes best' is a maxim I use to capture the importance of the mature integrative practitioner who, after several years of practice, is not wedded to theories difficult to apply to practice. The journey is on a continuum and only ends when therapists stop practising.

References

Aaron, R. (1937) *John Locke*. Oxford: Oxford University Press.

Ackerman, S.J. and Hilsenroth M.J. (2001) A review of therapist characteristics and techniques negatively impacting the therapeutic alliance. *Psychotherapy*, 38: 171–85.

Bedi, R.P., Davis, M.D. and Arvay, M.J. (2005) The client's perspective on forming a counselling alliance and implications for research on counsellor training. *Canadian Journal of Counselling*, 39: 71–85.

Benjamin, L. and Critchfield, K.L. (2010) An interpersonal perspective on therapy alliances and techniques. In J.C. Muran and J.P. Barber (eds), *The Therapeutic Alliance: An Evidence-Based Guide to Practice* (pp. 123–49). New York: Guilford Press.

Bradfield, B. (2012) Intersubjectivity and the knowing of inner experience: Finding space for a psychoanalytic phenomenology in research. *Journal of Humanistic Psychology*, 53(3): 263–82.

Buber, M. (1967) *A Believing Humanism: Gleanings by Martin Buber*. New York: Simon & Schuster.

Castonguay, L. and Beutler, L.E. (2006) Principles of therapeutic change: A task force on participants, relationships, and techniques factors. *Journal of Clinical Psychology*, 62(6): 631–8.

Castonguay, L., Constantino, M. and Holtforth, M. (2006) The working alliance: Where are we and where should we go? *Psychotherapy*, 43: 271–9.

Castonguay, L.G., Goldfried, M.R., Wiser, S., Raue, P.J. and Hayes, A.M. (1996) Predicting the effect of cognitive therapy for depression: A study of unique and common factors. *Journal of Clinical and Consulting Psychology*, 64: 497–504.

Fonagy, P. (2003) The developmental roots of violence in the failure of mentalization. In F. Pfafflin and G. Adshead (eds), *A Matter of Security: The Application of Attachment Theory to Forensic Psychiatry and Psychotherapy*. London: Jessica Kingsley Publishers.

Fonagy, P., Gergely, G., Jurist, E.L. and Target, M. (2002) *Affect Regulation, Mentalization and the Development of the Self*. New York: Other Press.

Frank, J.D. and Frank, J. (1991) *Persuasion and Healing* (3rd edn). Baltimore, MD: Johns Hopkins University Press.

Gale, C. and Schröder, T. (2014) Experiences of self-practice/self-reflection in cognitive behavioural therapy: A meta-synthesis of qualitative studies. *Psychology and Psychotherapy: Theory, Research and Practice*, 87: 373–92.

Hill, C.E. (2005) Therapist techniques, client involvement, and the therapeutic relationship: Inextricably intertwined in the therapy process. *Psychotherapy: Theory, Research, Practice, Training*, 42: 431–42.

Hubble, M.A., Duncan, B.L. and Miller, S.D. (2000) *The Heart and Soul of Change: What Works in Therapy* (4th edn). Washington, DC: American Psychological Association.

Kaufmann, W. (1992) *Freud, Adler and Jung: Discovering the Mind*, vol. III. New Brunswick, NJ: Transaction Books.

Lambert, M.J. and Barley, D.E. (2001) Research summary on the therapeutic relationship and psychotherapy outcome. *Psychotherapy*, 38: 357–61.

Lambert, M.J. and Bergin, A.E. (1994) The effectiveness of psychotherapy. In A.E. Bergin and S.L. Garfield (eds), *Handbook of Psychotherapy and Behaviour Change* (4th edn) (pp. 143–89). Oxford: Blackwell.

Lansford, E. (1986) Weakenings and repairs of the working alliance in short-term psychotherapy. *Professional Psychology: Research and Practice*, 17: 364–6.

Legrand, D. (2007) *Pre-reflective self-as-subject from experiential and empirical perspectives*. Available at: https://www.researchgate.net/profile/Dorothee_Legrand/publication/6303037_Pre-reflective_self-assubject_from_experiential_and_empirical_perspectives_Consciousness_and_Cognition_16_583-599/links/00b7d51d1ff192f636000000.pdf (accessed 3 June 2016).

Norcross, J. (1990) An eclectic definition of psychotherapy. In J.K. Zeig and W.M. Union (eds), *What Is Psychotherapy?* San Francisco, CA: Jossey-Bass.

Norcross, J., Levant, R. and Beutler, L. (eds) (2006) *Evidence-Based Practices in Mental Health*. Washington, DC: APA Press.

Nuttall, J. (2008) The integrative attitude – a personal journey. *European Journal of Psychotherapy and Counselling*, 10(1): 19–38.

Ogunfowora, B. and Drapeau, M. (2008) A study of the relationship between personality traits and theoretical orientation preferences. *Counselling and Psychotherapy Research*, 8(3): 151–9.

Orbach, S. (1999) *The Impossibility of Sex*. Harmondsworth: Allen Lane.

Petronzi, G.J. and Masciale, J.N. (2015) Using personality traits and attachment styles to predict people's preference of psychotherapeutic orientation. *Counselling and Psychotherapy Research*, 15(4): 298–308.

Rogers, C.R. (1951) *Client-Centered Therapy: Its Current Practice, Implications and Theory*. Boston, MA: Houghton Mifflin.

Rogers, C.R. (1957) The necessary and sufficient conditions of psychotherapeutic personality change. *Journal of Consulting Psychology*, 21: 95–103.

Safran, J.D. and Muran, J.C. (2000) *Negotiating the Therapeutic Alliance: A Relational Treatment Guide*. New York: Guilford Press.

Safran, J.D., Muran, J.C. and Shaker, A. (2014) Research on therapeutic impasses and ruptures in the therapeutic alliance. *Contemporary Psychoanalysis*, 50: 211–32. Doi:10.1080/00107530.2014.880318.

Sartre, J.P. (1973) *Existentialism and Humanism*. London: Methuen.

Schön, D.A. (1987) *Educating the Reflective Practitioner*. San Francisco, CA: Jossey-Bass.

Schürmann, I. and Mühlmeyer-Mentzel, A. (2016) *What Leads to Success in the Change Process from a Client Perspective? / ¿Qué es lo que conduce al éxito en el proceso de cambio desde la perspectiva del cliente?* Available at: http://dx.doi.org/10.1080/02109395.2016.1189211.

Stiles, W.B., Glick, M.J., Osatuke, K., Hardy, G.E., Shapiro, D.A., Agnew-Davies, P. and Barkham, M. (2004) Patterns of alliance development and the rupture-repair hypothesis: Are productive relationships U-shaped or V-shaped? *Journal of Counseling Psychology*, 51: 81–92.

Stolorow, R. and Atwood, G. (1996) The intersubjective perspective. *The Psychoanalytic Review*, 83: 181–94. Available at: http://icpla.edu/wp-content/uploads/2012/10/Stolorow-Atwood-The-Intersubjective-Perspective-Psychoa.-Review-1996.pdf (accessed 3 April 2017).

Stolorow, R. and Atwood, G. (1997) Deconstructing the myth of the neutral analyst: An alternative from intersubjective systems theory. *Psychoanalytic Quarterly*, 66(3): 431–49.

Wampold, B.E. (2011) *Qualities and Actions of Effective Psychotherapists*. Washington, DC: American Psychological Association.

Zahavi, D. (2005) *Subjectivity and Selfhood: Investigating the First-Person Perspective*. Cambridge, MA: MIT Press.

9   A portrait of a personal journey towards personal integration

Maria Luca

Introduction

In this chapter, I will present a portrait of a personal journey towards becoming an integrative psychotherapist, with a psychoanalytic base. Every journey has phases and I aim to present the impact of each phase on my model. The portrait will consist of:

1. my personal/subjective world, values, beliefs as well as ambiguities and con-fusion and their impact on my budding identity as an integrative therapist;
2. the philosophical, theoretical, research and clinical influences to becoming an integrative psychotherapist; and
3. the nuts and bolts or key principles informing my approach to practice.

The synthesis of these elements has contributed to my evolving, fluid sense of being an integrative psychotherapist. What I hope to be able to convey is what I consider to be the *sine qua non* of effective practice, which has developed through learning from my clients, theory, mistakes and research. These elements have all been integrated into my model. The chapter is not intended to present a full con-ceptualisation of these aspects, but an outline capturing the overview of my inte-grative model.

My personal world and life learning

At the time I first considered training as a psychotherapist, I had completed a bachelor's degree and had been working in a professional capacity for a number of years. I had also been married and divorced and had two young children, so I needed to find a way to navigate through their needs before I fully committed to training in psychotherapy. I was not aware that my own personal psychotherapy, to help me work through my divorce, had provided me with the incentive to embark on this quest until a few years into my psychotherapy training. As for the idea of psychotherapy *integration*, I had little knowledge or understanding of it. In fact, I had an adverse reaction to a module dedicated to integration. Having fallen in love with the psychoanalysis and existentialism modules, there was no space to open my mind to integration. It felt like an eclectic mixture of everything with little substance or power to capture me; I needed a glue to bind the parts into a coherent whole. I had received training in humanistic, psychoanalytic and phenomenological psychological theories and all of them made sense in their own unique ways in explaining what it is to be human. (All made fascinating bed-time reading!) My interest and curiosity in phenomenology and existentialism started during my undergraduate studies and led to much philosophical readings including Heidegger, Kierkegaard, Sartre and Husserl, as well as novelists such as Kafka, Dostoyevsky, Camus, de Beauvoir and others. Although I had some knowledge of psychoanalysis, it was during my psychotherapy training that I really delved into it. Every fibre of my being opened up to replenishing ideas, some enticing, others confusing; but, I was sure that becoming a psychotherapist was a quest I would follow. I enjoyed helping others all my life, so why not make a career of it?

Before entering psychotherapy training, I had some understanding of what brings people to therapy through early exposure to people's wounds, especially those of my immediate family. My mother was the embodiment of a paradox of strength and vulnerability. I learned how to see people and really pay attention to people's inner wounded child, driven by my own need and quest to understand my relationship to myself, my wounds and my relational patterns with others, starting with my parents. It took me many years after training to come close to developing an understanding. At the time, I could only go so far, because I had not yet reached the deepest recesses of my psyche. I lacked the psychological grammar.

My first therapist was a woman who practised psychoanalytically. I learnt to let her in and the emotional connection between us grew as the months went by. She evoked my experience with my maternal grandmother, who had been the most influential figure during my early years. As with my grandmother, I trusted my therapist whole-heartedly. It was, conceptually speaking, a positive transference relationship, important in the development of a working alliance. By the end of this relationship, I knew that she loved me. To get to the stage of feeling 'loveable', I had to face the shadow of my parents, which created emotional turbulence, particularly emotional pain in the process of unravelling painful memories, linking them to unconscious life choices as an adult and learning to make conscious decisions.

My early relationship with my father had taken a backstage during my therapy. He had been emotionally absent during my childhood, not unusual for Mediterranean fathers. My second therapist, whom I saw during my training, was a male Jungian analyst and my relationship with my father here took centre stage. This was another journey of self-discovery, sieving through some vague, translucent memories, and the hurt associated with them had begun. One of my trainers had mentioned the concept of the 'wounded healer' in a lecture and I had an immediate resonance with the term. My curiosity to learn more led to reading Rippere and Williams' (1985) *Wounded Healers: Mental Health Workers' Experiences of Depression. The Myth of the Untroubled Therapist*, by Marie Adams (2013), is a more recent compelling narrative of therapists' own wounded self. The idea that a key motivation to train as a psychotherapist is to heal one's own wounded self made sense to me. I have found that both clients in therapy and the general public assume that therapists are psychologically sorted. For me, this is an idealisation of psychotherapists. In fact, anecdotal evidence suggests that people's motivation to train in the caring professions is often driven by their own need to be nurtured and healed. Recognition of the therapist's own wounded self is paramount in empathising with clients' wounds, but also fundamental in distinguishing between subjective therapist responses to clients that arise from the wounded healer's psychopathology and those that are a direct response to clients' psychopathology, as well as a mixture of both.

Observing clients and knowing them purely cognitively, without becoming emotionally engaged with them, is pure objectification of them and not sufficient to helping the healing process. I have learnt through practice that emotional connection involving the therapist's subjectivity in the relational space is fundamental to successful therapy. Self-awareness is also a cornerstone to being a therapist who can be there for others. This is one of 14 qualities in effective therapists detailed by Wampold: 'The effective therapist is aware of his or her own psychological process' (2011: 5). Personal therapy, curiosity to understand oneself and professional development groups are some ways of developing self-awareness.

Learning to feel 'loveable' and embracing the notion of being 'good enough' were significant in having faith in my own ability to love, help and accept my clients. As Shamasundar poignantly put it: 'One cannot give what one does not have' (2008: 302). Having a positive experience of therapy myself had an immense influence on my valuing therapy as a genuinely helpful and rewarding career. It nurtured me, gave me a valuable experience, took me to the depths of my psyche and enabled me to take my own clients to the depths of their psyches.

I believe in therapy's power to heal. However, every client has a limit to how far they can travel therapeutically. This often depends on their ability to tolerate pain and whether they possess resilience and a level of psychological mindedness to engage in therapy. Hence, therapy is not suitable for everyone. Some clients benefit more than others from therapy.

By reflecting on and researching the key factors that influence reduced benefits of therapy for certain clients, I identified lack of client motivation, engagement and rigid defensiveness as three of the most relevant contributing factors. Resilience, strength and ability to tolerate pain determine the pace of therapy. For example, if my assessment indicates lack of resilience, then I would be careful to be gentle in softening clients' defences in my therapeutic attempt to access their deeper, wounded self, so understanding and working *through* can be worked *with*. The learning from observation, critique and questioning is immense. The knowledge from experience has helped me adapt my model to what works for individual clients.

In terms of therapist factors, I hold that the therapist's personality, ability to emotionally connect, motivation and engagement are the most influential in building the alliance that is the foundation of therapy. As Jørgensen highlighted, what is important is 'a particular kind of emotionally-charged relationship between the patient and the therapist that supports the patient's confidence in the therapist's competence and in his desire to help' (2004: 516).

Evidence from research on common factors (Hubble et al. 1999; Wampold 2011) substantiated my personal observations. Research has provided evidence that therapist factors have an important influence on therapeutic outcomes. Wampold rightly raised the question on what makes effective therapists when he argued that,

> The evidence that there are small or negligible differences among treatments that are intended to be therapeutic for particular disorders and the evidence that some therapists consistently achieve better outcomes than other therapists, in clinical trials and in practice, raises the unmistakably important questions: What are the qualities and action of effective therapists?
>
> (2011: 2)

As we saw earlier, Wampold (2011: 3) listed 14 qualities and actions of effective therapists. Of these, I consider interpersonal skills crucial and have focused on developing them in myself. According to him, effective therapists have a sophisticated set of interpersonal skills, including:

1. verbal fluency;
2. interpersonal perception;
3. affective modulation and expressiveness;
4. warmth and acceptance;
5. empathy;
6. focus on others.

One of my clients told me recently:

> I'm feeling terrible . . . The last three days have been awful; I was tempted not to come today then I thought, 'no, I'm not going to do what I normally do', which is keeping my vulnerability away from everyone. Therapy is working. I was telling a friend about you, about therapy . . . it's you (looking at me straight in the eyes) it's you . . . I feel that you feel me. I look at your face and I know . . . I just know you understand me (tears). I've never had that, ever, and had therapy before . . . (Gesturing with their hands, they described how my face is not empty of emotion) I trust you and I miss you when I'm not here. Your therapy room is a hug!

Another client, during the ending session when they were evaluating the positive benefits from their short-term therapy with me, said:

> It's you; you are a witch. You've been amazing. Despite sometimes being horrible to you, you tolerated me and understood my anger. I don't feel so angry any more. Thank you.

I don't take what my clients say to me about our relationships lightly. I think of different meanings and I share my understandings. These client comments were genuinely from their hearts, a gift to us both for creating a healing therapeutic environment.

These are two of many comments from clients on what they find helpful in therapy. It reconfirms my belief that emotional connection between client and therapist is that special foundation on which therapeutic effectiveness rests. I felt very close to these clients in those moments of moving into a space of immediacy, giving me what they valued in me – visibility, empathy, acknowledgement and visceral, intuitive understanding. Clients like to give something back to their therapist, perhaps unconsciously demonstrating that they too have valuable resources. Generosity of spirit in therapists encourages clients to be open with their own feelings towards their therapist. The therapy relationship is, however, a strange one. (Clients often say this.) We expect them to reveal their most intimate self, while we keep ours at bay and occasionally, through careful disclosures, give snippets of ourselves. I am not suggesting that therapists should reveal, but it is important to acknowledge that therapy is a strange relationship while considering sharing our feelings, thoughts, observations and understandings in a timely and appropriate fashion.

The nuts and bolts of developing an integrative model

My training, personal therapy, practice with clients, supervision and personal reflections enhanced my self-awareness and helped me unravel and understand ghosts from my past. I became a client to myself. Every single concept I learned, I was applying to myself, so I became the subject of rigorous case study research – to the point where I fitted into *every single category of the DSM*. I felt totally *pathologised*, not to mention frustrated that, as the subject of a case study I had imposed on myself, I had numerous diagnoses! Phenomenology provided respite by strongly opposing the idea of pathology. For example, I valued Buber's (1967) concept of the I–Thou relationship where therapist and client relate at different levels. The I–Thou being fundamentally relational confirmed what intuitively I had known, hence it helped me find the language for existing intuitive knowledge. This is one of the concepts that I have retained and is at the core of my approach to therapy.

However, I found a number of phenomenology's attempts to apply abstract philosophical concepts to practice insufficient. What I mean is that applied existential practice, just like applied psychoanalytic practice, in itself lacked a rich vocabulary and toolbox of qualities for me to feel they were rounded perspectives. So, what initially seemed to be a rescuing remedy became temporary relief, as I now began to find flaws in phenomenology and in other approaches. I was being pulled from pillar to post in my own mind, shifting from idealising humanism to psychoanalysis to phenomenology – and feeling unable to have a faithful allegiance to any of these approaches. I had, in my early days of training, fallen in love with each of these approaches in themselves. I embraced them with passion and I heartily welcomed them to my mind's eye. But within this intellectual infatuation, my rational mind was not ready to commit. What saved me were some reflections on the idea of a perfect parent, which most children believe they have, despite their parents' flaws. Some adults go to the other extreme of denigrating the parents they had previously idealised (in order to separate and develop their independent identity); I placed myself in the middle. So I thought, just like my parents had met some of my needs and my grandparents, other relatives, teachers and the environment had met others, it made sense that I could be my own architect and construct my own good-enough parent called 'integration'.

Big mistake!

There were many times when I wanted to give up. It was too challenging, too confusing, too energy-consuming. But being predisposed to my family's mottos of 'never give up', 'tolerate confusion and uncertainty', 'trust the journey', 'you will find light at the end of the tunnel' and 'failure is not an option until you exhaust all avenues' sustained me in putting the pieces of the puzzle together to develop a good-enough, coherent integrative approach. Little did I know that this was only the beginning of a journey of discontent.

Looking back, this was my process of deconstruction. It was a process of selecting what practice showed to be viable concepts and therapeutic qualities, then a process of reconstruction made up of hypotheses, theories and, most importantly, knowledge from experience. If my approach made sense therapeutically, I would continue formulating and reformulating until both the client and I felt our relationship was helping. My model evolved slowly but surely. Along the way, thinking back on my practice, I identified mistakes that I was not mature enough to recognise at the time. Patrick Casement's (2002) *Learning from My Mistakes* consoled my inner critic. Instead of a persecutory relationship with myself, where all the 'shoulds' and 'oughts' could have blocked me from taking therapeutic risks, I allowed myself to see the learning, which was developed from mistakes, that posed no harm to clients.

My integrative model is still evolving after 22 years of practice. This inevitable process of evolving as a psychotherapist requires psychological integration and psychological maturity. It also demands that the therapist is the gatekeeper of their own mental health and well-being and does not collude with clients' unrealistic or 'magical' expectations of therapy but empowers clients to be responsible for themselves. This does not mean that clients would not benefit from experiencing me as a new, idealised parent who helps them make reparation of their inner wounds. However, if the therapy gets stuck in this phase to the exclusion of the adult-to-adult phase where clients recognise their therapist's limitations and, by implication, their own, then clients are not helped to psychologically mature, accept limitations and take responsibility for their own lives.

Once the client's agency is activated, I have found that the work flows differently. Any idealised, erotic, eroticised or negative transferences are dissolved and the final phase of the work is more in sight. This extract from *Ithaka* by Cavafy, translated by Keeley and Sherrard (1992), captures the wisdom of any journey, including the journey to integration:

> As you set out for Ithaka
> hope the voyage is a long one,
> full of adventure, full of discovery.
> Laistrygonians and Cyclops,
> angry Poseidon—don't be afraid of them:
> you'll never find things like that on your way
> as long as you keep your thoughts raised high,
> as long as a rare excitement
> stirs your spirit and your body.
> Laistrygonians and Cyclops,
> wild Poseidon—you won't encounter them
> unless you bring them along inside your soul,
> unless your soul sets them up in front of you.
>
> Hope the voyage is a long one.
> May there be many a summer morning when,
> with what pleasure, what joy,
> you come into harbors seen for the first time;
> may you stop at Phoenician trading stations
> to buy fine things,
> mother of pearl and coral, amber and ebony,
> sensual perfume of every kind—
> as many sensual perfumes as you can;
> and may you visit many Egyptian cities
> to gather stores of knowledge from their scholars.
>
> Keep Ithaka always in your mind.
> Arriving there is what you are destined for.
> But do not hurry the journey at all.
> Better if it lasts for years,
> so you are old by the time you reach the island,
> wealthy with all you have gained on the way,
> not expecting Ithaka to make you rich.
>
> Ithaka gave you the marvelous journey.
> Without her you would not have set out.
> She has nothing left to give you now.
>
> And if you find her poor, Ithaka won't have fooled you.
> Wise as you will have become, so full of experience,
> you will have understood by then what these Ithakas mean.

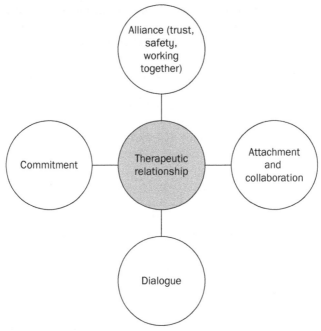

Figure 9.1   Elements of the therapeutic relationship

My developing model of integration

Guided by the words of Maslow that 'if you only have a hammer, you treat every-thing like a nail' (cited in Palmer, Dainow and Milner 2006: 89) and Polkinghorne's view that 'the large number of theories claiming to have grasped the essentials of psychological functioning provides *prima facie* evidence that no one theory is cor-rect' (1992: 158), I decided to choose those theories that held depth and the power to explain for my model, as seen in Figure 9.1.

For me, the therapeutic relationship is the cornerstone of therapy. Research using video of micro-momentary facial expressions recognisable across cultures has highlighted relational, intersubjective processes as being crucial to the thera-peutic relationship (Haggard and Isaacs 1966; Ekman and Friesen 1978; McCluskey et al. 1997, 1999). Increasingly, research has brought to the psychotherapy field useful knowledge of the interpersonal sphere, capturing the minute expressions of therapists, including warmth and attentive listening, which clients value (Hubble et al. 1999).

What clients also value is feeling safe and trusting of their therapist's ability to hold the space between them. Through collaboration – feeling involved and encour-aged to share their intimate selves, having their understandings about themselves received respectfully by therapists through genuine responsiveness – clients' self-esteem and resilience stand a better chance of developing. This is the process of developing an attachment that cements the therapeutic relationship. I've had clients whose previous experience of therapy they described as 'pointless' or even 'a waste of money'. Enquiring into these experiences, clients have shared with me that lying on the couch session after session, unable to see the face of their therapist, not hearing a sound from their therapist, felt abusive. I believe that access to the face is a building block to the development of the alliance. It is a mirror that speaks volumes, often without saying a word. It is through the face that a client sees and feels the warmth and empathy so important to the healing process. I accept that the free association experience emerging through lying on the couch can evoke strong transferences, which are helpful to understanding what from the past is transferred onto the therapist. This technique aids awareness of early patterns of relating, transferred onto the person of the therapist or indeed onto important others in the client's life. However, I have found that transferences will inevitably manifest with access to the face anyway. My personal preference is to engage in dialogue with my clients and allow silences where appropriate, but I do not subscribe to the idea that silence should prevail.

Theory: intersubjectivity

My resonance with the idea that therapists' and clients' subjectivities interact and engage and that the therapist cannot be a neutral observer is captured in the concept of *intersubjectivity*. The nucleus of ideas in the box that follows, which have influenced my integrative model, consists of relational perspectives in psychoanalysis and phenomenology.

- Attachment perspectives
- Object relations perspectives
- Humanistic/existential relational perspectives
- Phenomenological perspectives (social context, human condition, angst, constructing meaning)

At the heart of my developing integrative model is the theory of intersubjectivity, referring to Clarkson's (1995) person-to-person therapeutic relationship. Clarkson's transferential/countertransferential, reparative, developmentally needed and transpersonal types of relationship are influenced by the person-to-person dimension and cannot be understood purely as distinct from one another.

Chodorow (1989) theorised that humans have an innate ability and intrinsic need to relate to others as subject-to-subject. Stolorow and Atwood described the intersubjective space as a relational system where 'experience is continually and mutually shaped' (1996: 181). Implicit to this idea is the need for humans to relate with each other. Various researchers (for example, Trevarthen 1979; Bruner 1983;

Ramberg 2006; and Rochat and Passos-Ferreira 2008) have proposed a primary and a secondary intersubjectivity: 'There is a tight natural coordination between child and mother from the start of life, a kind of primary intersubjectivity . . . Later in the child's development, a so-called secondary intersubjectivity evolves' (Ramberg 2006: 21).

Primary intersubjectivity develops from birth up to the age of 5. The process of mirroring and imitation mechanisms forms the basis of intersubjectivity that consists of mutual recognition and reciprocal relations constituting sociability. Secondary intersubjectivity consists of joint attention, inter-exchanges, social communication and intentional co-experience. Rochat added a third level of intersubjectivity, the tertiary, which entails triadic recognition, projection, inter-exchanges and embarrassment and ownership (Rochat and Passos-Ferreira 2008).

In humanistic and existential conceptualisations, intersubjectivity is captured in ideas about relationality and relational depth (Mearns and Cooper 2005) and in Buber's (1970) notion of the I–Thou, which refers to the intersubjective relating. It is a subject-to-subject relating, as opposed to the I–It, which is subject-to-object relating. In human interactions, both modes of relating are inevitable. However, the former contains the elements of working together, dialogue, collaboration and recognition of the subject in otherness. Relationality has been at the heart of humanistic therapy since Rogers' (1957) person-centred therapy was introduced. Gendlin's (1990) moments of meeting between client and therapist take place through intersubjective relating and influence therapeutic progress. Mearns and Cooper used the concept of relational depth to capture the intersubjective space. They defined relational depth as a 'state of profound contact and engagement between two people' (2005: xii). My theoretical position integrates ideas from the humanistic, phenomenological and psychoanalytic perspectives. All three perspectives espouse intersubjectivity and the importance of the relational aspects of therapy.

To be able to appreciate the influences on people's psychological problems, we need theories of child development as well as an understanding of how life can weigh heavily on people's mental health and normal functioning. The existential/phenomenological position provides rich philosophical understandings about the givens of existence in general and the human condition in particular, such as human choice, freedom, angst and self-deception. However, to date, there is no systematic theory of child development and its influence on the human condition in this tradition. Psychoanalytic thinking, on the other hand, is replete with theorisations on child development.

Object relations theory (Klein, Winnicott, Fairbairn, Kohut, Mahler, Bowlby) has moved away from biological drives and placed importance on patterns of interpersonal relations. There are differences and flaws in each of the object relations theorists mentioned. Nonetheless, object relations theory's shift away from Freud's drive theory is fundamental to the notion of 'the relational' in therapy and is at the core of my personal integration. Fairbairn (1951 [1946]) introduced this notion early on in his works. As Rubens (1994) argued, Fairbairn's view of people was that by nature they are object-related. The self, in Fairbairn's view of humans, is in relation to another and the relationship in between. I also find Bowlby's (1969) attachment perspective particularly helpful in understanding psychological health and well-being and its opposite, psychological ill-health. I draw heavily on attachment perspectives to help me understand as a clinician how early attachments have positively and negatively impacted on my clients. Attachment theory (Bowlby 1969; Ainsworth et al. 2015) theorised that the bond in any relationship is influenced by the quality of the attachment experienced during child development with the primary caregivers. I regard early attachment experiences as ingrained in our psychological templates and containing early memories, including trauma. These memories are interpreted and symbolised uniquely by each individual and, rather than being fixed in time, they undergo unique transformations during the life span of individuals.

One of my therapeutic aims is to understand the client's early attachments and their unique interpretation and personal experience of their impact. Our template is a complex map that becomes activated through exposure to the human condition. What surfaces through the activation is the historical, evolved memory that has undergone subtle modifications over time. Therapy does not uncover fixed memories but *historically evolved* memories transmuted over time. It does not uncover truths, but within an empathic, psychologically conducive environment, constructs understandings that provide clients with a coherent, digested and well-organised experience that enhances awareness and clarifies choices. At the core of historically evolved experience is the actual experience that travels through the channels of time evolves and can be accessed therapeutically following activation.

Principles and therapist qualities: integrating elements of humanism and phenomenology

Models of therapy consist not only of theoretical perspectives, but also certain characteristics such as therapist values, qualities, beliefs, characteristics and technique. Here is a list of the characteristics key to my integrative model.

- Spontaneity and naturalness
- Core conditions (humanistic)
- Attentive and caring presence
- Challenge
- Revelation of subjectivity (in a timely fashion)

The principles underpinning the relational approach to therapy, as discussed in the previous section, include authentic engagement, dialogue, attunement and risk taking, which together facilitate the client's potential for optimal growth. The process of change takes place within a context that impacts on the therapy. To try and mould all clients in the same context is to deny them their uniqueness. Hence, my model embraces the client's lived experience, the social, cultural, racial, religious and economic context within which they function, and acknowledges the client's givens, including how they embrace and navigate through the angst of existence. Together we work to construct understandings that are empowering for the client, both in terms of increasing client self-awareness and clarifying their past and future choices.

A conducive psychotherapeutic environment consists of spontaneity and naturalness (Hubble et al. 1999), therapist qualities that move them away from the burden of constantly wearing a professional hat. Rogers' (1957) core conditions can contribute to a more authentic therapist attitude. Empathy, in particular, is for me the *sine qua non* for a climate of understanding, relationality and *agape* (Rogers' concept of love, not romantic love). According to Daly's (2014) phenomenological perspective, empathy is intertwined with intersubjectivity. Research (Greenberg et al. 2001; Warner 2001; Elliott et al. 2013) has shown that empathy is highly beneficial to positive outcomes. Greenberg and Pascual-Leone argued that 'Empathy, which predicts therapy outcome (Greenberg et al. 2001), seems to be particularly important in learning to self-soothe, restore emotional equilibrium, and strengthen the self' (2006: 616).

Empathy alone is not sufficient in restoring equilibrium and strengthening the self. Constructive challenge is also necessary to help clients focus on what they tend to avoid, because it is uncomfortable or painful, or something they'd rather not see, know about and take responsibility for, such as unwanted aspects in themselves, sometimes conveniently placed in others. Confronting avoidance in a therapeutically caring tone can help unravel and work through pain associated with early trauma. Unconditional positive regard should not be equated with avoidance of client challenge. Likewise, acceptance means relating to my client with respect as a human being, which does not equal colluding with behaviours and attitudes that may be detrimental to them and those they love and care about. An attentive and caring presence (Hubble et al. 1999) are necessary qualities for the development of empathy. Therapists who attend to the client's story with focus, interest and curiosity, displaying a caring attitude, are more likely to feel and appreciate what clients are experiencing.

A professional therapist reflects on their practice, makes note of what works for a client and uses therapist attitudes, qualities, approaches and techniques. My experience tells me that revelation of therapist subjectivity is soothing and reparative for the majority of clients. This revelation is evident through facial expressions, tone of voice, body posture, and verbal and non-verbal communications. I differentiate between personal disclosure and self-revelation. The former is akin to revealing some facts about the person of the therapist. For example, if I believe it is important in facilitating a client's process to respond to their question whether I am a mother or what my racial background is, I will provide the information. Revealing my subjectivity refers to sharing myself authentically through smiling, laughing and being serious with clients. It also involves sharing insights tentatively with clients throughout the process, starting with the assessment and formulation. I regard revelation of my subjectivity as a potent gift that encourages clients to engage in relationship with me and consider insights I offer as food for thought. This is a reciprocal process of therapist and client being receptive to one another. If clients are expected to reveal themselves, therapist revelation creates trust and reassures clients that the therapist is warm and human, holds them in mind and at the very least tries to understand them. For me, being authentic and transparent holds therapeutic promise and enhances the therapeutic alliance.

Therapeutic understandings form over time and undergo a navigation process that is mediated through dialogue between client and therapist and appropriate use of transference/countertransference. Revelation of therapist subjectivity is a craft that is fine-tuned with experience. It involves risk, especially if we get the understanding or interpretation wrong and upset our client. If we do not share our feelings and understandings with our clients in a timely fashion and we sit back expecting clients to do all the work on their own, we risk compromising empathy and perpetuating clients' isolation and frustration. Without risk and honesty there is no intimacy. The opposite argument to this assertion may be that excessive therapist involvement forges dependence and compromises client empowerment. Dependence and attachment between client and therapist are inevitable and part of the process of developing the alliance. An effective navigation of a client's process will reach a phase where the therapeutic couple prepare themselves for the ending of an attachment they had known from the beginning would one day come to an end. Dependence and empowerment do not cancel each other out. In addition to the five types of therapeutic relationship (Clarkson 1995), all therapists use tools and techniques. How these are applied is influenced by the therapist's personal integration model.

Clinical approach

Tools, skills and techniques

A therapeutic model contains tools and techniques that one uses if and when one sees fit. I carry my therapy toolbox with me at all times and, depending on my clients' presenting issues and the psychological interventions arising from my formulations, I will use what in my judgement are the appropriate tools for the individual client. Here are some examples.

- Formulations (formulating and reformulating understandings – a fluid process).
- Individualised approach (using tools, such as sharing written formulations with clients, exposure techniques, normalising, modifying negative beliefs and keeping a diary).
- Working with the transference and countertransference (Clarkson 1995).

The process of psychotherapy is uncertain and unpredictable. Although therapists may have an approximate prediction of how the therapeutic *process* may evolve based on their initial assessment and formulation, they cannot be certain on how the therapeutic *relationship* will evolve. We may have some hunches that make the future of this relationship 20 per cent predictable, but the rest is guesswork. The unpredictability may cause anxiety for some therapists. But remembering that trusting the unfolding process and having faith in ourselves that we will manage whatever appears in the consulting room is important for the placebo effect. Clients need to feel safe in their therapist's professional ability to help them during the turbulences of getting in touch with often unfamiliar and frightening emotions. The therapist's confidence in him/herself will aid the placebo, known for its importance in positive outcomes (Hubble et al. 1999). Developing psychological formulations and sharing these with clients is common in my practice. As discussed earlier, revelation of therapist subjectivity is soothing. I apply this principle to the sharing of formulations with my clients. The assessment is the first opportunity to create initial impressions, to bring together information about clients in a coherent understanding and to share these with clients.

My recommendation in terms of the psychological treatment is informed by the initial formulation. Tufekcioglu and Muran present a relational perspective:

> We believe that a collaboratively constructed case formulation must always be considered in the context of an evolving therapeutic relationship. Further, self-reflection and self-revelation on the part of the therapist are critical for a more elaborate and nuanced case formulation and for understanding the patient. This highlights the importance of attunement to the here and now and the evolving therapeutic relationship. From this attunement, the therapist's self-reflection and self-revelation can emerge further, which can lead to the patient's personal growth and increased self–other awareness.
>
> (2015: 469)

As this quote highlights, formulations are not fixed. With the deepening of the alliance, the therapeutic relationship is strengthened and, so too, the therapist's understanding about clients. It is a dance where synchrony between client and therapist evolves through a secure attachment, which has an increased potential to contain and navigate through difficulties and uncertainties.

There are numerous therapeutic techniques, skills and tools from the plethora of therapeutic approaches for the integrative therapist to choose from. I will not list all the tools out there but would encourage integrative therapists to inform themselves in terms of what research shows works well for certain problems. I start from the premise that my commitment to my clients is the foundation of the therapeutic relationship. This includes being flexible in my choice of tools that I believe might be helpful in facilitating my clients' processes. Each client is unique and formulations help in identifying specific tools and skills that are known to work effectively for certain problems. For example, I have used the CBT exposure technique to bring to the surface anxieties and fears that are otherwise inaccessible, but sometimes such techniques are sub-optimal, given the client's presenting needs.

Scenario from practice 9.1

A client had severe anxiety using the bathroom. She would spend hours in the bathroom imagining sharp objects flying around and landing in her genitalia. Terrified, she would obsessively check herself and try to remove these objects. This behaviour was symptomatic of child sexual abuse by an uncle. Talking about her experience and forming an alliance were not enough for her to get in touch with the associated feelings from her early trauma to allow me to help her modulate and work through them. I invited her to try using the toilet at my practice and time herself to be out within five minutes. The exposure to a room that so far had been triggering such terror was effective. She would leave the toilet within five minutes and enter the consulting room where she felt safe. I would then help her deal with the powerful feelings that had emerged.

Conclusion

To conclude this chapter, I want to remind that each one of you has a story to tell about your continuing evolution as a psychotherapist or psychologist. I have shared a snippet of mine and hope it resonates with some of you. In doing so, it has helped me organise aspects of my journey as pivotal to the evolution of my model as an integrative psychotherapist. Adhering to a purist model of psychotherapy has presented problems for me personally as there is always something missing from each model. The freedom to be the architect of my own personal integration is one I never take for granted. I have learned that some therapists' need to belong to a group may take precedence over celebrating and valuing difference, which does not equate to not having an identity. One can belong to a polymorphous group, each with its own colours and shapes, and feel rewarded. Finally, the words of Buber carry the wisdom of relationality in integration:

> The deciding reality is the therapist, not the methods. Without methods one is a dilettante. I am for methods, but just in order to use them, not to believe in them. Although no doctor can do without a typology, he knows that at a certain moment the incomparable person of the patient stands before the incomparable person of the doctor; he throws away as much of his typology as he can and accepts this unforeseeable thing that goes on between therapist and patient.
>
> (1967: 165)

Tools, skills and techniques can help reinforce the professional trust clients invest therapists with. They can help clients engage, to enhance the placebo and bring to the surface core psychological conflict. However, in themselves, they are not sufficient to produce positive outcomes, as the literature discussed highlights. Effective therapists need to develop what research shows to be the qualities and competences of effective therapists.

References

Adams, M. (2013) *The Myth of the Untroubled Therapist.* London: Routledge.

Ainsworth, M.D.S., Blehar, M.C., Waters, E. and Wall, S.N. (2015) *Patterns of Attachment: A Psychological Study of the Strange Situation.* Hove: Psychology Press.

Bowlby, J. (1969) *Attachment and Loss.* London: Basic Books.

Bruner, J.S. (1983) *Child's Talk.* New York: Norton.

Buber, M. (1967) *I and Thou.* New York: Charles Scribner's Sons.

Casement, P. (2002) *Learning from Our Mistakes: Beyond Dogma in Psychoanalysis and Psychotherapy.* London: Routledge.

Cavafy, C.P. (1992) *Collected Poems.* E. Keeley and P. Sherrard, trans. Princeton, NJ: Princeton University Press.

Chodorow, N.J. (1989) *Feminism and Psychoanalytic Theory.* New Haven, CT: Yale University Press.

Clarkson, P. (1995) *The Therapeutic Relationship in Psychoanalysis, Counselling Psychology and Psychotherapy.* London: Whurr.

Daly, A. (2014) Primary intersubjectivity: empathy, affective reversibility, 'self-affection' and the primordial 'we'. *Topoi,* 33(1): 227–41. http://dx.doi.org/10.1007/s11245-013-9206-7.

Ekman, P. and Friesen, W.V. (1978) *Facial Action Coding System.* Palo Alto, CA: Consulting Psychologists Press.

Elliott, R., Watson, J., Greenberg, L.S., Timulak, L. and Freire, E. (2013) Research on humanistic-experiential psychotherapies. In M.J. Lambert (ed.), *Bergin and Garfield's Handbook of Psychotherapy and Behavior Change* (6th edn) (pp. 495–538). New York: Wiley.

Fairbairn, W.R.D. (1946 [1951]) *Object-Relationships and Dynamic Structure in an Object-Relations Theory of the Personality.* New York: Basic Books.

Gendlin, E.T. (1990) The small steps of the therapy process: How they come and how to help them come. In G. Lietaer, J. Rombauts and R. Van Balen (eds), *Client-Centred and Experiential Psychotherapy in the Nineties.* Leuven: Leuven University Press.

Greenberg, L.S. and Pascual-Leone, A. (2006) Emotion in psychotherapy: A practice-friendly research review. *Journal of Clinical Psychology,* 62: 611–30. http://dx.doi.org/10.1002/jclp.

Greenberg, L.S., Watson, J.C., Elliot, R. and Bohart, A.C. (2001) Empathy. *Psychotherapy: Theory, Research, Practice, Training,* 38(4): 380–4.

Haggard, E.A. and Isaacs, K.S. (1966) Micromomentary facial expressions as indicators of ego mechanisms in psychotherapy. In L.A. Gottschalk and A.H. Auerbach (eds), *Methods of Research in Psychotherapy* (pp. 154–65). New York: Appleton-Century-Crofts.

Hubble, M.A., Duncan, B.L. and Miller, S.D. (eds) (1999) *The Heart and Soul of Change: What Works in Therapy.* Washington, DC: American Psychological Association.

Jørgensen, C.R. (2004) Active ingredients in individual psychotherapy: Searching for common factors. *Psychoanalytic Psychology,* 21(4): 516–40.

McCluskey, U., Hooper, C.-A. and Miller, L.B. (1999) Goal-corrected empathic attunement: Developing and rating the concept within an attachment perspective. *Psychotherapy: Theory, Research, Practice, Training*, 36(1): 80–90.

McCluskey, U., Roger, D. and Nash, P. (1997) A preliminary study of the role of attunement in adult psychotherapy. *Human Relations*, 50(10): 1261–73.

Mearns, D. and Cooper, M. (2005) *Working with Relational Depth in Counselling and Psychotherapy.* London: SAGE.

Palmer, S., Dainow, S. and Milner, P. (eds) (2006) *Counselling: The BAG Counselling Reader*, vol. 1. London: SAGE.

Polkinghorne, D.E. (1992) Postmodern epistemology of practice. In S. Kvale (ed.), *Psychology and Postmodernism.* London: SAGE.

Ramberg, L. (2006) In dialogue with Daniel Stern: A review and discussion of the present moment in psychotherapy and everyday life. *International Forum of Psychoanalysis*, 15(1): 19–33.

Rippere, V. and Williams, R. (eds) (1985) *Wounded Healers: Mental Health Workers' Experiences of Depression.* London: Wiley.

Rochat, P. and Passos-Ferreira, C. (2008) From imitation to reciprocation and mutual recognition. In J.A. Pineda (ed.), *Mirror Neurons Systems: The Role of Mirroring Processes in Social Cognition.* New York: Humana Press.

Rogers, C.R. (1957) The necessary and sufficient conditions of therapeutic personality change. *Journal of Counseling Psychology*, 21: 95–103.

Rubens, R.L. (1994) Fairbairn's structural theory. In J.S. Grotstein and D.B. Rinsley (eds), *Fairbairn and the Origins of Object Relations.* New York: Guilford Press.

Shamasundar, C. (2008) Some personal reflections relating to psychotherapy. *Indian Journal of Psychiatry*, 50(4): 301–4.

Stolorow, R.D. and Atwood, G.E. (1996) The intersubjective perspective. *Psychoanalytic Review*, 83: 181–94.

Trevarthen, C. (1979) Communication and cooperation in early infancy: A description of primary intersubjectivity. In M. Bullowa (ed.), *Before Speech: The Beginning of Interpersonal Communication* (pp. 321–48). Cambridge: Cambridge University Press.

Tufekcioglu, S. and Muran, J.C. (2015) Case formulation and the therapeutic relationship: The role of therapist self-reflection and self-revelation. *Journal of Clinical Psychology*, 71(5): 469–77.

Wampold, B.E. (2011) *Qualities and Actions of Effective Therapists.* American Psychological Association Education Directorate. Available at: http://www.apa.org/education/ce/effective-therapists.pdf.

Warner, M. (2001) Empathy, relational depth and difficult client process. In S. Haugh and T. Merry (eds), *Empathy.* Ross-on-Wye: PCCS Books.

10 Embodiment, integrative therapy and psychopathology

Maria Luca

Introduction

This chapter will trace the concept of embodiment historically and propose that it is a foundational principle in integrative practice. It will trace the historical conceptualisations of the term with reference to Merleau-Ponty and explore how therapists' and clients' mind and body work in unison in the therapeutic relationship and how the relationship is influenced by the cultural context. Embodiment is one way of understanding a particular dynamic of the mind–body relationship in human subjectivity. One way of understanding embodiment was found as early as 1890 in the work of William James:

> What kind of an emotion of fear would be left if the feeling neither of quickened heartbeats, nor of shallow breathing, neither of trembling lips nor of weakened limbs, neither gooseflesh nor of visceral stirring, were present, it is quite impossible for me to think.
>
> (James 1890, cited in Damasio 1994: 129)

As this passage suggests, there is a corresponding relationship between mind and body; there is no hierarchical importance between them but a single experience between the senses and the mind. From this point of view, there is a prototype theory of embodiment in James' work.

Damasio traced James' idea of embodiment to his readings of Spinoza. Damasio (2003), in a systematic study of emotions, refers to Baruch Spinoza's theory of embodiment, in particular, that consciousness (and bodily actions) reflect mind and body as two aspects of one order – mind and body are different attributes of a single essence, a single *thing*, rather than being distinct substances as in Descartes' interactionism. From this perspective, mind (and body) are essentially embodied.

Spinoza's notion of freedom as self-determination is pivotal to his view of the mind. Similar to the idea of the mind being embodied, in Merleau-Ponty's works, body is a source of meaning (van Wolputte 2004).

Mind and body in the Western tradition

In the Western paradigm, the attempt to psychologically examine the relationship between mind and body and in particular 'the work of Pierre Janet, and the emergence of psychoanalysis at the turn of the century, led to the discovery of the role of emotions in the pathogenesis of mental disorders, and eventually also to the formalization of psychosomatic medicine' (Taylor et al. 1997: 3). Psychosomatic medicine developed as a result of the limitations of the medical model to explain the aetiology of psychosomatic phenomena such as people presenting with physical symptoms with no organic causes.

Perspectives on health and illness are constructions of a perceived reality in a given socio-political, religious and cultural context. Phenomena such as somatisation (now replaced by medically unexplained symptoms, MUS) are constructs of an objective, medicalised model of illness behaviour, much more complex and subjective than our scientific theories allow us to understand. These phenomena are contingent upon health professionals' constructions of clinical realities, as well as the constructions of people labelled as 'ill'. The culture with which an individual identifies and from which they seek standards of behaviour shapes their understanding of bodily states and determines acceptable ways for the expression of, for instance, distress. This raises a fundamental question: 'Is the body invariant across history and culture, or is it the product of social constitution?' (Couzens Hoy 1999: 3). Integrative therapy is concerned with understanding the person in the context of culture, not just intra-psychically.

Other ideas of mind seem to attempt to integrate the Spinozistic notion of embodiment. The notion of 'objective subjectivity' proposed by Fonagy (Fonagy and Target 2002) shows that subjectivity arises out of a hierarchical order in the process of mental and reflective development leading to the optimal level of mentalised affectivity. Thus, the theory of mentalised affectivity that takes place within the interaction and early environment resembles ideas on embodiment, albeit within an attachment perspective.

For Merleau-Ponty (1968), the human body is a subject and an intending entity. Body is subject and subject is body. Intentionality refers to body–subject deep-level engagement with its world. Intending is associated with exercising agency and autonomy, as well as choice. Hence, intentionality suggests the ability to reflect, think and choose. Merleau-Ponty explored embodiment at two levels: the *phenomenological* and the *cognitive unconscious*. At the first level, individuals are conscious of their feelings and actions, while at the second level, sensorimotor and other bodily-oriented inference mechanisms inform their processes of abstract thought and reasoning. By employing the term 'embodiment', Merleau-Ponty 'stresses the unity of the two phenomena' (Langdridge 2005: 90). Embodiment is a concept that argues against dualism and puts forward a unitary perspective of mental health and illness.

Merleau-Ponty's concept of embodiment, as applied to intersubjective development challenged the dominance of dualism by arguing that 'knowledge of ourselves, and others, is given through our interconnectedness' (Langdridge 2005: 87). In a paper entitled 'The Child's Relations with Others', Langdridge (2005) elaborates on

Merleau-Ponty's criticism of child development theories discussed in his *Phenomenology of Perception* by arguing that Merleau-Ponty's theory of embodiment places the focus on the immediate lived experience and, to this end, is a theory of understanding the body in terms of a total system and not as a separate group of sensations. The implications of the phenomenology of embodiment for our understanding somatisation are implicit in the notion of 'lived experience' and 'lived body'. If in somatisation individuals focus purely on the bodily sensations, then this could be described as 'dis-embodiment' or 'dis-embodied consciousness'. The individual is preoccupied with the objective body and ignoring or unable to reflect on the *phenomenal* body, or the body as it appears to consciousness. Thus experience remains partially devoid of the affective component that comes from experiencing oneself in totality. Damasio describes this embodiment process as:

> The overall function of the brain is to be well informed about what goes on in the rest of the body, the body proper; about what goes on in itself; and about the environment surrounding the organism, so that suitable survivable accommodations can be achieved between the organism and the environment.
>
> (1994: 90)

The aim of Damasio is to create a synthesis between affects, the self and the brain and, along Spinozistic lines, to create a theory of an embodied mind (Fonagy et al. 2002: 81). Although the analysis of embodiment is preliminary, the exploration of the tenets of the theory provides a sketch for a better appreciation of a philosophy that describes humans as beings-in-the-world and consciousness as a dialectical relationship between the objective and the phenomenal world. It is not certain whether the aim of the philosophy of embodiment's attempt to tackle the Cartesian mind–body problem has been achieved. What is apparent in the theory of embodiment is that it provides a means of integrating 'mind' and 'body' by placing consciousness in the lived experience and being-in-the-world.

It is important that therapists who acknowledge intersubjectivity as central to therapeutic relationships also consider how embodiment can positively enable integration of mind–body both in therapists and clients. Integration of the therapist's self is a journey of personal development and involves knowing oneself in an embodied fashion. That is, always addressing the therapeutic question of how the mind affects the body and vice versa so that therapists can understand their affective and countertransferential responses to clients (whether these present as ideas or bodily responses, such as feeling nauseous in response to a client's narrative) and help clients also to reach a holistic way of understanding themselves that can lead to integration of the self.

Psychotherapists have long been interested in the mind–body connection and the role each plays in health and illness. The historical tendency to split mind and body, managing the former with psychological treatments and the latter with medical treatments, is still prevalent in contemporary medical practice and, to a degree, in psychological therapies. Materialism or biological determinism, with its restrictive biological model of illness and disease, can be understood as resting on the idea that physical pain is caused by material factors and therefore taking for granted the influence that psychological factors may have on sensory experience.

In contrast to materialism, one might explore Descartes' dualist interactionism, which separated mind and body into independent and essentially distinct substances that causally interact. Descartes maintained that most aspects of affective states are primarily somatic. Until the nineteenth century, a unitary view of illness prevailed, and diagnosis often meant diagnosis of a patient rather than of a disease. The replacement of this unitary view by the notion of diseases having a bodily location led eventually to the conceptual separation of mind from body. Cartesian dualist theorising and its implications are criticised by Taylor et al.: 'In our view, Cartesian dualism and interactionist theory have [made] limited progress in understanding the role of emotions in health and illness' (1997: 4, cited in McWhinney et al. 1997: 2).

Bayer and Malone also argue that this dualist ontology appears to be 'endemic within western culture' (1998, cited in Shaw 2003: 11). The criticism by the authors cited here of separating mind–body was intended to draw attention to the contemporary clinical practices where the body is treated by medicine and the mind and emotions by psychological treatments. The problem arising from these practices is that bodies are not separate from subjectivities, therefore individuals are not treated holistically.

Sociocultural perspectives

Sociocultural perspectives on health and illness emphasise the influence of culture on the expression of psychological distress and how the body becomes a medium for such expression (Csordas 1994). Cultural and anthropological perspectives argue that there is an inter-dependence between culture and subjective experience (Csordas 1994; van Wolputte 2004). The anthropologist Csordas conceptualises the body and bodily experience within a cultural phenomenological perspective. The central tenet of Csordas' theory is his phenomenological critique of the body and its associated cultural meanings encapsulated in his theory of embodiment.

Rack also provides examples of what he calls 'culture-bound syndromes' and the meanings associated with them. These show the strong influence of culture on the construction of meaning and its inherent association with the body. One such example is 'Susto (Latin American) means temporary loss of the soul from the body as a result of stress' (1982: 148), which resonates with Western notions of dis-embodiment, a kind of not inhabiting one's body, implying depersonalisation. Such culture-bound meanings attached to the body are illuminated also by other anthropological studies. The meaning of bodily functions, flesh and body symptoms, varies from culture to culture (Herdt 1981). In Sambian rituals, for example, the body is central to the regulation of relationships between women and men who regard some body fluids with suspicion. Herdt's research also highlights how the body becomes a place for the expression of fears and anxieties and is at the centre of cultural idioms constructed about the self.

It was not until the mid-twentieth century that social psychology, theories of culture and phenomenological perspectives on embodiment shed new light on our understanding of constructions of the body and health. As Csordas eloquently puts it: 'Beginning in the early 1970s, and with increased energy in the late 1980s, the body has assumed a lively presence on the anthropological scene, and on the stage of interdisciplinary cultural studies' (1994: 1). He goes on to argue that the body can be understood as a 'seat of subjectivity' and this, he says, is a challenge to 'theories of culture in which mind/subject/culture are deployed in parallel with and in contrast to body/object/biology' (1994: 9). Csordas' assertion is a critique against the separation of the body-subject.

Guimon refers to the important contribution of phenomenology in trying to unite the corporeal aspect of being with consciousness, which led to the concept of the 'lived experience'. He cites Ortega's concept of the 'intrabody', referring to the experience the individual has of their internal invisible organs and that the body must be seen as a 'feeling body'. In the same context of the lived experience, Zuazo refers to Dolto whose idea of physical illness 'implies that the person speaks with the body (and often of the body), and does so because that body is the symbolic incarnation expressing some cognition and emotion that have a sense of language and communication' (Dolto 1994, cited in Zuazo 1997: 56). These perspectives attempt to ascribe a unity between body and mind by suggesting that the two co-exist, co-depend on one another and are constantly in relation with one another.

Merleau-Ponty with his theory of 'embodiment' placed emphasis on the unity of consciousness as a phenomenon inseparable from being-in-the-world (a world consisting of subjects and objects). In his study on perception, he constructs the body as a unified entity where, he argues, 'we must therefore try to avoid saying that our body is *in* space, or *in* time. It *inhabits* space and time' (1962: 139). This notion affirms the importance of mind and body existing in relation to one another. Embodied, integrative practice should therefore approach clients' presenting problems not as distinctly physical or psychological, but as manifestations of a single and unified body–mind.

Embodied subjectivity: bridging the dualist gap?

Consciousness comprises of the lived experience. As Merleau-Ponty explicates, 'man is in the world, and only in the world does he know himself' (1962: xi). Embodiment in Merleau-Ponty's philosophy means experiencing and knowing the world reflectively and through the living body-subject. His account of embodiment distinguishes between the *objective* body, which is the body regarded as a physiological entity, and the *phenomenal* body, which is not just some body, some particular physiological entity, but 'my body as I experience it'. The distinction between the objective and phenomenal body, is central to understanding the phenomenological treatment of embodiment. Embodiment is not a concept that pertains to the body grasped as a physiological entity. Rather it pertains to the phenomenal body and to the role it plays in our object-directed experiences.

(*The Cambridge Dictionary of Philosophy*, 1999)

Merleau-Ponty's 'reversibility' thesis (1968) implies that the objective and the phenomenal body are two sides of the same coin and that knowledge and understanding of this are subject to our perception. Thus, the body senses and is being sensed. The central feature of Merleau-Ponty's phenomenology is his challenge to notions of objective thinking and the Cartesian and empirical ideas of knowledge. For Merleau-Ponty, the reflective analysis required for objective thinking is not sufficient in understanding human subjectivity. Lived experience, he argues, is a totality of our external and internal perceptions, which are products of a continuous interaction between the phenomenal body and the pre-objective world (1962: xi). Implicit in Merleau-Ponty's thought is that human beings are social and cultural through participation in the world, a notion similar to Husserl's (1965) 'lifeworld'. Thus, subjects are made via their engagement with others and their environment, an idea emphasised throughout this book. Thus, knowledge cannot be detached from others, culture, language and history; it is the product of participation and dialogical engagement with the world. It is in this orientation towards the world that one's human existence is concretised as an intentional entity through the body. We learn about ourselves through interaction with others and through our perception of our actions. It is in this context that we learn and adopt cultural behaviour. From this perspective, culture is a given and has a fluidity that is immanent in human subjectivity. Therefore culture and intersubjectivity are closely connected and part of an indivisible whole.

This notion of human subjectivity was the subject of extensive discussion at a lecture given by Trevarthen (1996) on the 'Psychobiology of Sympathy'. Trevarthen demonstrated, with visual images, how infants engage with others very early on and learn to distinguish adult signals and respond in ways that maximise belonging to the group. He argued that language knowledge, among other learning, is a construction of collaborative inventions mediated by culture. This view advocates that self and other are in dialectic relations, culturally influenced and shaped through sympathetic interaction that involves sensitive and affective understanding of the other. This idea resembles the concept of the *corps proper*, regarded as one of the seminal ideas of Merleau-Ponty. This is the place where subject–object are not in opposition but in unity. It is a place where the intersection between the world and being occurs. In tribute to Merleau-Ponty, van Wolputte cites the following expression in contemporary literature on the body: 'We all have and we all are a body' (2004: 251); this could be described as 'dis-embodiment' or as 'dis-embodied consciousness', preoccupied with the objective body and ignoring or unable to reflect on the phenomenal body. Thus experience remains partially devoid of the affective component that comes from experiencing oneself in totality.

The embodied integrative therapist

Integrative psychotherapy embraces an attitude towards the practice of psycho-therapy that affirms the inherent value of each individual and places the individual in context. It is a unifying psychotherapy that responds appropriately and effect-ively to the person at the affective, behavioural, cognitive and physiological levels of functioning, and addresses the spiritual dimension of life and how culture influ-ences the psychological make-up of individuals. From this vantage point, it is *embodied*.

It has been argued that the capacity to mentalise is necessary for the regulation of affects (Fonagy et al. 1997) and the capacity for regulation of affects provides the grounds for mentalisation. For alexithymic patients, the ability to tolerate, con-tain and verbalise affects is fundamental to psychological equilibrium (Taylor et al. 1997: 260). In contrast to these ideas, the cross-cultural and anthropological per-spectives call for a better understanding of illness behaviour. They advocate for greater sensitivity among health professionals of cultural and social idioms of dis-tress, the meaning of symptoms in relation to cultural norms and the perceived causes and explanatory models (Kirmayer and Robbins 2005). The meaning of ill-ness is also a principle for greater understanding of the sick role, particularly con-cerning psychosomatic phenomena in the cognitive–behavioural model. Beck et al. (1979) coined the term 'schema' to encapsulate the course of development, knowl-edge acquired about the world and how this is stored internally in the form of stable mental structures. From this perspective,

> Psychological disturbance manifests itself through a consistently nega-tive, maladaptive bias in how events concerning the self, others and the world are interpreted. Beliefs become rigid and inflexible and information that could contradict these perceptions is filtered out.
>
> (Corrie and Milton 2000: 14)

In other words, individuals, either through habit or survival mechanisms, adopt negative attitudes, which would not be shared by others, but are associated with their own individual learned behaviours or early traumatic experiences that influ-ence them. The clinical implications of the models of affect regulation and mental-isation are twofold: (1) clinicians as affect-regulators; and (2) clinicians as empathic synchronisers.

In the first instance, clinicians are called upon to facilitate the process of regu-lating and modulating emotional pain and distress. This rests on the assumption that regulation of affective states would achieve a decrease in the arousal and sub-sequently in somatic/psychological symptoms. This would help patients cope better with the psychological distress that may be the result of disability brought about by the illness. Interactive moments can either promote or diminish therapeutic activity depending on the level of the therapist–client emotional attunement that acts in the service of an affect-balancing, receptive central system. Similar to the 'affective synchrony' (Schore 2001: 45) in the caregiving environment, which promotes healthy growth, the therapeutic environment can be 'affectively synchronised' or be the agent of affective disharmony and friction. Likewise, a mind–body synchrony pertains to psychological health whereas a mind–body split pertains to pathology.

In the second instance, as empathic synchroniser, the integrative therapist, in contrast to Freud's (1900 [1953]) suggestion that the unconscious sources of affect must be settled and forgotten (Schore 1994: 443), employs empathy and not neutrality. Empathy, as far as Stern (1985) is concerned, is important as a mechanism that gains access to the patient's inner world, so that they can act as affect regulator (in Schore 1994: 465). But empathy is not purely a mind or emotion empathy. It is felt in the therapist's body and communicated through physiological signals as well as words. It is therefore embodied. Hence the two features of affect regulator and empathic synchroniser closely correspond with one another in an embodied fashion.

Spezzano supports the idea of therapists as affect regulators. He asserts that:

> The analytic relationship heals by drawing into itself those methods of processing and regulating affect relied on by the patient for psychological survival and then transforming them. The mechanism of these transformations is the regulation of affect in a better way within the analysis than it was previously managed by the patient.
>
> (1993: 215–16)

In therapeutic work, therapists become the regulators of clients' overwhelming and often unregulated emotions through helping clients process, digest, distinguish between and understand their emotions (including sources and triggers). This process enables clients to internalise the therapist as regulator, so they can develop the function of regulating their emotions themselves.

In Schore's words, conducive therapy requires an affectively interacting therapist:

> The ability to autoregulate affect allows for an advance in the individual's adaptive functions – a broadened affect tolerance, an expansion of the affect array, and an improved capacity to regulate psychobiological state transitions and to recover from disruptive affective states.
>
> (1994: 464)

This idea of an affectively-interacting therapist is also a challenge to the classical psychoanalytic approach of abstinence and neutrality. Schore's perspective presents therapists as engaging, involved and open to being emotionally and physically affected and infected by the patient. What is transparent from the evaluation of therapeutic stances from recent contributions is not just a theoretical shift but a change in clinical approach.

Although there is no explicit clinical model developed as a direct result from Merleau-Ponty's concept of embodiment, Langdridge suggests 'enactment'.

He believes that not all understanding resides in language and for this reason 'people may realise previously disavowed experiences and give voice to them: without incorporation of bodily factors such as posture, comportment and gesture people may never come to realize fundamental aspects of their being-in-the-world' (2005: 95–6). This postulation has implications for the embodied therapist, in so far as they would need to acknowledge non-verbalised experiences in their clients and help give voice to them. To achieve this, they need to listen to their body and their instinct, to what emerges in the intersubjective space they inhabit with their clients.

Alongside Spinoza's notion of freedom as self-determination, which is pivotal to his view of the mind, the embodied integrative therapist has a responsibility to try and understand their client's mind through reconciling the mental phenomena with the material world. The client lives in the world, encounters the world and acts upon the world, but fundamentally their being-in-the-world, their mind–body beingness, is one and the same dialectical process.

Embodiment and psychopathology

Phenomenology has given the living body as it exists within an environment a central function: that of uniting mind and brain. Concepts of embodiment, from the phenomenological as well as from the dynamic systems points of view, are opposed to mind–brain identity models. Instead, they regard both subjective experience and brain processes as being inseparably linked with the environment (Fuchs and Schlimme 2009: 573). By implication, psychopathology is an emergent disruption in the individual's being-in-the-world. In postulating a new account of mental illness, Fuchs and Schlimme (2009) argue that:

> Embodied concepts of mental illness should, on the one hand, describe and understand the patient's being-in-the-world by using phenomenological methods, whereas, on the other hand, they should investigate the circular interactions of mind, brain, organism and environment in the cause and maintenance of psychiatric disorders . . . phenomenological and ecological concepts of embodiment could be conjoined to enable a new, advanced understanding of mental illness.
>
> (2009: 574)

Conclusion

The embodied practitioner approaches the body as one of being in unity with consciousness. For example, if a patient complains of tightness in her chest, has had medical investigations that found no organic causes, but continues to feel she may be having a heart attack, her therapist would encourage her to think what else this bodily symptom might represent in her lived experience. The client's subjective experience and her brain mediate to produce the cognition, 'I may be having a heart attack.' Enabling the client to think about alternative explanations to the tightness in her chest may help her integrate cognitions with affects and to be able to mentalise. Likewise, if a therapist suddenly develops a headache during a session with a client, it is helpful to try and understand this not purely as of itself, 'I'm having a headache', but consider its manifestation as a product of the interaction and what the client might be feeling psychologically that the therapist experiences physically.

References

Beck, A.T., Rush, A.J., Shaw, B.E. and Emery, G. (1979) *The Cognitive Therapy of Depression*. New York: Guilford Press.

Corrie, S. and Milton, M. (2000) The relationship between existential-phenomenological and cognitive-behaviour therapies. *European Journal of Psychotherapy, Counselling and Health*, 3(1): 7–24.

Couzens Hoy, D. (1999) Critical resistance: Foucault and Bourdieu. In G. Weiss and H. Fern Haber (eds), *Perspectives on Embodiment*. London: Routledge.

Csordas, T.J. (ed.) (1994) *Embodiment and Experience*. Cambridge: Cambridge University Press.

Damasio, A. (1994) *Descartes' Error: Emotion, Reason and the Human Brain*. London: Macmillan.

Damasio, A. (2003) *Looking for Spinoza: Joy, Sorrow and the Feeling Brain*. Orlando, FL: Harcourt.

Fonagy, P., Gergely, G., Jurist, E.L. and Target, M. (2002) *Affect Regulation, Mentalisation, and the Development of the Self*. New York: OTHER Press.

Fonagy, P. and Target, M. (1997) Attachment and reflective function: Their role in self-organization. *Development and Psychopathology*, 9: 679–700.

Freud, S. (1900 [1953]) *The Interpretation of Dreams*. Standard Edition, vols 4–5. London: Hogarth Press.

Fuchs, T. and Schlimme, J.E. (2009) Embodiment and psychopathology: A phenomenological perspective. *Current Opinion in Psychiatry*, 22: 570–5.

Guimon, J. (1997) From the body schema to the body image. In J. Guimon (ed.), *The Body in Psychotherapy* (pp. 5–18). Basel: Karger.

Herdt, G.H. (1981) *Guardians of the Flutes: Idioms of Masculinity*. New York: Columbia University Press.

Husserl, E. (1965) *Phenomenology and the Crisis of Philosophy*, Q. Lauer, trans. New York: Harper Torchbooks.

Kirmayer, L.J. and Robbins, J.M. (eds) (2005) *Current Concepts of Somatization*. Washington, DC: American Psychiatric Press.

Langdridge, D. (2005) The child's relations with others. *Existential Analysis*, 16(1): 87–99.

McWhinney, I.R., Epstein, R.M. and Freeman, T.R. (1997) Rethinking somatization. *Annals of Internal Medicine*, 126: 747–50.

Merleau-Ponty, M. (1962) *Phenomenology of Perception*. London: Routledge.

Merleau-Ponty, M. (1968) *The Visible and the Invisible.* Evanston, IL: Northwestern University Press.

Rack, P. (1982) *Race, Culture, and Mental Disorder.* London: Tavistock.

Schore, A.N. (2001) The effects of early relational trauma on the right brain development, affect regulation, and infant mental health. *Infant Mental Health Journal,* 22(1–2): 201–69.

Schore, A.L. (1994) *Affect Regulation and the Origin of the Self: The Neurobiology of Emotional Development.* Hillsdale, NJ: Lawrence Erlbaum Associates.

Shaw, R. (2003) *The Embodied Psychotherapist: The Therapist's Body Story.* London: Routledge.

Spezzano, C. (1993) *Affect in Psychoanalysis: A Clinical Synthesis.* Hillsdale, NJ: The Analytic Press.

Stern, D. (1985) *The Interpersonal World of the Infant.* New York: Basic Books.

Taylor, G.J., Bagby, R.M. and Parker, D.A. (1997) *Disorders of Affect Regulation: Alexithymia in Medical and Psychiatric Illness.* Cambridge: Cambridge University Press.

Trevarthen, C. (1996) The psychobiology of sympathy: Infants teach us how human brains in human bodies make sense together. Lecture given on 10 May 2006 at The Centre for Child Mental Health, London.

The Cambridge Dictionary of Philosophy (1999) (2nd edn) General Editor: Robert Audi. Cambridge: Cambridge University Press.

van Wolputte, S. (2004) Hang on to your self: Of bodies, embodiment, and selves. *Annual Review of Anthropology,* 33: 251–69.

Zuazo, J.I. (1997) The body and distance in psychopathology. In J. Guimon (ed.), *The Body in Psychotherapy* (pp. 52–7). Basel: Karger.

11 Assessment in integrative practice

Maria Luca

Introduction

Psychological assessments and formulations are important clinical aspects in psychological therapies. They provide a necessary structure for clinicians and contribute to a thought-out and systematic approach to understanding clinical phenomena, such as symptoms, emotional concerns and destructive behaviours, and help therapists tailor individualised treatment plans with a choice of interventions.

Assessments commonly take place in therapeutic settings, such as the National Health Service (NHS) and charities. Formulation is a tool that psychologists tend to use more than psychotherapists or counsellors. Psychological therapy services usually have their own model of assessment and independent practitioners have the freedom to develop their own model. Bateman and Holmes state: 'There are two strands in the assessment interview: an empathic attempt by the analyst to grasp the nature of the patient's predicament, and a more distanced effort to sum up his strengths and weaknesses' (1995: 139). Empathy requires immersion into the client's subjectivity, whereas a distanced effort requires stepping outside immersion and taking a more objective, thought-out understanding. Case formulations, meanwhile, have their origins in clinical psychology with a rich heritage that 'can be traced back to the 1950s and the emergence of the scientist-practitioner model' (BPS 2011: 4). Although formulations have long been associated with the discipline of clinical psychology, they have only recently been given space in psychotherapy and counselling psychology trainings. A clinical case formulation is a 'conceptual scheme that organizes, explains, or makes clinical sense out of a large amount of data and influences the treatment decisions' (Lazare 1976, cited in Ingram 2006: 3). Hence, formulations consist of concepts that explain the client's situation and psychological way of being and help practitioners choose unique and individualised psychological interventions and tailor-made treatments.

A number of professional bodies in the UK, such as the United Kingdom Council for Psychotherapy (UKCP), the British Association of Counselling and Psychotherapy (BACP), the British Psychological Society (BPS) and the Health and Care Professions Council (HCPC), regard assessments as part of the range of professional competencies. Formulation is a key competency for clinical psychologists, while professional psychotherapy-accrediting bodies and counsellors have not embraced it as such. Professional training institutions recognise the importance of teaching assessment skills and increasingly of teaching formulation, and most now provide specific training in these skills.

Assessments are normally carried out face-to-face in one session, although some therapists carry out extended assessments over a few sessions before they formulate. If the client is very reticent, therapists could recommend a prolonged assessment before developing a formulation and recommending an appropriate psychological intervention. I use different assessment templates to guide the initial assessment. These cover important areas that therapists need to explore to obtain relevant client information to help formulate. (Appendix 1 provides two assessment templates for guidance.)

Models of practice and therapists' paradigms

Clarity of paradigm helps the integrative practitioner have a foundation and play with theoretical ideas until they are in a position to select the parts that will complete the pattern. Integrative trainings have a responsibility to expose trainees to a variety of perspectives to help with the process and evolution of personal psychotherapy integration. Integration is gaining momentum in psychotherapy and counselling psychology, but also in clinical psychology where there are calls for trainings to 'broaden the curriculum to encompass a range of theories of psychological change and therapies as they might be applied across a diverse range of patient groups' (Lewis et al. 2010: 5). They refer to broadening the skill base and the treatment options by assessing a wider range of patient functions and characteristics. This broadening of perspective and skill base can help 'tailor individualised treatment plans with the maximum likelihood of success' (Wampold 2001, in Lewis, Habib and King 2010: 5).

Any model of practice rests on the therapist's set of beliefs, assumptions and values concerning the human condition and what it is to be human; they rest on an epistemology. Saferstein found

> specific differences in the personal style of the therapist according to the therapist's epistemic assumptions (rationalist versus constructivist). Additionally, therapist epistemology was a significant predictor of their emphasis on the working alliance (Bond subscale), as well as their use of specific interventions (cognitive-behavioral versus constructivist).
>
> (2006: vii)

Hence, clarity of paradigm is important to prevent difficulties in integration. The integrative psychotherapist implicitly or explicitly rests their views on their epistemological position and exposure to a variety of perspectives on the human condition.

Paradigms and epistemology

What do we mean by paradigms and epistemology? Following Guba and Lincoln:

> A paradigm may be viewed as a set of basic beliefs that deals with ulti-
> mates or first principles. It represents a worldview that defines, for its
> holder, the nature of the 'world', the individual's place in it, and the range
> of possible relationships to that world.
>
> (1994: 107)

My paradigm or epistemological position is influenced by constructivism, which can be understood as postulating that individuals are proactive in their personal constructions of reality. From this point of view, knowledge is comprised of meaning-making processes where the individual is in charge of organising their experiences. Constructivists believe that knowledge should not be understood as conforming to a reality that is single, stable or external, and assert that individuals' feelings and actions cannot be meaningfully separated from human thought (Saferstein 2006). Applied to the topic of intersubjectivity, for Chodorow (1989), this maintains the intrinsically relational construction of the self and the human need to connect with other subjects. In my view, this plays a big part in the assessment consultations, as these lay the foundations for the alliance and an evolving relational therapy relationship. Granvold noted: 'The development of a quality therapeutic relationship with such characteristics as acceptance, understanding, trust and caring is a prime objective of constructivists' (1996: 350). These characteristics are typical of the Rogerian core conditions of empathy, acceptance, congruence and unconditional positive regard, which are at the centre of all humanistic therapies.

My paradigm both as a therapist and as a researcher is what we might call *abductive* (bottom-up/experiential). I mean by this looking inside the phenomenon (client narrative, data, interactions with therapist) and, with a receptive attitude, inviting 'it' to speak to me. Once I hear the sounds and meaning of the narrative/story/data, they will land on my subjective map and be shaped by this map. I can then try to disentangle the meanings of the story and how my subjective map reshapes, reconstructs or even avoids/rejects them. What we hear as therapists is only a representation of the story. Relational knowing is a dynamic developed through relational engagement between people who impact on each other and, as a result, develop a unique perspective. I treat assessments and formulations as collaborative endeavours that co-create a meaningful understanding of the client and of their problems. Reflection on the process of relating between the therapy participants is key in assessments and formulations.

Reductive assessments and formulations do not serve the relational world. On the contrary, they reduce the client to a cause and effect situation that objectifies them and deprives them of their agency. Cause and effect fall within the determinist paradigm. Probst argues:

Social workers, committed to working with the whole person, need to look beyond the limited epistemology of the DSM . . . This may be especially important when working with clients whose cultural or spiritual backgrounds rely on different ways of conceptualizing illness, health, personhood, and help. Clinicians unused to examining and thinking critically about their own cognitive assumptions will not have the acuity or flexibility necessary for serving their clients.

(2015: 40)

Probst therefore embraces practitioner flexibility and reflexivity (thinking about their thinking), and this approach applies to any psychological health practitioner. Clients and therapists are subjectively involved in the therapeutic process.

In the psychological therapies field, humanistic/existential, integrative and relational psychodynamic modalities come under the constructivist umbrella. However, all therapists have in-built biases (Probst 2015), causing oversights and blocks in metacognitive actions. Therefore, at the core of integrative practice is 'the willingness and ability to reflect on one's own thinking processes and to critically examine one's own assumptions, beliefs, and conclusions' (Berner and Graber 2008: S7). A respectful therapeutic relationship is one where the agency of the client and therapist is at the core of their relationship and understood as such.

For the purposes of simplifying paradigm/epistemological positions, I will provide a summary below. (For a basic review of some epistemological positions, I refer the reader to Guba and Lincoln 1994.) For simplicity, there are two polarities in epistemology.

Key terminology
Positivism and objectivism

There is an external, objective reality that can be known directly by analysing our perceptions. In post-positivism, the knower is influenced by a cultural context but can arrive at knowing an objective reality by striving to mitigate any bias arising from this context.

Subjectivism and interpretivism

There may be an external, objective reality, but knowledge is best understood as internally constructed and inherently subjective. It depends on things like the context, coherence, reliability and justification and should be viewed holistically. The knower cannot be separated from what is known.

In the middle of the two polarities, and applied to the therapeutic domain, sits constructivism.

> **Key terminology**
>
> **Constructivism (especially social constructivism)**
>
> Knowledge about the social world is different from knowledge about the phys-
> ical world. Focusing on the former, it is socially constructed, always belonging
> and being judged relative to a particular context. The way we experience one
> another is relative to certain (subjective) constructs but is experienced as
> objective by the people concerned.

The following excerpt highlights the nuances of social construction: 'Constructions are not more or less "true", in any absolute sense, but simply more or less
informed and/or sophisticated. Constructions are alterable, as are their associated
"realities"' (Guba and Lincoln 1994: 111). Judging from Guba and Lincoln's assertion, they are stressing that constructions are not about truth as typically understood and can be changed depending on realities changing. This is the paradigm
most contemporary relational/integrative psychotherapists and psychologists
employ to understand knowledge, which is seen as stemming from human interaction and relationship.

Increasingly, psychotherapy trainings have a broad curriculum that exposes
trainees to a variety of theories, perspectives and practice skills. Being exposed to
different assessment formats and formulations for psychotherapy trainees is also
important to widening perspective and aids the development of individualised treatment plans.

Integrative assessments

Although each discipline in the psychological therapies field (psychotherapy and
counselling, counselling psychology, clinical psychology) view assessments with
their discipline-informed lenses, generally assessments share a common purpose:
they bring together a clear history of the patient's lived experience, their relationship
patterns, health, successes, struggles, traumas, symptoms, behaviours, strengths
and functioning or non-functioning aspects (to name but a few) that help pull
together information to understand the client and their individual lived experience
as they and the therapist collaboratively perceive it. Assessments also evaluate risk
of harm to self and others, providing clinicians with an in-road to a psychological
formulation tailored with a specific approach and interventions to manage risk and
provide a safe, professional therapy that meets the individual patient's needs. Assessments help clinicians evaluate whether the referral is appropriate for the approach
and type of intervention offered and provide the nexus for referring on to a more
appropriate type of psychological service.

The issue of diagnosis

Some clinicians rely on the *Diagnostic and Statistical Manual of Mental Disorders* (DSM-V) (American Psychological Association 2013) to help them put together assessment reports and formulations. Although the use of the DSM-V in mental health settings is pervasive, there are arguments against it, mostly due to reliance on a diagnosis. Bazzano asserted that the 'humanistic tradition of counselling and psychotherapy had, and still has, very good reasons for being suspicious of diagnosis' (2011: 21). Davies' (2013) study of the original construction of the DSM-V highlights the unscientific, naïve approach adopted by the group of psychiatrists who developed it. He highlighted the impact on the mental health field when diagnostic criteria are assumed to be based on scientific principles. His thesis concludes that psychiatry and the indiscriminate use of the DSM-V does more harm than good. Sturmey also draws attention to the 'limitation in diagnosis predicting the most effective treatment for each client is that many clients meet diagnostic criteria for more than one diagnosis' (2009: 5). In other words, tailoring our treatments based on the diagnoses to which a client's presenting problems most conform can result in a treatment package that does not address the full range of the client's issues or the multifaceted diagnoses for which they are liable.

Therefore, clinicians who use the DSM-V for diagnostic criteria need to be mindful and tentative, not adopting labels as ultimate truths but as hypotheses to be explored. Historically, starting with Rogers, humanistic psychotherapists have been anti-diagnosis. In Rogers' view, having knowledge of diagnostics is unnecessary for good therapy. Although Rogers paid little attention to diagnosis, he advised, if it is used, that it must be client-centred, giving primacy to the client's process and secondary importance to the therapist's knowledge. He advocated that diagnosis is 'a process which goes on in the experience of the client, rather than in the intellect of the clinician' (1951: 223). In this process, the therapist encourages the client to explore and disentangle their distress, rather than cognitively explaining it. Cooper describes this as a process of 'conceptualizing, and engaging with people in a deeply valuing and respectful way' (2007: 11). That is, it is a way of respectfully working with the intersubjective dynamic of the therapeutic relationship, rather than imposing an analysis from outside of this space.

Roth and Fonagy support the use of the DSM-V for the classification of psychological disorders, while recognising its limitations. They discuss cases where patients present with psychosocial difficulties (for example, unemployment or divorce) that are not categorisable under the DSM-V. In their view, the use of the DSM-V 'reflects the belief that no treatment will work for all problems, and that it is important to verify which interventions are most likely to be effective for which type of disorder' (1996: 360). Their perspective encourages clinicians to be more tentative in categorising under the DSM, while choosing interventions known to be effective for certain problems. Assessment therefore provides the body of data to help practitioners formulate.

Whether we endorse or object to using the DSM-V, we can now answer the question: what do we mean by integrative assessment? Whereas some modalities' approach to assessments is to reach a diagnosis independently of clients, integrative therapists who are informed by a constructivist epistemic style collaborate and elicit clients' own understandings of themselves. Integrative assessments, therefore, are co-constructed.

Personal models of integration

As mentioned in Chapters 3 and 4, there are various models of integration: common factors, technical eclecticism, theoretical integration, assimilative integration and personal integration (Norcross and Goldfried 1992). Practitioners need to arrive at their own personal model, which can be influenced by existing ones. Whichever they choose, it will be unique to them, as subjectivity mediates all that we create and construct.

The process of arriving at an integrative model first needs to make sense to the individual. Models of psychotherapy are constructions of reality; they are narratives and stories we construct using our subjective lenses to make sense of the world. Second, it is important that the model is informed by research on what works for whom (Roth and Fonagy 1996; Hubble et al. 1999). For the purposes of this chapter, I will apply the theory of personal integration developed by Nuttall who emphasises that 'no one school is more efficacious than another' (2008: 24) and describes his process of personal integration thus:

> I moved from a conceptually naïve position of seeking an ideal system, to one of accepting psychotherapy integration as something necessarily personal and contextual and, therefore, at the profession level, pluralistic. It represented a developmental process. Firstly of adding parts together, then of seeing wholes or higher order patterns, whilst throughout there was a dialogue with the outside world, with other disciplines and social artefacts.
>
> (2008: 32)

Nuttall's description of his journey to integration is common among therapists who search for ideal systems. It is important for therapists to embark on a developmental journey, letting go of dogma and opening themselves to the idea of integrating what resonates for them personally that can also make sense to others.

Integrative practitioners' principles of relationality and intersubjectivity are at the heart of the integrative assessment model they develop. Nuttall's view captures recent research evaluations of different therapy treatments approved by NICE (2009) that show no marked differences in effectiveness. Through many years as a lecturer on an integrative training programme for psychotherapists, I observed how trainees in the early stages of their training, in order to feel safe, look for comfort in seeking ideal systems that provide certainty and perfection in their clinical practice. Keeping an open mind while having faith in oneself to arrive at a point of knowing that evolves out of the intersubjective encounter, the struggle to make sense and being prepared to discard unfounded hypotheses, is a difficult position for trainees. By implication, trainees often prematurely attach themselves dogmatically to a particular approach, presenting it as superior to other approaches. This position can compromise the fluidity of the relational space and indeed the growth of the trainee. Paradoxically, the foundations of intersubjectivity and relationality would be denied if therapists rigidly and dogmatically hold on to ideas of superior perspectives, while claiming relationality in their approach.

Hence, integrative practitioners:

- first and foremost need to be clear on their paradigm (set of beliefs and assumptions about the world);
- need to adopt ongoing reflection on the use of their self and the nurturing of their self as this can foster connection; a therapist's vulnerability is often the cornerstone of empathy;
- need to be exposed to a variety of theoretical perspectives, to make sense of these and to choose the ones they most resonate with;
- need to give primacy to the intersubjective, relational value of therapy and base their formulations and understandings on what emerges through interaction with clients; and
- know that integration focuses on the client's understanding of their difficulties and the placebo (client's belief in therapy to help them) (see Wampold 2001: xii).

Maintaining hope, even in the face of client hopelessness, is fundamental for successful therapy. In the words of Yalom, 'instilling and maintaining hope is crucial in any psychotherapeutic treatment and will help to keep the patient in therapy' (1995, cited in Jørgensen 2004: 520–1). A hopeless therapist, who gives up on the client, destroys the placebo with implications for the alliance and the risk of an impasse. Therefore, the integrative therapist's attitude requires nurturing faith and commitment to the therapy endeavour and owning their expertise, while recognising and valuing the growth of the therapist's self. These are fundamental principles that use the placebo effect, contributing to an engaged, effective therapy tailored for the individual client's needs.

The way in which the integrative practitioner conceptualises client problems presented at the assessment interview would be informed by the use of self, the client's understanding of self, the integrative attitude, and the practitioner's epistemological position and chosen perspectives that form their integration model. Assessments provide the necessary data for individual formulations that capture the essence of the client's problems and identify an appropriate treatment plan with a set of interventions linked to knowledge of what works for whom (Roth and Fonagy 1996).

The fictional scenario that follows highlights the therapist's hypothesis and reflections that helped her devise an initial formulation following the assessment.

Scenario from practice 11.1

A new potential client's mother left a lengthy voicemail message for a therapist, explaining her 23-year-old daughter's problems in minute detail and asking whether the therapist could offer a date for an initial consultation for her
daughter. The therapist contacted the mother indicating that she would be
happy to arrange an initial consultation if the daughter would be able to make
direct contact. The therapist reflected on the mother's long, protracted voicemail message and wondered whether she overshadowed her daughter (hypothesis), not encouraging her to be autonomous and take initiative. The therapist
wondered why the daughter had not made contact directly as this would show
evidence of motivation and responsibility, good indicators for therapeutic
engagement. Four days later, the therapist received a call from the daughter
asking to be seen.

The client's demeanour when she arrived for the assessment was
sheepish and anxious and she spoke in such a gentle tone, she sounded
much younger than her years. She explained that she does not take initiative, that her mother does everything for her and that she had found it difficult to make contact with the therapist if it hadn't been for her mother
pushing her into it.

It transpired at the assessment that the client had suffered from chronic
anorexia and self-harm for many years, to the point of near death. She then
had to drop out of university as her mental health had reached a point of
being unable to get out of bed. The mother had to give up her job for months
to keep her daughter alive. She had been seen in two different hospitals but
found the therapists ineffective and stopped attending after a couple of
sessions.

The therapist hypothesised that at the core of the client's illness was an
enmeshed relationship with her mother who could not listen and totally col-
onised her daughter. The mother continued to make calls to the therapist
who advised she would not be able to discuss her daughter's therapy with her
and that it was entirely up to her daughter to share her therapy experience
directly.

The therapist's initial insistence on the client making direct contact to
arrange an appointment and tackling the mother's anxiety worked on two levels:

1. By not colluding with the client's mother to treat her as a child, the
    client developed faith in the therapist. If the therapist could tackle
    the client's overpowering mother, then there was hope she, too,
    might be able to do this one day.
2. The therapist shared her initial hypothesis with the client on what
    she perceived to be an enmeshed relationship between the mother

and daughter and how this may have impacted on her taking control through anorexia and releasing her anger through self-harm. The therapist also invited her to share her own view of her problems. This helped the client develop trust in the therapist's ability to understand through collaboration, not colonisation, what was going on behind her illness and helped the development of an alliance.

As this scenario illustrates, assessments are opportunities to forge trust and engagement in clients. These are the relational dynamic aspects of assessments. In addition, having a clear idea about important components of assessments covering a wide range of areas about the client provides a structure for practitioners and a framework that helps pull together important information and develop insight.

Integrative therapy engages with individual subjectivity through the channel of intersubjectivity. Collaborating and eliciting clients' views about themselves help enhance the alliance and give depth to the therapeutic relationship. Assessments help unify fundamental aspects of the client's self and articulate the understanding of the experience through the assessment report. The process therefore relies on the therapist's ability to tune in, be receptive, empathise and open themselves to feeling an approximation of what the client is feeling, so they can access the subjectivity of the client and understand the meaning of the client's problems.

Important components of integrative assessments

Every assessment consultation aims to identify relevant information such as family and individual history, traumas, developmental issues, needs, expectations from therapy, fears, symptoms and problematic behaviours, life patterns, relationship patterns, resilience and ego strength. What the client is most concerned about should form the focus of the assessment. Our therapeutic objective is to engage the client as much as possible during the assessment consultation through listening, empathising, constructively challenging and making tentative statements of understanding to develop the alliance. It is important that the assessor encourages the development of dialogue and collaboration to help clients feel safe to disclose their most intimate self. Assessments provide the foundation for the development of a formulation that makes sense of this information and of the individual client.

What follows, in Table 11.1, is a description of components in assessments, while in Appendix 1 you can find an assessment form that can be used as a template for developing your own model.

Table 11.1 List of important components in assessments

Get a sense of the person	Identify any substance abuse and addictive behaviour in the client and their family members	Obtain information on education and work history	Contextualise symptoms (i.e. cultural, social, economic context)	Get a feel of how the client relates to self, others and the world	Assess capacity for self-reflection and psychological insight (necessary for in-depth analytic/exploratory work). If these capacities are low, then an extended assessment with an in-built review is recommended, before recommending supportive work that is more suitable	Help devise initial hypotheses to be explored in therapy, which can help revise and reformulate
Get a sense of the problems the client presents with	Be aware of any physical illness/impairment and impact on psychological well-being	Obtain information on the client history of intimate relationships (i.e. when, how long for, what happened for relationship to end)	Ascertain the goals and expectations the client brings to therapy	Get a sense of how the client relates to you as the assessor (using your affective, felt sense can help you make sense of this)	Identify attachment style and how this manifests in current relationships	

(Continued)

Table 11.1 Continued

Engage client in sharing what concerns them most	Know the client's sleeping patters (insomnia, dreams)	Identify any children, ages and type of relationship client has with them	Evaluate level of motivation to pursue therapy	Assess ego strength and resilience (this will determine to what extent the client can cope with pain, and regression) and assess whether they will stay or leave	Provide the client with a taste of what therapy can be like (helps make decisions on therapy)	Help devise an initial psychological formulation and treatment plan
Identify any early traumas	Identify any psychiatric involvement in the client's and in family members' history	Know what type of relationship and early attachments they had with early caregivers including extended family members	Evaluate level of ambivalence in starting treatment. (If ambivalent it is useful to have more than one assessment interview)	Assess whether the client is suitable for the type of intervention and approach you can offer (i.e. short-term supportive work, long-term exploratory work). Consider other possibilities, including referring on		

The debate on assessment

I share my initial understanding about the client at the assessment, giving them an opportunity to respond to and engage in thinking with me and involve themselves collaboratively in co-creating meanings and understandings. This approach to assessments sets the foundations for a therapy relationship of trust, safety, collaboration, authenticity and transparency. Although assessments are useful in bringing information together on clients and making sense of it, there are arguments against them such as:

- they label people;
- they are medicalised due to diagnostic labels used;
- they will tell you very little about the person;
- therapists should be able to work with any type of problem;
- ideas that a model would benefit anyone wanting help;
- if a client starts therapy and we realise they are not suitable, we could refer them on so we do not need assessments.

Despite some therapists' arguments against assessments, they provide essential information about the client and are opportunities to develop initial understandings and identify client concerns, expectations and hopes, while enabling client and therapist to decide whether they wish to work together. Assessments can be meaningful stories about a person and do not need to be medicalised or intended to develop a diagnosis.

For me, integration is synonymous with awareness of self, flexibility, questioning and ongoing reflection until the clinician arrives at their own model of assessing, using the key principles and constructs of their integrative model. Clarity of paradigm and approaching each assessment interview as unique to the clinical encounter itself are important factors. Integrative assessments rest on these principles. Clients and therapists are subjectively involved in the therapeutic process. Both client and assessor meet as the individuals they are, which means that every assessment consultation evolves as a unique intersubjective encounter. We see this idea in the following:

> The patient brings his hopes and his fears to the assessment consultation, the assessor his skills as an experienced psychoanalytic psychotherapist based on his particular theoretical orientation. But both patient and assessor also meet as the individuals they are, which means that every assessment consultation evolves as a unique intersubjective encounter.
>
> (Tonnesmann 1998, cited in Cooper and Affillé 1998: 8)

Conclusion

I approach assessments with an open mind. Experience tells me that clients may not be very forthcoming with important information at the assessment stage. It is therefore important to build on the assessment once further information is revealed. This will impact on the initial formulation, which also needs to be revised until the therapist reaches a point of saturation (feels they have sufficient relevant information to contextualise the chosen intervention and approach, while constantly reviewing whether it works).

A number of template assessment forms are included in the appendices, and clinicians can build on a template to create their own. It is appropriate here to echo the words of Lewis, Gould, Habib and King: 'the integrated approach to clinical assessment is a prerequisite to an integrated approach to psychological therapy' (2010: 6). I would refer the reader to Ingram's (2006) *A Coherent Integrative Assessment*, which provides a framework that includes standards for assessment, hypotheses and therapists' understanding of these.

References

American Psychological Association (2013) *Diagnostic and Statistical Manual for Mental Disorders* (5th edn). Arlington, VA: American Psychological Publishing.

Bateman, A. and Holmes, J. (1995) *Introduction to Psychoanalysis: Contemporary Theory and Practice*. London: Routledge.

Bazzano, M. (2011) Reclaiming diagnosis. *Therapy Today*, November 2011, www.therapytoday.net.

Berner, E.S. and Graber, M.L. (2008) Overconfidence as a cause of diagnostic error in medicine. *The American Journal of Medicine*, 121(1): S2–S23.

BPS (British Psychological Society) (2011) Guidelines on the use of psychological formulation. https://www1.bps.org.uk/system/files/Public%20files/DCP/cat-842.pdf (accessed 14 January 2018).

Chodorow, N.J. (1989) *Feminism and Psychoanalytic Theory*. New Haven, CT: Yale University Press.

Cooper, M. (2007) Humanizing psychotherapy. *Journal of Contemporary Psychotherapy*, 37: 11–16.

Davies, J. (2013) *Why Psychiatry Is Doing More Harm Than Good*. London: Icon Books.

Granvold, D.K. (1996) Constructivist psychotherapy. *Families in Society: The Journal of Contemporary Human Services*, 77(6): 345–59.

Guba, E.G. and Lincoln, Y.S. (1994) Competing paradigms in qualitative research. In N.K. Denzin and Y.S. Lincoln (eds), *Handbook of Qualitative Research* (pp. 105–17). Thousand Oaks, CA: SAGE.

Hubble, M.A., Duncan, B.L. and Miller, S.D. (1999) *The Heart and Soul of Change: What Works in Therapy*. Washington, DC: APA.

Ingram, B.L. (2006) *Clinical Case Formulations: Matching the Integrative Treatment Plan to the Client*. Hoboken, NJ: Wiley.

Jørgensen, C.R. (2004) Active ingredients in individual psychotherapy: Searching for common factors. *Psychoanalytic Psychology*, 21(4): 516–40.

Lewis, A.J., Gould, E., Habib, C. and King, R. (2010) *Integrative Assessment in Clinical Psychology*. Sydney: Australian Academic Press.

NICE (2009) *Depression: Treatment and Management of Depression in Adults. Clinical Guideline 90.* London: National Institute for Health and Clinical Excellence. Available at www.nice.org.uk

Norcross, J.C. and Goldfried, M.R. (eds) (1992) *Handbook of Psychotherapy Integration.* New York: Basic Books.

Nuttall, J. (2008) The integrative attitude – a personal journey. *European Journal of Psychotherapy and Counselling,* 10(1): 19–38.

Probst, B.H. (2015) *Critical Thinking in Clinical Assessment and Diagnosis.* London: Springer.

Rogers, C. (1951) *Client-Centered Therapy: Its Current Practice, Implications and Theory.* Boston, MA: Houghton Mifflin.

Roth, A. and Fonagy, P. (1996) *What Works for Whom: A Critical Review of Psychotherapy Research.* London: Guilford Press.

Saferstein, J.A. (2006) The relationship between therapists' epistemology and their therapy style, working alliance, and use of specific interventions. Dissertation, University of Florida.

Sturmey, P. (2009) *Clinical Case Formulation: Varieties of Approaches.* London: Wiley-Blackwell.

Tonnesmann, M. (1998) Foreword. In J. Cooper and H. Affillé (eds), *Assessment in Psychotherapy.* London: Karnac.

Wampold, B.E. (2001) *The Great Psychotherapy Debate: Models, Methods and Findings.* Taylor and Francis e-library.

12 Formulation in integrative practice

Maria Luca

Introduction

There is a distinction between diagnosis and formulation. The former attaches an existing DSM-V label to the cluster of presenting issues; the latter involves clients collaboratively in drawing together understandings of the presenting client problems (Macneil et al. 2012): 'The concept of clinical case formulation advocates for collaboratively working with patients to identify idiosyncratic aspects of their presentation and select interventions on this basis' (Macneil et al. 2012: 1).

Psychological formulation therefore uses the information from the assessment to organise and make sense of the problems; this forms the basis of the initial formulation. Often clinicians begin formulating during the assessment and continue building on their initial formulation as the treatment progresses.

Historically, formulations focused on providing an explanation of the causes of presenting problems (precipitants) and maintaining factors, which lead to specific therapeutic interventions (Butler 1998). The integrative perspective on formulations places clients in the context of their social world, including their unique combination of culture, values and beliefs. It embraces the relational idea of collaboration, sense-making and meaning-making, a collaborative endeavour to construct a story that makes sense to the therapy dyad. A formulation can best be understood as co-constructing the personal meaning of the client's life story. It is a 'process of ongoing collaborative sense-making' (Harper and Moss 2003: 8), which summarises the client's core problems in the context of psychological theory and evidence and thus indicates the best path to recovery. Unlike diagnosis, formulations are not about making expert judgements, but about working closely with the client to develop a shared understanding, which is likely to evolve over the course of the therapeutic work. Therefore, formulation is the process of making sense of a person's difficulties in the context of their relationships, social circumstances, attitude to self and others, life events and their reaction and management of them. It is a personal narrative that a mental healthcare professional draws up in collaboration with an individual.

Clients are the holders of knowledge about themselves. They might not have psychological understanding of this knowledge, or the ability to reflect and make sense of it. But it is imperative that we involve clients in the process of formulating and choosing a therapeutic way forward, which involves specific interventions, models, skills and length of therapy. Without the client's cooperation, involvement and motivation, the formulation and indeed the therapy relationship would be compromised.

Integrative formulations

Formulations help clinicians develop co-constructed understandings of the client and their unique problems/concerns. They act in the service of decisions about the most appropriate plan of action and treatment strategy, which includes specific interventions. Historically, the limits of diagnosis led to the development of formulations within the profession of clinical psychology. The benefits of formulations are that they focus on the uniqueness of the client and avoid placing them in a given box/diagnosis, which helps more with prognosis as it is based on the clinician's and client's collaboration.

Subsequently, as seen by the growing number of publications on formulations, including from the humanistic field (Eells and Lombart 2003; Eells 2007; Johnstone and Dallos 2014; Johnstone 2018), the psychotherapy and counselling psychology fields are increasingly embracing formulations. Some (Antaki et al. 2005) advocate diagnostic formulations, but the perspective from most of the literature argues for individualised, collaborative formulations, integrating clients' views. However, Eells argues for a balance 'between an individual and general formulation. Humility is an asset in this respect. The match between any model and any individual is inherently imperfect, and the formulation is never more than an approximation of the individual in distress' (2007: 22). What Eells is postulating is that there will always be a gap in the therapist's model and the individual client, concluding that absolute understanding cannot be reached. Eells' assertion confirms the constructivist notion that therapists are aiming for constructing a viable understanding of clients and that truth and fact are open to interpretation.

The psychological therapies field is now supported by many research studies on effective interventions rooted in formulations for specific mental health issues, providing clinicians with a knowledge base to draw on. Roth and Fonagy's (1996) work is a good example of this. The success of formulations is discussed by Green whose position is similar to Eells, stating that the success of individualised formulations is associated with capturing the subjective world of the individual as opposed to attaching fixed diagnostic labels to individuals:

> The use of formulation to describe an individual's difficulties in terms of 'working hypotheses' has been a successful project within the profession of clinical psychology due to its focus on individualised understanding and choice of interventions. This constructionist perspective to formulations does away with labels altogether and reverts to passages of descriptive writing that aim to capture something of the individuality of a person's distress.
>
> (2013: 24)

However, for formulations to be meaningful and effective, it is important that they move beyond description and use theory to conceptualise the client's problems. In addition, according to Sim et al., 'case formulation is a topic of interest in psychotherapy not only in its utility as a conceptual and clinical tool but also because of its potential as a research tool into the outcomes of psychotherapeutic work' (2005: 289). Sim et al. are promoting the use of formulations for psychotherapy as a valuable tool that could also help research identify outcomes of certain therapeutic work.

The approach to formulations can vary depending on the clinician's approach. For example, Hinshelwood advocated that psychodynamic formulations consist of 'three areas of object-relations (the current life situation, the early infantile relations and the transference relationship)' (1991: 166).

The literature on formulations has established their importance as a clinical tool. However, as Hinshelwood asserted, the approach to formulations would inevitably be associated with the therapist's modality. The recognition that formulations are important research tools is confirmed by Kendjelic and Eells: 'Psychotherapy case formulation is recognized as a core psychotherapy skill by diverse practitioners and researchers' and they state that 'some researchers have found that therapy guided by a case formulation improves treatment outcome' (2007: 66).

An integrative approach to formulations must be guided by the therapist's clinical approach and conceptual underpinnings. The therapeutic relationship, with emphasis on developing the alliance, needs to be the focus in formulations, too. To activate client engagement and motivation, as early as the assessment session, integrative practitioners need to consider using interpersonal skills, such as the humanistic core conditions and interpersonal perception (see Chapter 9). These skills aim to create a climate of trust and safety that encourages clients to openly share their problems, views and perspectives on their presenting problems. The essential features of an integrative formulation can be seen in Table 12.1.

Table 12.1 Features of an integrative formulation

A summary of the client's key issues	A summary of the client's personal perspective on the issues (i.e. causes and general understanding)	A conceptualisation of the client's presenting problems, including the core issue, and how these may relate to one another	Devise a treatment plan with types of interventions rooted in the client's psychological processes and a rationale of how these interventions will help the client
A summary of the client's therapeutic goals/ expectations	A summary of the client's relational pattern including with the therapist	Using theory, explain how the issues are maintained by the client (for example, lack of trust in themselves or fear of psychological exposure) (these are hypotheses to be tested)	As new material emerges and hypotheses are tested, re-formulate and consider adopting and/or revising interventions based on the revised formulation

Formulations are not fixed; they should be imbued with fluidity and elasticity. New client problems and concerns may come to light in the process of therapy, so practitioners need to review treatments and revise their formulations. This may necessitate a modified approach and new interventions. Initial formulations map the key issues and identify the core conflict and client concern, which helps practitioners to reflect on useful aspects of the client's life and have an idea of the types of interventions with which it might be useful to begin the work. As therapy progresses, practitioners develop deeper insight into their client, thus the need to revise and reformulate. In-built reviews can help the process of reformulating. Integrative formulations emphasise the usefulness in involving clients in the review process.

A brief history of formulations

Formulation was a significant development within clinical psychology from 1969 onwards, when the term first appeared in the professional regulations. It continues as a core training competency mandated by the Division of Clinical and Counselling Psychology of the BPS (BPS 2011). Although today many therapy approaches embrace formulations, humanistic approaches to psychotherapy have a varied and uneasy relationship with case formulation and assessment, as they associate these with diagnosis, as we saw in Chapter 11. The person-centred approach, developed by Rogers (1951), questioned the benefits of diagnosis. Person-centred practitioners are concerned about assigning labels, which they consider potentially damaging or unhelpful in therapeutic practice. Other, more integrative humanistic approaches (Elliott et al. 2004) use their own theoretical concepts for assessment, diagnosis and case formulation and approach this process experientially and as a joint venture between the therapist and the client. Client empowerment and transparency are important principles in all humanistic approaches, even though therapists might put them into practice in different ways. A conference paper by Hoffman and Hoffman (2017) indicated that existential–humanistic therapists viewed conceptualising client problems, case formulation and treatment planning as a collaborative, ongoing process. Within the context of humanistic psychotherapy, intersubjectivity is seen as the process of co-creation: the therapist and the client co-create meaning and experience on the basis of both of their subjective experiences, with all that it entails. Assessment and case formulation in this philosophical framework require the therapist to remain reflective, interested and questioning about their own psychological process and the sociopolitical context and environment (Summers and Tudor 2000). Integrative therapists treat the understanding that emerges in the assessment and formulation as co-constructed with the client.

A formulation can be understood as both an event and a process, and it summarises and integrates a broad range of biopsychosocial causal/associated factors. It is recognised as a conceptual and clinical tool based on testing hypotheses, because a diagnosis alone does not focus on the underlying causes of a patient's problems. Case formulation can fill the gap between diagnosis and treatment. It can provide insights into the integrative, explanatory, prescriptive, predictive and therapist aspects of a case (Sim et al. 2005).

Fowlie and Sills (2011) developed a comprehensive list of integrative principles underlying case formulations influenced by a relational perspective. In this list, they highlight the centrality of the therapeutic relationship and taking into consideration the therapist's subjectivity in creating meanings. They also stress the importance of looking at the reality of the adult in the client, rather than a purely developmental view.

Definitions of formulations

Definitions of formulations vary, so I will give some examples to demonstrate the wide range of definitions available.

- Ingram defines formulation as 'the creation of an individualized conceptual framework for a single, unique client' (2006: xxi). Formulations begin with hypotheses, which provide in-roads for exploration.
- Persons argued that 'The therapist can never be certain her hypothesis about the underlying mechanism is correct and must always be prepared to revise or change it in the face of evidence. This is a continuous process; in fact, assessment and treatment are a continuous process of proposing, testing, re-evaluating, revising, rejecting, and creating new formulations' (1989: 55).
- In Butler's words, 'A formulation is not an expert pronouncement, like a medical diagnosis, but a "plausible account"' (1998: 1).
- Ross's poignant account of formulations supports this idea. He suggested that formulation 'involves selecting the highlights of a person's life: the important people or events that shaped the person into a unique individual. It is not a summary of a case although it involves summarized aspects of a case' (2000: 1).

The psychology of integrative formulations

In tandem with integrative assessments, as discussed in Chapter 11, the approach to integrative, relational formulations incorporates a two-person psychology in looking at how meaning is constructed in the context of the relationship. The client and the therapist bring with them their own experiences, context and individuality and the interaction between them is the product of both. Two-person psychology stems from the psychoanalytic perspective of the concept of intersubjectivity.

> Intersubjective systems theory seeks to comprehend psychological phenomena not as products of isolated intrapsychic mechanisms, but as forming at the interface of reciprocally interacting worlds of experience.

> Psychological phenomena . . . cannot be understood apart from the inter-subjective contexts in which they take form.
>
> (Atwood and Stolorow 1984: 64)

To be able to develop clear and useful formulations, integrative clinicians must know,

> what to do (and what not to do) in order to create a strong alliance at different phases of the treatment. They must rely on an implicit or explicit understanding of the client's problems and how to treat them. Such understanding will be based on case formulation derived from preferred theoretical orientation(s). Thus, the therapist's language and methods . . . will be nested within favored theories.
>
> (Castonguay 2000: 265)

In other words, there are multiple ways of integrating, therefore, the onus is on the therapist to select theories, concepts and interventions that resonate with their values and paradigms and most importantly derive from experience and knowledge on what works for whom, especially for the client.

An example of a formulation

This fictional case example will illustrate the importance of using the therapist's agency in formulating, which activates the client's agency and helps create a collaborative approach to formulation.

Scenario from practice 12.1

Mr Belluci, a 35-year-old man originally from Italy, referred himself for therapy due to depression and feelings of frustration in his relationships with women. He could not sustain a romantic relationship and had sex mostly with high-class prostitutes, getting into what he described as enjoying aggressive women and being controlled by them. He mentioned having had some psychoanalytic sessions in the past analysts, which he found helpful. He occasionally sees one of these analysts whom he likes when in Italy, but feels it is time he has consistent and regular psychotherapy in his new home of London to deal with his problems.

Previously, he was diagnosed with ADHD, as well as bipolar disorder. He presented with dark thoughts, emotional heaviness and a hedonistic lifestyle and was concerned that he had surrendered to the idea that this will always be the status quo. He was fearful that any attempts to develop and sustain a normal intimate relationship would be sabotaged by the part of him that is destructive. Mr Belluci had developed an addiction to adrenalin and dopamine and his chosen lifestyle accommodated this.

He described his childhood as stressful with some traumatic events, characterised by constant fights between him and his mother, following by making up and re-establishing their closeness. His relationship with his father was good and continues to be supportive, according to the client. Mr Belluci spoke initially of his relationship with his mother as intense and overwhelming, both needing her close but also hating her over-involvement in his life. His mother was described as fragile, emotionally volatile and presenting with hysterical outbursts. She also suffered from OCD.

In developing the initial formulation with Mr Belluci, a collaborative approach was used, where the therapist shared some initial thoughts (hypotheses) on his presenting issues, inviting him to respond and share what he thought was going on. The therapist and client together arrived at the hypothesis that his tendency to fear intimate romantic relationships was associated with anxiety linked to a loss of masculinity. In paying prostitutes, he retained some control, despite being passive during sex. He believed that 'ordinary' women would not tolerate his need to be passive sexually and added that he would feel like a boy, not a man, anyway.

Mr Belluci demonstrated a tendency to interpret intimacy and commitment in romantic relationships as potentially boring and emasculating. He felt that the type of woman he expected to choose as a partner would not be aggressive and controlling, like the women he pays for sex. This expectation created a double bind for Mr Belluci, keeping romantic relationships at bay, or when in a romantic relationship, feeling bored. Without the ability to tolerate what seemed to be a paradox between his sexual and emotional needs, the client arrived at the conclusion that he would always be in this predicament of preferring sex with women he pays, while harbouring the need for an emotionally intimate relationship.

The therapist and client explored the question of whether there might be a solution to his predicament, bringing his sexual and emotional needs together in relationships. The client could see how, by keeping his sexual and emotional needs separate, he was protecting himself against the threat of feeling overwhelmed and controlled by a woman. The therapist shared her thoughts tentatively, wondering whether Mr Belluci's need to be controlled felt much more powerful than his need to be in control of himself, which left him in the double bind. He felt that this formulation resonated with him as he often felt like a child with aggressive, controlling women, which he enjoyed within the safety of a transaction. Nonetheless, he needed to feel 'like a man', like his father in romantic relationships, which motivated him to seek therapy.

The therapist and client agreed that a therapeutic way forward was to address the presumed mechanisms by exploring the double bind and the associated feeling of impasse in Mr Belluci. The therapist and client agreed to review progress after five months and revise the formulation. The therapist initially provided an empathic presence to help establish a therapeutic alliance; she also integrated interpretation based on transference with some psychoeducation to normalise the emerging anxiety in Mr Belluci.

Mr Belluci expressed feeling overwhelmed with the intensity of therapy and it was agreed to change the pace. The therapist acknowledged the client's feelings and praised his honesty about therapy. She noted that he seemed to wait passively for instructions from her and she interpreted this as part of his habitual need for women to control him. Although Mr Belluci understood his passivity as an aspect of his need to be looked after, his need to mature and take control of his life was not as strong, which left him unable to sustain himself in romantic relationships due to his fear of loss of self. Because he really enjoyed being controlled by women he paid, as well as continuing his hedonistic lifestyle, his desire to psychologically mature and take responsibility continued to be low in his priorities.

In exploring this further, Mr Belluci looked thoughtful and frustrated. He said he expected that therapy would help him change his habits (albeit it seemed) without him having to take an active role in the process. His therapist challenged him on his stance and he agreed to be more committed and actively help himself to achieve his therapeutic goals.

By reviewing progress and reformulating, therapist and client were able to identify the obstacles to progress. In particular, it helped the therapist to adopt new interventions, such as challenging and focusing Mr Belluci on understanding and processing his anxieties. This helped bring the client out of his habitual comfort zone, which contributed to the double bind.

Sharing formulations with our clients

It is important that we think through whether sharing our formulations with clients will facilitate the therapy or in some way cause an impasse. Each client is unique, with particular sensitivities and reactions, therefore, deciding to share our formulation must rest on our knowledge and understanding of each client. I have found that sharing my written formulations with some clients as a tentative story put together based on our dialogue invites reflection and further involvement in the process of understanding. Clients with whom I have shared formulations often mull over, respond in the affirmative or engage by reformulating aspects that in their view do not quite capture who they are. Some clients are satisfied to see that the therapist continues to think about them outside sessions, something that validates and enhances their self-worth. This is a dynamic ongoing process that can be repeated over the course of treatment. Johnstone and Dallos (2014) draw attention to how sharing formulations with clients could be potentially harmful. I would not personally share formulations with a client who may have paranoid tendencies or seems rigidly defensive and unlikely to treat the formulation as food for thought, a story that can be revised. Doing so might be too risky in that the client may feel excessively conscious and exposed. I would instead consider sharing at a much later stage of therapy, if indeed I feel the client is more receptive. With these issues in mind, it is important that the language used in formulations is simple and client-friendly.

The use of the therapist's self and reflection in formulations

It is not the purpose of this section to evaluate the vast body of literature on effective ways therapists' use of self is utilised to understand the intersubjective therapeutic process. The purpose and what will be explored are an overview of the principles guiding a postmodern way of using self to achieve effective practice. The movement towards a new, postmodern psychology gave rise to a climate of therapists learning from the experience of being with clients and reflecting on how the self of the therapist may be impacting on the process. The tradition of the (reductive) case study as a means of understanding psychopathology and psychotherapy process was first introduced by Freud and Breuer (1895). Formulations are on par with intersubjectivity, as they acknowledge how the therapeutic interaction is a meaningful construction and cannot be reduced to events in the past. However, the past, just like the present, is taken into consideration.

It is now widely acknowledged that professional practice aims to 'give primacy to experience and meanings and treat the human subject with respect' (Hoshmand and Polkinghorne 1992: 60). Practitioners increasingly recognise the value in collaborative work in devising formulations as this demonstrates respect for the client as the expert of their life. Unlike diagnoses, formulations are hypotheses to be tested through reflection, which helps the process of reformulating.

A comparative study by Eells and Lombart into case formulation and treatment concepts among novice, experienced and expert cognitive–behavioural and psychodynamic therapists found that modality, level of experience, and expertise were predictors in case formulation and treatment preconceptions. A key finding from this study is that experts 'were more likely than other therapists to believe that the patient was able to achieve therapeutic change independent of the actions taken by the therapist' (2003: 200). This suggests that more experienced therapists recognise more readily the client's own autonomy and capacity for self-healing. The study also showed differences between the modality groups that the authors ascribe to the influence of theoretical underpinnings.

Formulations that draw heavily on theory, without client involvement and understanding of the presenting issues, risk becoming dogmatic and alienating of clients. Given that formulations are hypotheses developed in collaboration with clients, they are essentially fluid. They tell a story, which is an amalgam of the practitioner's and client's language that can be revised as therapy progresses.

It is expected that integrative therapists, in their journey of developing a personal integration model, will also create an integrative formulation model that complements the way they work.

Conclusion

I have been using psychological formulations for several years. In my experience, they are indispensable in terms of focussing on the uniqueness of individual clients; in helping therapists draw together a coherent summary of clients' problems, aetiology and strengths; and in guiding therapists to choose suitable approaches and psychological interventions for each client. The indispensability of formulations is summarised thus: 'a psychotherapy case formulation is an integrative tool. In the hands of a psychotherapist who knows how to construct and use it, a case formulation is indispensable' (Eells 2007: 25).

As the treatment draws to a close, it is important to carry out a client evaluation of their experience of therapy. This will help clinicians to better understand what their clients value most and any areas for improvement. I use a standard evaluation form, which can be found in Appendix 2.

References

Antaki, C., Barnes, R. and Leudar, I., (2005) Diagnostic formulations in psychotherapy. *Discourse Studies*, 7(6): 627–47.

Atwood, G.E. and Stolorow, R.D. (1984) *Structures of Subjectivity: Explorations in Psychoanalytic Phenomenology and Contextualism*. London: Routledge.

Butler, G. (1998) Clinical case formulation. In A.S. Bellack and M. Hersen (eds), *Comprehensive Clinical Psychology*. Oxford: Pergamon.

Castonguay, L.G. (2000) A common factors approach to psychotherapy training. *Journal of Psychotherapy Integration*, 10(3): 263–82.

Eells, T.D. (ed.) (2007) *Handbook of Psychotherapy Case Formulation* (2nd edn). New York: Guilford Press.

Eells, T.D. and Lombart, K.G. (2003) Case formulation and treatment concepts among novice, experienced, and expert cognitive-behavioral and psychodynamic therapists. *Psychotherapy Research*, 13(2): 187–204.

Elliott, R., Watson, J.C., Goldman, R.N. and Greenberg, L.S. (2004) *Learning Emotion-Focused Therapy: The Process-Experiential Approach to Change*. Washington, DC: American Psychological Association.

Freud, S. and Breuer, J. (1895) *Studies on Hysteria*, vol. 3. A. Strachey and J. Strachey, trans. 1991. London: Penguin Books.

Fowlie, H.S. and Sills, C. (2011) Introduction. In H.S. Fowlie and C. Sills (eds) *Relational Transactional Analysis: Principles in Practice*. London: Karnac.

Green, H. (2013) Psychiatric diagnosis vs. psychological formulation: A plea for synthesis. *Clinical Psychology Forum*, 246: 23–25.

Harper, D.J. and Moss, D. (2003) A different kind of chemistry? Reformulating 'formulation'. *Journal of Clinical Psychology*, 23: 6–10.

Hinshelwood, R.D. (1991) Psychodynamic formulation in assessment for psychotherapy. *British Journal of Psychotherapy*, 8(2): 166–74.

Hoffman, L. and Hoffman, H.P. (2017) *An Existential-Humanistic Approach to Case Conceptualization and Treatment Planning*. Available at: https://www.researchgate.net/publication/318793034_An_Existential-Humanistic_Approach_to_Case_Conceptualization_and_Treatment_Planning. (accessed 4 May 2018).

Hoshmand, L.T. and Polkinghorne, D.E. (1992) Redefining the science-practice relationship and professional training. *American Psychologist*, 47(1): 55–66.

Ingram, B.L. (2006) *Clinical Case Formulations: Matching the Integrative Treatment Plan to the Client*. Hoboken, NJ: Wiley.

Johnstone, L. (2018) Psychological formulation as an alternative to psychiatric diagnosis. *Journal of Humanistic Psychology*, 58(1): 30–46.

Johnstone, L. and Dallos, R. (2014) *Formulation in Psychology and Psychotherapy*. Hove: Routledge.

Kendjelic, E.M. and Eells, T.D. (2007) Generic, psychotherapy case formulation training improves formulation quality. *Psychotherapy: Theory, Research and Practice*, 44(1): 66–77.

Macneil, C.A., Hasty, M.K., Conus, P. and Berk, M. (2012) Is diagnosis enough to guide interventions in mental health? *BMC Medicine*, 10: 111–13. http://www.biomedcentral.com/1741-7015/10/111.

Nuttall, J. (2008) The integration: A personal journey. *European Journal of Psychotherapy and Counselling*, 10(1): 19–38.

Persons, J.B. (1989) *Cognitive Therapy in Practice: A Case Formulation Approach*. New York: W.W. Norton.

Rogers, C. (1951) *On Becoming a Person*. London: Constable.

Ross, D.E. (2000) A method of developing a biopsychosocial formulation. *Journal of Child and Family Studies*, 9(1): 1–6.

Roth, A. and Fonagy, P. (1996) *What Works for Whom: A Critical Review of Psychotherapy Research*. London: Guilford Press.

Sim, K., Gwee, K.P. and Bateman, A. (2005) Case formulation in psychotherapy: Revitalizing its usefulness as a clinical tool. *Academic Psychiatry*, 29(3): 289–92.

Summers, G. and Tudor, K. (2000) Cocreative transactional analysis. *Transactional Analysis Journal*, 30(1): 23–40.

13 Embodied, integrative supervision

Maria Luca

Introduction

Supervision in psychological therapies is regarded as a requirement by professional bodies in the UK (see UKCP 2012; BPS 2017) but is often conducted with little or no training. More recently, professional bodies have introduced a requirement that, to supervise, a therapist must complete a recognised supervision training course that meets professional standards. The view that supervision is a core competency and should warrant professional training is now prominent:

> Clinical supervision is one of the professional activities often performed by psychologists. Yet, the majority of clinicians have not received formal training and supervision in this area of competence (Scott, Ingram, Vitanza, and Smith 2000), most likely because their trainers did not view supervision as a core competence on a par with other core competencies such as assessment and intervention.
>
> (Falender et al. 2004: 774)

Supervision has been the subject of much research. One study by Ellis et al. (2015) has found an alarming number of supervisees are receiving either inadequate or harmful supervision. The study in the Republic of Ireland compared results with studies in the United States and suggested the following results (Table 13.1).

These are alarming findings, particularly in light of the important functions of supervision such as support, professional development, safe practising and encouragement for therapists, especially for those in private practice who often work in isolation. According to Orlinsky, Botermans and Ronnestad (2001), who interviewed 4,000 psychotherapists of different modalities about what influenced their development, there was considerable agreement on what facilitates or impedes therapists' professional development. Among the main positive influences was formal supervision as the second most influential factor with 66 per cent rating it as a highly influential factor in their professional development. The study highlights that supervision is fundamental to professional development.

Table 13.1 Comparison of Republic of Ireland and US supervision

	Republic of Ireland (%)	United States (%)
Percentage of supervisees categorised as currently receiving inadequate supervision	79.2	69.5
Percentage of supervisees categorised as currently receiving harmful supervision	40.3	25.2
Percentage of supervisees who, at some point in their careers, have received inadequate supervision	92.4	86.4
Percentage of supervisees who, at some point in their careers, have received harmful supervision	51.7	39.7
Percentage of supervisees who reported receiving exceptional supervision from their current supervisors	51.0	55.0

Source: Data from Ellis et al. (2015).

The embodied supervisor

As a therapist and supervisor, my allegiance lies within postmodern epistemology (Polkinghorne 1983; Kvale 1992; Elliott et al. 1999). The key perspective in postmodernism is that human consciousness is not passively mirroring the world as in the subject–object dichotomy where a therapist or supervisor is the subject and the client is the object of observation. Instead, I regard therapeutic practitioners and their clients as relational, active agents operating within social contexts, engaging with each other and co-creating meanings. Merleau-Ponty (1962) postulated that the world exists before we come to know it and the lived world is pre-reflective. Embodiment from this perspective is not just about the body as a physiological entity, but a living, interacting body experiencing and knowing the world reflectively and through the living body-subject (relationship between the body and the mind).

> For Merleau-Ponty the reflective analysis required for objective thinking is not sufficient in understanding human subjectivity ... Subjects are made via engagement with others and their environment. Thus knowledge cannot be detached from culture, language and history; it is the product of participation and dialogical engagement with the world.
>
> (Luca 2007: 66)

Hence it is inconceivable to have a mind without a living body and a body without a living mind. My supervisee's being in its totality encounters my being, we both impact on one another and through this dialogical, experiential engagement we connect. The outcome of this process often involves the transformation not only of the supervisee but also the supervisor. Being a therapist or supervisor is a journey to help others develop but, most fundamentally, it is a continuous journey of self-development, both challenging and rewarding.

I will now briefly describe a personal practice experience to highlight how I've come to understand bodily communications and resonant bodily responses (Bownas and Fredman 2017), which have taken a foundational place in my integrative supervision practice.

Scenario from practice 13.1

During my time as a trainee psychotherapist, I experienced a memorable bodily response to a client in a number of our sessions. The client's mother had been murdered when she was only 3 by her father, who was consequently imprisoned. The client presented with frequent heavy menstrual bleeding over more than the monthly cycle. Medical investigations revealed no organic cause to this symptom and she was referred for long-term psychotherapy. She engaged well but, in the initial stages of therapy, avoided discussing her early traumas. The therapeutic atmosphere was devoid of emotional connection and I was unsure whether this client was suitable for exploratory, long-term work. Six months into therapy, the client started to weep during sessions and found it difficult to speak. The therapeutic atmosphere was heavy and I was aware of my feeling nauseous, which appeared only during sessions with this client. I also occasionally developed migraines and experienced aura in my peripheral vision. I listened attentively, wondering whether my client felt overwhelmed, frightened or perhaps had difficulty naming her feelings. It would take me 30 minutes to an hour to recover from my nausea and headaches following the end of each of our sessions.

I asked myself what might have brought on my nausea and migraines, which I explored in my own therapy and in supervision. An early memory from when I was 6 years old sprang to mind in one of my therapy sessions: it was dark and I was at home alone with my younger sister. My parents were down the road working at their café. (It was common practice in the village during that time to leave children in bed asleep and for a parent or neighbour to occasionally check on them.) During the night, I heard a big bang and woke up frightened but felt unable to move from my bed. My limbs were frozen, my mind racing. I began to cry quietly so as not to wake my little sister. I felt nauseous, something I had previously experienced only as motion sickness when in a car or bus. Luckily, there was a pot in the bedroom so I used it to collect my vomit. For the first time, I saw zigzag lights around my eyes and thought of a villager who was blind, wondering if I, too, was going blind. This thought was terrifying. The ordeal lasted for what felt like hours, until my parents returned home; I cried tears of relief when I saw them. I could not speak, all I could do was cry.

> Thinking back on my bodily response of nausea and migraine during therapy with my client, it seemed to me that my client was unconsciously communicating her fear through projective identification, to which I responded with my own map of bodily resonance.

This bodily dialogue with my traumatised client has provided the impetus for me to learn more about embodied therapy and embodied supervision, concepts I have been working with since then. For the practising therapist, supervision can help illuminate the therapeutic encounter through embodied and relational practice. However, it is important that supervision looks beyond the pattern, style and meanings of the client's narrative. Encouraging therapists to understand their own bodily and emotional responses to clients' style of narrative reflects embodied supervision practice.

The role of the relational integrative supervisor

All therapists and supervisors are informed by certain values and principles that guide our work (Nuttall 2018). Mine have evolved over the last 22 years of practising as a therapist and supervisor. At the core of my integrative approach to therapy and supervision is the intersubjective relationship. Creating an empathic, warm atmosphere is for me a fundamental principle, rooted in the humanistic psychology of Rogers (2003). This helps build an alliance that will see the supervisory relationship through difficult processes that manifest from time to time. Collaboration with my supervisee is another important principle. Like the general practitioner who needs to listen attentively to the patient in order to develop a more accurate diagnosis, I encourage the supervisee to reveal who they are, what their strengths and competences are and what gaps and learning ambitions they harbour. Getting to know the person of the supervisee requires involving my entire being (i.e. listening attentively with my emotions, bodily felt sense, cognition and intuition). This sets the foundations for a deeper understanding of the supervisee, knowing them more intimately, but also understanding their relational propensity towards me. Buber's (1970) I–Thou is a concept at the heart of relationality, where supervisee and supervisor relate to each other as subjects and not as object–subject. The ability to listen attentively and understand oneself is linked to the ability to tune into others' being.

Like clients, supervisors have their own style of narrative, personality and leanings to be more or less cognitively or affectively orientated; therefore, awareness of self is fundamental. For example, if I tend to evoke specific reactions in my supervisees, such as fear of judging them, I take stock of this and try to identify the contribution my personality and approach have on supervisee reactions to me. This awareness helps own my contribution rather than holding the supervisee solely responsible for the supervisory dynamic developed through our interaction.

Spinelli (2005) identified two aspects in therapy that run in parallel fashion with supervision. These are 'being', involving the relational aspects of therapy, as discussed earlier, and 'doing', involving therapy tasks and goals. The former are on a continuum; relational depth deepens as the supervisory relationship goes through stages of anxiety, an alliance develops and trust allows for a more honest relationship, not in a linear fashion but in a more circular back and forth fashion. The latter are identified in the initial stages of the supervision agreement and are reviewed as the supervisory relationship evolves.

Once an alliance has developed, the supervision relationship establishes the foundations of trust, safety and collaboration, so that more risk can be taken to reveal areas that may feel uncomfortable to the supervisee. As the holders of experience and knowledge, supervisors are often idealised by supervisees, a dynamic that in my experience can cause an impasse. If supervisees are not encouraged to step outside their comfort zone, where they hide their perceived inadequacies and protect themselves against anticipated criticism, their professional development is compromised. Supervisor-appropriate self-disclosure of mistakes can encourage supervisees to take more risks, which would open them to deeper understanding and emotional connection in the supervisory relationship. As Clarkson (2003) highlighted, there is a growing body of research that suggests the therapeutic relationship is more significant than the therapist's theoretical orientation to clinical outcomes. Orlinsky et al.'s (1994) study also emphasised the importance of the therapist–client relationship. The authors argued that the value of this is so consistently replicated in studies that it can be considered a fact. In my experience, building the supervisory relationship and a strong alliance can help withstand potential conflicts between supervisee–supervisor.

My model of integrative supervision is individualised. I approach each supervisee as a unique individual with a unique personality and developmental needs. Following my understanding of the kind of relationship that has evolved between the supervisee and myself as supervisor, I will time my supervisory interventions depending on the readiness and receptivity of the supervisee.

The role of supervision is to ensure that the practitioner's work is up to ethical and professional standards, which involves monitoring the growth and development of the supervisee, enabling the supervisee to develop their therapeutic skills and deepen their reflective function. Supervision in psychotherapy and the related disciplines is a growing field, as Gilbert and Evans explain: 'recent years have seen the development of sophisticated models of supervision . . . these models provide conceptual frameworks for supervision, a discussion of developmental stages in supervision as well as a focus on the tasks and functions of supervision' (2000: 1).

What is often overlooked in the literature on the supervisory role that focuses on competence frameworks are the salient, relational dynamics that make for an authentic, rewarding supervisory experience for both supervisor and supervisee. Relational dynamics are central to the integrative approach to supervision.

The relational integrative supervisor's aim would be first and foremost to engage the supervisee in a process of developing a trusting, safe relationship, establishing an alliance where difficult issues can openly be explored. Fostering an alliance involves relational aspects (engaging our subjectivity) pivotal in the early stages and necessary thereafter in supervisory relationships. Supervision with a focus on evidence-based practice and the intellectual theorisation of clients misses out on what Hargaden (2016) describes as a supervisory relationship based on mutual respect and reciprocity, providing an atmosphere for emotional and intellectual development. Integrative supervision needs to consider Nuttall's view that the integrative quest 'should be viewed more as a way of being, constantly becoming and unfolding, rather than something with a determined and sedimented end' (2017: 24).

Reflection on my own experience as a supervisee psychotherapist with different supervisors tells me that what helped me grow were times when my supervisor's approach was not narrowed down to reflection and exploration of client material as independent of me, the therapist. Instead, it included a display of curiosity and an invitation to think about my feelings for the client and how my own subjectivity played a part in how the therapy evolved. This approach is based on intersubjective ideas where two subjectivities (therapist–client and supervisor–supervisee) come together, creating a third element that constitutes the unique relationship. It applies not only in the dyadic dynamic created between therapist and client but also in the relationship between supervisor and supervisee. This set of dynamics interacts in supervision and needs space for reflection and exploration. Supervision that is critical of any intimacy that develops from an interpersonal, intersubjective approach between therapist–client and supervisor–supervisee resembles a structure without foundations.

The unconscious in the therapeutic relationship

Motivation to reflect on the work that is fundamental to growth is a product of a supervisory experience *with a heart*. I believe that transference and countertransference are useful concepts for eliciting unconscious feelings in supervision; this process helps supervisors and supervisees identify what may be going on between them that may be unconscious and enacted in the supervisory relationship. It is not always helpful to rest our understanding of the supervisory relationship purely on feelings accessible to consciousness. I believe that the notion of the I–Thou (Buber 1970) relating of healing through meeting (Kavanagh 2017), that captures the here and now immediate engagement, becomes enriched when aspects of our subjectivities we are not fully aware of are brought to the fore, explored and understood. This process creates relational depth in the supervisory experience, motivation and a quality of aliveness necessary for professional intimacy that maintains engagement.

Supervisees come to supervision expecting that the supervisor has reached a level of seniority and competence in their field, in order to positively impact on their development. This seniority comes with responsibilities, including creating a climate conducive to the I–Thou type of relating that has the potential for nurturing growth in supervisees. Constructive challenge of supervisees' possible ethical and

competence-related practice issues and validation of good practice are also fundamental aspects of integrative supervision.

The relational context

Relational, integrative supervision is not about a set of techniques; it is about an
intersubjective relationship and a process. Hargaden postulates that a relational
approach to supervision is that

> we do not help people with theory, but with our selves. It is our personal
> relational abilities for emotional engagement, discernment, nuanced
> attunement and perhaps most of all our integrity that will inform how we
> work with people who are suffering, as well as how we engage with rela-
> tional theories.
>
> (2016: 1)

Therefore, who the supervisor is, their interpersonal skills, ability to reflect and
engage emotionally, and how experienced they are will influence the degree of relationality they can demonstrate in the supervision relationship.

What makes for an effective supervisor? What supervisees appreciate, according to research, is relationally sensitive supervisors (Friedlander and Ward 1984).
As DiMino and Risler explained:

> As the literature on training supervisors continues to increase, there appears
> to be some agreement that the quality of the relationship matters in supervi-
> sion as it does in treatment, and that the supervisor's sensitivity to the needs
> of the supervisee is intimately related to the success of the work.
>
> (2012: 62)

To achieve supervisee satisfaction, supervisors need to tap into their inner resources
to first understand the supervisee's needs (attunement), be sensitive to the supervisee's fears and anxieties, create space to air them and navigate through initial emotional blocks until the alliance allows for more openness and disclosure. If a
supervisee anticipates judgement from the supervisor, they may close down and
not share material that gives power to the supervisor to judge them with.

Supervisee growth from a relational perspective

The supervisory relationship is central to the supervisee's growth. As Frawley-O'Dea
and Sarnat postulate: 'The richest and ultimately most useful supervision takes
place when, in addition to more traditional supervisory tasks, the relational vicissitudes of the supervision are examined by both parties as the process unfolds' (2001:
62). The authors explicate relationality by proposing that:

In a relational model, the supervisor's authority derives from her capacity to participate in, reflect upon, and process enactments, and to interpret relational themes that arise within either the therapeutic or supervisory dyads . . . She sees herself as an embedded participant in a mutually influencing supervisory process.

(2001: 41)

Enactments are rooted in the supervisee's and supervisor's unconscious, forming a unique dynamic in the supervisory relationship. For example, a supervisee may idealise the supervisor to the extent that the supervisor may become invisible as a person and unreal, producing a supervisor countertransference response of feeling flattered, omnipotent or perhaps disappointed that a person-to-person, here and now relationship is being compromised. Nonetheless, initial idealisation can potentially facilitate the placebo effect (belief and trust in the supervisor's expertise), associated with positive outcomes in therapy as well as in supervision. However, it also has the possibility to take the supervisory dyad to a level of unreality, creating the risk of avoidance of real issues, thus becoming a detriment to creative work. Once the alliance is established, the supervisor has the responsibility to acknowledge idealisation and attempt to introduce the person-to-person here and now relationship of collegiality.

As a relational supervisor, I have found that the therapy transference–countertransference dynamics are also at play in supervisory relationships both in individual and in group supervision. In the latter, the added dynamics of rivalry between supervisees could transport the supervision task to a fight for 'specialness' with the implication of diverting focus away from the supervisory task. In these supervisory situations, it is wise for supervisors to acknowledge and interpret the dynamics so the traditional supervisory tasks are not compromised. Under these conditions, I have found it necessary to explore and make explicit any transference–countertransference dynamic. I am clear that there is a delineation between therapy and supervision; however, there is a fine line that connects the two together. If a powerful supervisee transference hinders real engagement, then I see it as my responsibility to facilitate awareness and create space for reflection, a growth-inducing process that on occasion becomes necessary when the supervisee has not yet developed sufficient understanding of their unconscious dynamics and how these play a part in the supervisory relationship.

Setting the framework

Contracting and agreeing the supervisory framework is a necessary process in supervision. Professional bodies make this a requirement for accredited supervisors. A clear frame sets the foundations for a professional relationship. Supervisors are exposed to colleagues' and supervisees' perspectives on how to understand clients, as well as the library of articles and books they read to help shape their ideas. Integrative supervisors are more open to integrating principles, ideas and skills from various theoretical perspectives, particularly those whose training exposes them to a variety of modalities. Integrative supervision consists of a unique lens and angle of vision, a fusion or clash of personalities and character traits that together form the nucleus of unique subjectivities. It starts with persons and figuring out what kind of person you are as a supervisor and what kind of person your supervisee is. It involves not merely unique perspectives, but unique personalities that fit or clash in an embodied engagement.

I embrace the maxim that as a supervisor part of my role is to help the supervisee trust the process and feel safe to share even the most taboo subjects, such as sexual attraction. Further, it is my responsibility as a supervisor to nurture growth, branching out by opening up and clarifying new ideas and constructively challenging the supervisee to let go of their dogmas, through opening themselves to challenging their perspectives, and through considering the value and contribution of other perspectives. This process involves an expansion of self.

The hallmark of integrative supervision

> It has been said that the hallmark of successful supervision is the resolution of conflict that occurs naturally because of the power imbalance between supervisor and supervisee.
>
> (Mueller and Kell 1972, cited in Nelson and Friedlander 2001: 384)

There are various ideas and research papers on the hallmark of supervision, one of which is illustrated by this quote. A useful vantage point to start thinking about the hallmark of *integrative* supervision is to return to the relational system discussed by Stolorow and Atwood (1996). For me, the hallmark of integrative supervision is the initial bonding experience that very much depends on building trust and the supervisory alliance. Mehr, Ladany and Caskie's research validates the value of the therapeutic alliance: 'The findings provided further empirical support for the relationships between higher counseling self-efficacy and less trainee anxiety, stronger supervisory working alliance and less trainee anxiety, and stronger supervisory working alliance and higher willingness to disclose' (2015: 44). Disclosure is fundamental to the clinical and professional development of the supervisee. Where, for example, supervisees, due to personal fears and moral aptitudes (Luca 2016), fear disclosing personal feelings (e.g. of sexual attraction), it is important that supervisors are aware of this and help supervisees identify psychological blocks to disclosure. It is also necessary for supervisors to question whether they contribute to supervisees' lack of disclosure and to take steps to overcome their own biases and moral attitudes around certain therapy material. A research study by Luca (2017) on experienced existential and integrative therapists' views on facilitative conditions in the handling of a taboo subject in clinical supervision identified the following as important: supervisory alliance; containing and supporting; normalising sexual attraction; creating a contemplative, open atmosphere; and constructively challenging.

It is fundamental to help supervisees feel safe to say what they feel and reveal their client work openly. Research has highlighted that more supervisee disclosures are made when safety and trust are established. Kreider (2014) suggests that supervisor disclosure explains the level of supervisee disclosure. Other factors associated with high quality supervision include those identified by Martin et al.: 'Supervisor–supervisee matching and fit, supervisory relationship and availability of supervisor for support in between clinical supervision sessions appeared to be associated with perceptions of higher quality of clinical supervision received' (2015: 413).

Without these foundational dynamics in place, resolution of conflict becomes difficult if not impossible. Supervision will involve conflict, often associated with the supervisory power imbalance, lack of collegiality or understanding on the supervisor's part, or difference in interpreting and understanding client material. These could manifest in transference and countertransference experienced by the supervisory dyad or group.

Supervisors and supervisees hold their own unique perspective, so the conceptual sense they make of a client's world will be informed by these perspectives. It is to be expected that no two individuals, even those belonging to the same modality, will arrive at a shared understanding on all aspects mentioned. What we understand is *subjective*. Engaging in dialogue until some rapprochement has been reached is more fruitful than arguing about whose perspective is more accurate and closer to the truth. This process is necessary for the formation of the alliance and the establishment of safety. All supervisees are anxious about exposing their perceived incompetency to supervisors whose responsibility is not just supportive and educative but also evaluative. In what follows I will present a scenario to highlight conflict in a supervisory dyad.

Negotiating conflict in supervision

Scenario from practice 13.2

David was an intelligent, thoughtful, charming and motivated individual. We met during a conference a year before he completed his psychotherapy training. Three years later, and following his disappointment with his clinical supervisor, he asked me to take him on for supervision. At the outset, he mentioned that the reasons he wanted me as his supervisor were due to the respect he felt for me as an academic, that he had read my books and learned a great deal from them; he also said that he liked my clinical insights and warmth. He added that although he had considered asking me to supervise him before he started work with his previous supervisor, he feared I might have high expectations of him and that he might feel inadequate in light of my experience and competence. I said I respected his openness and hoped that our work together would be of benefit to him, both professionally and personally.

In the initial supervision session, I sensed David's excitement and motivation and felt positive about this new professional relationship. As our work progressed, David's enthusiasm and charm were expressed through directly commenting on how much he enjoyed working with me, that I am perfect for him and how lucky he is to have me as his supervisor. The transference was idealised and we both enjoyed the sessions. He was so hungry for my insights and I responded in kind, giving him more and more of my supervisory food. I felt flattered, but mindful of what might lie beneath David's flattery and idealisation of me. I increasingly sensed through David's presentations of client material that he had difficulty working with negative client feelings and I believe he unconsciously tried to elicit validation from his clients. The focus of his supervision seemed to gravitate around showing me how competent he is and how valued he felt by his clients. Any attempts on my part to encourage him to think about client material that contained negative transference were met with a dismissive attitude.

David's practice seemed to lack flexibility; he dreaded not being liked. His charming and seductive personality seemed to be covering a narcissistic fragility that could not handle disappointing others, just like he could not handle disappointing me with his perception that I would have high expectations of him. I reflected on the parallel process at play between David and his clients and David and me. My understanding of the idealised transference helped me get a glimpse of David's internal world, where if he charmed and seduced others, he would minimise the anticipated criticism. By engaging defensively (idealisation is often a defence against anxiety), David partly closed off his receptive sensors and only allowed positive views of him from others. I wondered about David's fears and thought long and hard on how to approach him with my understanding without further reinforcing his defensiveness. I would use gentle invitations to draw David's attention to what I thought were his blocks, but his idealisation of me continued.

Eventually, David made some noticeable changes in his attitude to clients, which allowed the work to go into more depth. Sessions with David increasingly felt false and I sensed some animosity from him towards me. Checking whether he felt dissatisfied was met with attempts to reassure his supervisor that he thought highly of her. The conflict became prominent in our work and the impasse even more so.

Six months into our work, I said to David that I would like to share something with him that might be difficult but necessary in terms of moving beyond what I perceived as an impasse. I started sharing my genuine view of him, starting with his strengths and competences and then shared my view of his relational approach towards me that seemed to block any constructive feedback. David immediately responded by saying how much he valued our work. In a trembling voice, he asked me to be honest with him. I briefly pointed out that I felt his idealisation of me might be masking envy, competitiveness and anger, but also providing a shield from anticipated criticism, a factor I felt appeared prominent in his therapy work. This, I said, may be blocking a more authentic and fertile supervisory relationship, which could more effectively meet his developmental needs as a professional.

Sharing my understanding with David was a catalyst. He became anxious and defensive initially. Although my urge was to reassure him and rescue myself from a compounding sense of conflict between us, I remained silent, giving him space to think about what I said. In my silence, I wondered whether I enjoyed the idealisation and if it might have been more appropriate if I had addressed it earlier in our work. He was pushing back tears and I felt an overwhelming sadness, which I shared with him. David composed himself and went on to disclose early personal experiences with his parents, which helped us make sense of his tendency to idealise authority, then denigrate them like he did with his two therapists, his previous supervisor and potentially myself. He listened attentively and seemed to mull over my understandings of the dynamics between us.

About a year into our work, I suffered an illness and was off work for two and a half months. David contacted me a couple of times to check how I was and ascertain when I planned to return to work. In the meantime, I had given him the names of a couple of supervisors to consult during my absence. After the third session following my return, David was able to express his anger associated with my absence. I wondered whether my illness, a symbol of my vulnerability, challenged David's idealised view of me. A new phase began where David became highly critical of my input and had difficulty thinking about what I was saying. I encouraged him to consider whether my illness had robbed him of his idealisation of me as a strong and resilient person. He was able to hear this and understand his need to see only the strong aspects of myself and deny my vulnerability. This contributed to the negative transference beginning to resolve itself, opening the way for a real person-to-person relating.

Conclusion

On reflection, I feel that the traditional aspects of supervision alone cannot deal with apparent conflicts rooted in an individual's psychological traumas that get repeated in supervision. So we need to recognise the limitations of supervision and consider adding a therapeutic aspect of helping the supervisee identify relational blocks to supervision manifested in idealised and negative transference. Supervisors can also encourage supervisees struggling with themselves to return to therapy to help them with their particular traumas and relational difficulties these pose in supervision and their therapeutic practice.

References

Bownas, J. and Fredman, G. (2017) *Working with Embodiment in Supervision: A Systemic Approach.* London: Routledge.

British Psychological Society (2017) *Practice Guidelines* (3rd edn). London: British Psychological Society.

Buber, M. (1970) *I and Thou.* New York: Charles Scribner's Sons.

Clarkson, P. (2003) *The Therapeutic Relationship.* London: Whurr.

DiMino, J.L. and Risler, R. (2012) Group supervision of supervision: A relational approach for training supervisors. *Journal of College Student Psychotherapy,* 26(1): 61–72.

Elliott, R., Fischer, C.T. and Rennie, D.L. (1999) Evolving guidelines for publication of qualitative research studies in psychology and related fields. *British Journal of Clinical Psychology,* 38: 215–29.

Ellis, M.V., Creaner, M., Hutman, H. and Timulak, L. (2015) A comparative study of clinical supervision in the Republic of Ireland and the United States. *Journal of Counseling Psychology,* 62(4): 621–31.

Falender, C.A., Erickson Cornish, J.A., Goodyear, R., Hatcher, R., Kaslow, N.J., Lenenthal, G., Shafranske, E. and Sigmon, S.T. (2004) Defining competencies in psychology supervision: A consensus statement. *Journal of Clinical Psychology,* 60(7): 771–85.

Frawley-O'Dea, M.G. and Sarnat, J.E. (2001) *The Supervisory Relationship: A Contemporary Psychodynamic Approach.* New York: Guilford Press.

Friedlander, M.L. and Ward, L.G. (1984) Development and validation of the supervisory styles inventory. *Journal of Counselling Psychology,* 31: 541–57.

Gilbert, M.C. and Evans, K. (2000) *Psychotherapy Supervision: An Integrative Relational Approach to Psychotherapy Supervision.* London: Open University Press.

Hargaden, H. (2016) *The Art of Relational Supervision.* London: Routledge.

Kavanagh, S. (2017) A description and critical evaluation of the philosophy, values, psychotherapeutic theories and methods that guide my work as an integrative psychotherapy practitioner. *The British Journal of Psychotherapy Integration,* 13: 77–91.

Kreider, H.D. (2014) Administrative and clinical supervision: The impact of dual roles on supervisee disclosure in counselling supervision. *The Clinical Supervisor,* 33(2): 256–68.

Kvale, S. (1992) Postmodern psychology: A contradiction in terms? In S. Kvale (ed.), *Inquiries in Social Construction: Psychology and Postmodernism* (pp. 31–57). Thousand Oaks, CA: SAGE.

Luca, M. (2007) Working with the phenomenon of somatisation: psychodynamic and cognitive behavioural therapists' conceptualisations and clinical practices. Unpublished thesis. University of Kent.

Luca, M. (2016) Trainee therapists' moralistic reactions and defensive handling of client sexual attraction in therapy. *Journal of Psychotherapy and Counselling Psychology Reflections,* 1(1): 27–34.

Luca, M. (2017) Clinical supervisors' handling of sexual attraction in the work of therapists they supervise. *Journal of Psychotherapy and Counselling Psychology Reflections*, 2(1): 3–10.

Martin, P., Kumar, S., Lizarondo, L. and VanErp, A. (2015) Enablers of and barriers to high quality clinical supervision among occupational therapists across Queensland in Australia: Findings from a qualitative study. *BMC Health Services Research*, 15: 413. doi:10.1186/s12913-015-1085-8.

Mehr, K.E., Ladany, N. and Caskie, G.I.L. (2015) Factors influencing trainee willingness to disclose in supervision. *Training and Education in Professional Psychology*, 9(1): 44–51. http://dx.doi.org/10.1037/tep0000028.

Merleau-Ponty, M. (1962) *Phenomenology of Perception*. London: Routledge.

Nelson, M.L. and Friedlander, M.L. (2001) A close look at conflictual supervisory relationships: The trainee's perspective. *Journal of Counselling Psychology*, 48(4): 384–95.

Nuttall, J. (2017) Out in the open air: The quest for integration. *The British Journal of Psychotherapy Integration*, 13: 15–29.

Nuttall, J. (2018) 'Supreme values reside in the soul': Reflections on values and psychotherapy. *Journal of Psychotherapy and Counselling Psychology Reflections*, 3(1): 3–8.

Orlinsky, D.E., Botermans, J.F. and Ronnestad, M.H. (2001) Towards an empirically grounded model of psychotherapy training: Four thousand therapists rate influences on their development. *Australian Psychologist*, 36(2): 139–48.

Orlinsky, D., Grawe, K. and Parks, B. (1994) Process and outcome in psychotherapy – *noch einmal*. In A. Bergin and S. Garfield (eds), *Handbook of Psychotherapy and Behavior Change* (4th edn) (pp. 270–376). New York: Wiley.

Polkinghorne, D.E. (1983) *Methodology for the Human Sciences*. Albany, NY: SUNY Press.

Rogers, C.R. (2003) *Client Centred Therapy*. London: Constable and Robinson Ltd.

Scott, K.J., Ingram, K.M., Vitanza, S.A. and Smith, N.G. (2000) Training in supervision: A survey of current practices. *The Counseling Psychologist*, 28(3): 403–22. http://dx.doi.org/10.1177/0011000000283007.

Spinelli, E. (2005) *The Interpreted World: An Introduction to Phenomenological Psychology*. London: SAGE.

Stolorow, R.D. and Atwood, G.E. (1996) The intersubjective perspective. *Psychoanalytic Review*, 83: 181–94.

UKCP (2012) *UKCP Supervision Policy*. London: Karnac.

14 The integrative therapist in the professional context

Maria Luca

Introduction

Embodiment, a term central to Merleau-Ponty's phenomenology, is a concept that attempts to tackle the Cartesian gap left by a dualism of mind and body by merging it into a unitary system. From this perspective, it is postulated that the world exists before we come to know it and the lived world is pre-reflective. This idea suggests that the world out there, external to subjectivity, exists and is not known to us until we think about it and learn to represent it through language. The relevance of embodiment for this chapter is the idea that the therapist will encounter the world, including specific psychotherapy contexts, act on it and develop a dialectical relationship with it, all of which are captured through language. Embodiment in this sense requires an integration of the body in the mind and the mind in the body in a social context (Overton et al. 2008).

Postmodernism in psychotherapy and psychology

There are debates on the meaning of postmodernism. One critique is provided by Kvale, who postulates that 'postmodern thought replaces a conception of a reality independent of the observer with notions of language as actually constituting the structures of a perspectival social reality' (1992: 2). In this way, ideas about social reality are social constructions. Human beings relate to the world around them and construct meanings and symbolic thoughts to represent it.

The philosopher Allan Bloom (1988: 173) asserted that 'the self is the modern substitute for the soul'. We might understand this through the lens of postmodernism, where the traditional idea of an immaterial soul as being the seat of our personal identity has been replaced with the postmodern notion of socially constructed 'selves'.

Postmodern Psychology, a useful blog, provides a critique of Foucault, who argues that 'each of us is "a being which is at least partially subjected to socially produced constraints and divisions"' (Foucault 2003: 142). He sees 'the modern-day notion of the self [as] bound up with, and inseparable from, the workings of social structures and institutions' (2003: 141). There is, therefore, no distinction 'between public and private selves implied by the concept of human nature nor can the individual be reduced to individual consciousness' (2003: 141). Foucault makes explicit how as social beings we are impacted and limited by the social world we live in. He discusses the modern-day idea of self as intertwined with one's social and institutional structures.

Ideas about knowing ultimate truths are replaced with ideas of socially constructed realities. Pluralism questions absolute truth and uses multiple approaches, methods and tools to construct understandings and knowledge. In the context of pluralism, single or pure modalities of therapy fall short of appreciating the complexities of reality.

Gergen believes that, to progress, psychology must embrace postmodern dialogues: 'If psychologists can replace a defensive posture with more productive participation in the postmodern dialogues, psychological inquiry can be transformed in ways that will deeply enrich our endeavors' (2001: 803). The idea of pluralism, as Gergen suggests, is conducive to dialogue that transforms experience and enriches individuals. So postmodernism emphasises the importance of dialogue, values subjectivity over objectivity and denounces notions of objectivity and absolute truth.

Psychotherapy and psychology in a postmodern context recognise that the therapy relationship is an intersubjective and socially constructed endeavour. The impetus is to place the enquiry within an epistemology of the 'double hermeneutic' (Rennie 2000) where therapist and client engage in an intersubjective encounter, they interpret their world according to their lived experience and, through their interaction, help co-construct and shape understanding of social phenomena.

The postmodern psychotherapist is required to have, at the very least, a developed awareness of self and others and to have processed and worked through their own personal issues. Awareness and regulation of the therapist's own mental states are the building blocks to helping clients develop this function. Semerari et al. (2003), as discussed in Chapter 8, addressed the importance of knowing and regulating mental states. Their theory of metacognitive functions builds on Fonagy and Target's (1997) concept of mentalisation but focuses on the functions rather than the contents involved in metacognition. Metacognition is described by Wells and Purdon as: 'the aspect of information processing that monitors, interprets, evaluates and regulates the contents and processes of its organization' (1999, cited in Semerari et al. 2003: 240).

Like mentalisation, metacognition is a concept referring to a cognitive ability to reflect and know and thus regulate all aspects of the personal experience in relation to the interpersonal dimension. This involves not only knowing oneself, but being able to know another, not simply through self-interest or egocentric motivation, but through 'decentration', a term used to describe 'the ability to comprehend another individual's mental state from a non-egocentric perspective' (Semerari et al. 2003: 244).

The therapist's self

Metacognitive contents refer to the individual's capacity to recognise specific thoughts and emotions as aspects of one's mental state and the ability to 'comprehend behaviour in terms of intentionality' (Semerari et al. 2003: 241). The concept of metacognitive functions, on the other hand, refers to the ability to translate recognition of mental states into performing certain operations. Metacognition describes a process of abstraction, with reflection being central, whereas metacognitive functions describe the application of abstract knowledge to carry out tasks, which are informed by knowing the current state of one's mind. The successful execution of tasks relies on the ability to make use of the knowledge derived from reflection. This concept resembles a component of Damasio's neuroscientific perspective of self-regulation, putting forward the idea that following reflective knowledge 'suitable survivable accommodations can be achieved between the organism and the environment' (1994: 90). The main thrust of postmodern theorising is that without the capacity to self-regulate and to reflect on the experience, the individual is prone to have an incoherent experience. It is within this theoretical context that the postmodern integrative psychotherapist operates.

Husserl's concept of the 'lifeworld' denotes that:

> To live as a person is to live in a social framework, wherein I and we live together in community and have the community as a horizon. Now, communities are structured in various simple or complex forms, such as family, nation, or international community. Here the world 'live' is not to be taken in a physiological sense but rather as signifying purposeful living, manifesting spiritual creativity – in the broadest sense, creating culture within historical continuity.
>
> (1965: 150)

This notion brings into sharp focus a key idea as to how therapists, whatever their theoretical orientation, operate in a phenomenological lifeworld where they interact with the patient in an embodied fashion: engaging holistically, using their own and their client's bodily felt sense.

This brings us to the professional context of psychotherapy and psychology.

The professional context

Increasingly psychological therapies, since the early 1990s, have undergone significant changes. More and more short-term therapy is now offered both in the National Health Service (NHS) and in voluntary organisations. The implication for therapists is the pressure to show evidence of positive outcomes within a short space of time; the pace of therapy has increased enormously and the notion of being with our clients in silence (as therapeutic) has also been greatly compromised. Another important implication is that clients who cannot afford private therapy only receive what is offered, even if it is not what they need or what is most appropriate to the presenting problems and the psychological formulation. The socio-economic environment currently influences assessments and formulations, as these too are shaped by what is *possible*, not by what is the *most appropriate* therapy treatment.

Efficacy, outcomes and effective treatments are factors that mediate the survival of specific therapeutic approaches. To survive within this current context, psychotherapy researchers have joined forces with psychology researchers and turned their attention to measuring and evaluating therapy interventions so that they could become approved by the National Institute for Health and Care Excellence (NICE) and become mainstream. Historically, psychotherapists were anti-measurement, especially in the context of the notion that subjectivity and intersubjective relationships can never fully be known or measured. Quite often, treatments that become mainstream are those that have research evidence to substantiate their claims, but research relies on funding, which is not readily available to those who do not have a solid history of it behind them – a vicious circle results. Psychotherapy falls within this category in comparison to psychology and the field of Cognitive–Behavioural Therapy (CBT). However, some therapy interventions outside CBT have succeeded in gaining recognition by NICE. For example, evidence reviewed for the NICE depression guideline (2009), which compared CBT, psychodynamic and person-centred therapy in routine NHS settings using CORE, showed that all were effective and about as effective as each other with the same intake of severity and chronicity.

The professional context of psychotherapy provision includes the guidelines by professional bodies that accredit therapists. In the UK there are several, including the UK Council for Psychotherapy (UKCP), the British Association for Counselling and Psychotherapy (BACP), the Psychoanalytic Psychotherapy Association (PPA), the British Psychoanalytic Council (BPC) and the British Psychological Society (BPS). The key elements in professional guidelines include confidentiality, respect, non-exploitation and record-keeping.

The professional context is characterised by and influences professional attitudes, behaviours and conduct. What follows is a discussion of key principles and guidelines in the context of psychotherapy.

Client records

Over the years professional organisations have revised their practice guidelines. One example is the BACP's *Ethical Framework for the Counselling Professions* (2018). Prior to this update, the BACP (2009) issued the following guidance on record-keeping: 'Practitioners are advised to keep appropriate records of their work with clients unless there are good and sufficient reasons for not keeping any records.'

Jenkins highlights the implications of a lack of clear record-keeping:

> The issue of recording has recently been highlighted by professional organisations. The Health Professions Council (HPC) struck off a clinical psychologist from the HPC Register in 2010, on the grounds of failure 'to maintain adequate patient records', in the context of working in a multidisciplinary team.

(2012: 24)

Table 14.1 Types of records

Client details (age, gender, ethnicity, eligibility for counselling service as employee, patient, etc.)	Letters and correspondence	Counsellor's process notes	In-session material (e.g. diaries, diagrams, therapeutic writing)	Name of person to notify client in the event of therapist illness or death
Personal details (address, phone number, etc.)	Email contact	Counsellor's personal diary	Case summary, assessment and formulation notes	Any communications with other professionals (e.g. GP or psychiatrist)
Record of attendance and non-attendance	Record of consent to counselling	Notes of supervision		

Both the UKCP and the BACP provide several examples of practitioners not complying with the requirement for record-keeping. However, not keeping records is no longer an option. The UKCP guidelines on records say very little on the types of records that should be kept except: 'The psychotherapist agrees to keep such records as are necessary to properly carry out the type of psychotherapy offered' (2018: 8.1) and that 'The psychotherapist commits to store and dispose of any personally identifiable records or data securely in order to protect the client's confidentiality' (2018: 8.2). The purpose of keeping records by therapists is to maintain professional responsibilities through evidence, to support therapeutic work.

Table 14.1 features a list I have developed on types of records, while Table 14.2 offers useful guidelines for the security of records.

Therapists should make sure that the records include basic demographic information; a mental status examination and diagnosis or presenting problem (does not need to be DSM diagnosis, can be familial, developmental, etc.); fee agreement; and treatment plan. If relevant, include risk factors, medical and other issues relevant to treatment and request for information.

The following example scenario is of a client suing a pharmaceutical company for side-effects of anti-depressant medication.

Scenario from practice 14.1

The client work had ended, but two years later the therapist received a letter from the client's lawyer. The letter came with a signed client consent form, requesting all records kept by the therapist under the Data Protection Act to be used in court to support the client's claim against a pharmaceutical company for suffering anxiety and depression as a result of taking Paroxetine. The therapist advised the lawyer that the records might not support such a claim, as they contain information that indicated prior childhood traumas, depression and anxiety prior to the client taking medication. The law firm insisted that they still wanted the records. The therapist complied, even though they had not been subpoenaed by the court. They did not receive any further communications from the lawyer or the client.

Due to the fact that the client had signed a request to access their records under the Data Protection Act, the therapist felt that they had a legal obligation to provide the records and it was then at the discretion of the client and their legal representatives to decide if these would be submitted to the court to support their claim.

Table 14.2   Security guidelines for records

Store hard copy records in a safe, locked place that is reasonably protected from theft, intrusion, fire, earthquake, water damage and unauthorised access	Gifts from clients, therapists or from third parties to therapists, such as loans of books or CDs	Out-of-office experiences, such as home visits, attending weddings or funerals, going on hikes, taking a client to a medical appointment, adventure therapy and clinically meaningful incidental/chance encounters
Protect your computer records by use of password, virus protection, firewall and access log. Back up regularly and store your back-up disks off site in a secure location. Print hard copies of very important documents and use access log if necessary	Extensive use of touch or self-disclosure (rationale)	E-therapy, phone therapy or any other telehealth practices, including a special disclosure if these practices are the basic mode of therapy
Enter clinically relevant and meaningful information in the clinical records. Detail clinically meaningful contacts, including important phone calls and important or clinically significant collateral contacts. Include in records the date and type of services provided, fees, charges, payments, balances and copies of third-party billing	Recording or videotaping of sessions	Dual relationship: the nature, extent, etc.

Ethical practice

Psychotherapy and psychology trainings are required by professional bodies of which they are members or by which they are accredited to ensure a good standard of training is offered regarding ethical practice. Although there are variations among professional organisations, the key principles on ethics appear to coalesce (UKCP 2009; BPS 2017):

- demonstrating respect, including of the client's autonomy;
- having the client's best interests at heart;
- integrity (e.g. honesty, clarity, fairness);
- not exploiting clients for sexual, emotional, or financial gain;
- avoiding dual relationships, which requires clear boundaries;
- bringing no harm to clients;
- understanding legal responsibilities;
- ensuring behaviour outside the therapy is professional;
- ensuring competence and qualifications are not misrepresented;
- challenging and/or reporting colleagues engaged in professional misconduct.

Confidentiality

Respecting client confidentiality is a fundamental requirement for the development of a trusting relationship. The professional management of confidentiality concerns the protection of personally-identifiable and sensitive information from unauthorised disclosure. (Disclosure may be authorised by the client or the law.) Disclosures must be made with the client's consent.

Confidentiality in therapeutic contexts is within bounds. It has limitations, especially if there is a risk of suicide or harm to self or others. Issuing a therapeutic agreement/contract signed by both therapist and client that makes this and other therapy givens clear to clients is good practice. What is fundamental for trust and the alliance is for therapists to be explicit with clients at the outset on the limits of confidentiality and of sharing records with other professionals. It is good practice in the majority of cases to share the records first with the client and to obtain their consent. This provides the opportunity for understanding and compliance rather than leaving clients to imagine what their therapist has shared about them with people outside the therapy relationship. A positive implication is that therapists are encouraged to be non-judgemental and clear in their records.

Courts can order disclosure of client material without a client's permission; however, therapists can request from the court not to disclose if they deem such disclosure harmful to the client. As the duty of confidentiality is not absolute, there might be circumstances where the public interest in maintaining confidentiality is outweighed by the public interest in disclosing specific information. Such circumstances may include where disclosure is necessary to avert a real risk of a danger of death or serious harm to others or for the prevention or detection of serious crime. Even then, such disclosure is permissible only if made to someone with a proper interest in receiving the information.

There are a number of publications (Jenkins 2007; 2012; Bond and Mitchels 2014) discussing all aspects of the Data Protection Act, confidentiality, records and situations where therapists can breach confidentiality. These are additional useful resources for all practitioners.

Contracts

Contracting in psychotherapy is not only good practice, it is also a requirement. Clients have a right to be given clear and accurate information about the practitioner's level of experience, qualifications and competence and the approach/model of practice.

The UKCP guidelines include the following on contracting in therapy:

> The psychotherapist agrees to at the outset explain to a client, or prospective client, their terms, fees and conditions and, on request, clarify other related questions such as likely length of therapy, methods of practice to be utilised, referral or termination processes.
>
> (2017: 6.1)

It is therefore important that therapists focus on developing professional standards through further training and the use of clinical supervision. Therapists require client consent before they undertake any assessment or apply any psychological interventions – clients could be asked to sign a psychotherapy agreement/contract that informs them of the assessment, interventions and records. In contracting, therapists also need to be mindful of diversity, including age, ability, culture, gender and sexuality. Therapists are expected to show integrity, honesty and professionalism and avoid superficiality, exaggeration of skills and competences. Contracts should also make the terms of engagement explicit, including the fee and how absence may impact on the fee. For example, some therapists charge clients for absence whereas others do not, mostly if clients give 24-hours' notice. Confidentiality and any limits should also be made explicit, as should therapist availability and holidays and responsibilities in the event of emergencies, termination and the recommended notice period (and how this may affect the therapy and the fee).

Competence

Therapist competence refers to therapist attributes and the extent of the knowledge and skills the therapist has to bring about expected outcomes (Fairburn and Cooper 2011). Recognising limits of competence and practising within the boundaries of competence is ethical practice. Professional bodies expect therapists to avoid deception through misrepresentation. Claiming to possess certain qualifications or implying competence a therapist does not possess is one example. All professionally accredited therapists are required to provide evidence of continuous professional development and of supervision to ensure the maintenance of competence and good standards.

We will now return to the integrative principle of reflection that enhances good therapeutic standards.

Pre-reflection, reflection and meta-reflection

The practice of integrative psychotherapy places substantial emphasis on reflection and on understanding different levels of knowing. There are different levels of consciousness and levels of reflection. It is therefore part and parcel of responsible, ethical practice that therapists reflect on the professional context, a lifeworld inseparable from the therapeutic relationship.

The pre-reflective level is characterised by what could be defined as raw, unprocessed experience of being in the world. This is what is often referred to as the concrete level of experience whereby consciousness is far from translucent, as Kaufmann (1992) argues. In contrast to Kaufmann's 'foggy mind', the reflective level is about a transparent mind. Fonagy et al. capture this idea in their concept of 'mentalization'. They state that 'mentalization involves both a self-reflective and an interpersonal component' (2002: 4). So the therapist not only reflects on the self, but also on the self in relation to the client.

Conclusion

It is a well-established idea in therapeutic circles that reflective action is transformational. It refers to a process of drawing out pre-reflective knowledge (requiring intentionality) and scrutinising its contents – these are then transformed into metabolised understanding. To achieve this transformation, the therapist would need to be equipped with the capacity to move away temporarily from the raw and reflective knowledge into meta-reflection; this would rest on the individual's ability to exercise their agency not just cognitively but also affectively; to process the subjective and intersubjective dynamics; and to think about how the professional context impacts on the development of a coherent, meta-reflected understanding. This idea refers to the directing of attention on the contents of experience and thinking about and experiencing them at different levels.

Agency requires deliberation and intentionality, qualities found in individuals focusing on particular aspects of living in the world. Without interest and desire on the part of therapists in any given activity, both being sources of affective vitality in humans, the goal of achieving meta-reflective awareness would be hindered. Clinical understanding is enhanced by meta-reflection, a process that is nurtured in supervision, the subject of exploration in Chapter 15, and in case discussions among colleagues.

References

BACP (2018) *Ethical Framework for the Counselling Profession*. London: BACP.

Bloom, A. (1988) *The Closing of the American Mind*. New York: Simon & Schuster.

Bond, T. and Mitchels, B. (2014) *Confidentiality and Record Keeping in Counselling and Psychotherapy* (2nd edn). London: SAGE.

Damasio, A. (1994) *Descartes' Error: Emotion, Reason and the Human Brain*. London: Macmillan.

Fairburn, C.G. and Cooper, Z. (2011) Therapist competence, therapy quality, and therapist training. *Behaviour Research and Therapy*, 49(6–7): 373–8.

Fonagy, P., Gergely, G., Jurist, E.L. and Target, M. (2002) *Affect Regulation, Mentalization, and the Development of the Self*. New York: OTHER Press.

Fonagy, P. and Target, M. (1997) Attachment and reflective function: Their role in self- organization. *Development and Psychopathology*, 9: 679–700.

Foucault, M. (2003) *The Birth of the Clinic*. London: Routledge.

Gergen, K. (2001) Psychological science in a postmodern context. *American Psychologist*, 56(10): 803–13.

Husserl, E. (1965) *Phenomenology and the Crisis of Philosophy*, Q. Lauer, trans. New York: Harper Torchbooks.

Jenkins, P. (2007) *Counselling, Psychotherapy and the Law* (2nd edn). London: SAGE.

Jenkins, P. (2012) Data protection in private practice. *Private Practice*, Winter: 24–7.

Kaufmann, W. (1992) *Freud, Adler and Jung: Discovering the Mind*, vol. III. New Brunswick, NJ: Transaction Books.

Kvale, S. (1992) *Psychology and Postmodernism*. London: SAGE.

Merleau-Ponty, M. (1962) *Phenomenology of Perception*. London: Routledge.

NICE (2009) *Depression in Adults: Recognition and Management*. Clinical guideline CG90. London: NICE.

Overton, W.F., Muller, U. and Newman, J.L. (2008) *Developmental Perspectives on Embodiment and Consciousness*. New York: Taylor and Francis.

Postmodern Psychology (2017) *What is Postmodern Psychology?* Blog. http://postmodernpsychology.com/ (accessed 4 August 2017).

Rennie, D.L. (2000) Grounded theory methodology as methodical hermeneutics – reconciling realism and relativism. *Theory and Psychology*, 10(4): 481–502.

Semerari, A., Carcione, A., Dimaggio, G., Falcone, M., Nicolò, G., Procacci, M. and Alleva, G. (2003) How to evaluate metacognitive functioning in psychotherapy? The metacognition assessment scale and its applications. *Clinical Psychology & Psychotherapy*, 10: 238–61.

UKCP (2018) *Ethical Principles and Code of Professional Conduct*. Available at: https://www.psychotherapy.org.uk/wp-content/uploads/2018/10/UKCP-Ethical-Principles-and-Code-of-Professional-Conduct.pdf. (accessed 5 December 2018).

15 Training and research on integrative therapy

Claire Marshall

Introduction

Chapter 14 explored embodiment and how we might conceptualise this in relation to therapeutic practice. Particular attention was paid to the qualities of reflexivity and the implications this has for the therapeutic relationship. This chapter will explore how we might address integration in our classrooms and research projects.

Integrative therapy: points of contact and degrees of convergence

Integration can be done through alignment with or employment of various systems or frameworks of understanding, briefly summarised as:

- *Technical eclecticism.* This involves selecting what is most useful from a variety of paradigms (i.e. the imminent practical question of which intervention to select).
- *Theoretical integration.* This emphasises theory, in particular uncovering the overlaps and aspiring toward coherence (one example is Clarkson's (2001) relationship model).
- *Assimilative integration.* This involves adapting theories to form a 'host' model or the therapist's own approach to the work (e.g. self-psychology).
- *Complementary integration.* This is based on the premise that one paradigm can compensate for the lack in another and, while theoretically they are held as separate, within therapy they can be combined (e.g. Cognitive–Behavioural Therapy (CBT), Dialectical Behaviour Therapy (DBT), Cognitive Analytic Therapy (CAT) or Eye Movement Desensitisation and Reprocessing (EMDR) with psychodynamic therapy).
- *Integration on the basis of common factors.* These factors are those that span across all modalities, which invariably leans towards relationally mediated elements (Nuttall 2008; Orlans and Gilbert 2011).

I posit that therapeutic integration does not exist. Or rather, what are often treated as separate therapeutic models or approaches are not distinct entities – they are not 'purist' in this sense. There is perhaps some alignment, some interweaving thread, some shared agreement on what constitutes the psyche, what contributes to human distress and what interventions should be used when working with particular distress. Yet aside from these overlaps, there are many disparities, many differing (sometimes contradictory) opinions. It is not uncommon for therapists to draw on ideas across disciplines and train in one specialism, which they use to inform the work relating therapeutic theory and practice. Moreover, often an author will be associated with the beginning of a historical period or the 'founder' of a particular psychological approach (such as Freud in psychoanalysis) and thereafter their contemporaries will take issue with one aspect of the theory or put forward another perspective that elaborates what has been said. This building on theory might seem as if knowledge is constructed in a linear, sequential fashion. This is often how knowledge construction is thought of. Alexander (2004) maintains that pedagogy is not merely the event of teaching, it is similarly the narratives within which this teaching is located. Through recognising and deconstructing some of the tacit narratives that give rise to the learning project itself (and thus the teaching project), the pedagogue, or more precisely the andragogue, depending on whoever the student happens to be, can begin to appreciate what is required to negotiate the meaning-making venture with learners.

Plateaus, rhizomes and ruptures

Deleuze, a philosopher, and Guattari, a psychiatrist, propose an alternative conceptualising structure. In their seminal work *Mille Plateaux* (*A Thousand Plateaus*) they describe the notion of the *plateau*. A plateau in geology is an area of highland, usually flat, open country. Applied to writing, plateaus might be understood as text that begins possibilities without offering structured conclusions, and these are always in the middle, as their writing lifts up ideas and leaves them in the air. They compare literary plateaus to 'mountains', which have lucid beginnings, middles and endings and a clear purpose. Plateaus enable continuous expansion and communication between many levels. Plateaus also aid encounters between incompatible fields. The authors describe the notion of *arriving and departing* rather than *beginning and ending*. They criticise hierarchical systems of categorisation, proposing instead a move towards interconnectedness and flexibility (Deleuze and Guattari 2004). Although much of the content of mainstream psychological theory is positivist in its tacit assumptions, drawing on objectivist epistemologies that prioritise causal, linear explanations of an observable reality, the way in which these theories tend to arise in psychology lends itself to the concept of a plateau.

Deleuze and Guattari (2004) use the concept of a *rhizome* to describe the interconnected nature of knowledge and ideas, society, people and history, among other aspects of existence. They suggest these aspects of existence are often thought about in terms of roots and trees. They argue this is an incorrect metaphor of the world as it is not a straightforward structure, but rather better understood through a series of endless possibilities and interactions connected with one another. This, rather than understanding existence as roots and trees, is more accurately represented as rhizomes (a plant stem with a mass of roots and shoots). A rhizome is comprised of many multiplicities. Rhizomes are ordered by principles of connection, as connections can and should be made at any point.

Another principle is that of *rupture*. Rupture allows for new ways of expression and, although the rhizome may break, it will retrace an old line or carve out a new one. Rhizomes are also a type of *Nomadic thought*. Nomadic thought promotes flow and freedom, without fixed boundaries or territories. Nomads can be members of the same tribe yet produce different, unpredictable possibilities. Nomadism is based on free movement, choice and a constant process of becoming. Thus, Nomadic thinking opens up a clearing in everyday existence that engenders inventiveness, inspiration and originality. This mode can also inspire confrontation and critique. It is always in constant movement. Where the tree is defined by splitting and binary dualism, the rhizome is one of a continual becoming in multifaceted amalgamations. This metaphor can be used as a framework to construct how we engage with integration, as clinicians, as researchers and as teachers. The human experience is rhizomic, not tree-like. Therefore, to engage with experience holistically we might be flexible, open to dynamic interplays initiating at random points and in a continual process of unravelling and coming back together. This will be unpacked further, later in the chapter.

Engaging with the philosophical underpinnings of psychotherapeutic paradigms in the context of contemporary issues

The contemporary context in Europe and the USA broadly favours coherence, unity, self-authorship and self-sufficiency. The economic crisis has meant that experience is often seen through a prism of worth, output and efficiency. These dominant discourses inform mainstream psychology and psychotherapy, in the way it is conceptualised, legitimised and funded. The socio-political and economic driving factors behind service provision and delivery not only impact upon how efficacy is measured, services are modelled and interventions are delivered, but also on the way clients (and clinicians) construct their identities. As Gergen argues:

> Without the recognition by the medical profession, courts of law, insurance companies, and the media, therapists could scarcely claim to be offering 'help'. All these institutions grant the therapeutic community their legitimacy as 'healers' and invite the public to respond positively to therapeutic practice. In effect, the therapist's words carry the enormous symbolic weight of the cultural surrounds.

(2011: 276)

In the same vein, we form identity from the discourses that are available to us (Burr 2015). It follows that clients will co-construct their understanding of not only what it means to be human but what it means to be human *with a specific experience*, in relation to the assumptions (both implicit and explicit) of contemporary culture. We as clinicians are positioned – whether in alignment with the dominant discourses, in opposition to these, or some variation therein. The current climate asks us to practise within a system that calls for justifications (for example, to extend the length of therapy); 'progress' and 'personality' are measured through psychometrics; screening tools are used to quantify experience (e.g. risk and distress); psychiatric diagnosis and medication often reduce 'madness' to neurobiological origins and locate maladaptation in behaviour (Bentall 2004; Szasz 1976); and 'mental health' care has been deinstitutionalised (when, in reality, 'care in the community' often translates into further social isolation). Arguably, such established orthodoxies and systemic configurations are insufficient and can at times echo and perpetuate the events that gave rise to the difficulties experienced by clients in the first instance. This phenomenon is self-sustaining, as Herman writes:

> Fifty years ago, Virginia Woolf wrote that 'the public and private worlds are inseparably connected . . . the tyrannies and servilities of one are the tyrannies and servilities of the other'. It is now apparent also that the traumas of one are the traumas of the other . . . The fate of this field of knowledge depends upon the fate of the same political movement that has inspired and sustained it over the last century.
>
> (1993: 32)

Public health provision means that interventions are measured on the basis of efficacy. This assumes that distress is quantifiable. Also embedded herein is the assumption that distress has a price. These contemporary issues are not only the backdrop against which therapeutic paradigms operate; economics and cultural understandings of the human subject intimately construct the therapeutic relationship. Funding is allocated to therapeutic paradigms that can demonstrate value for money and, above all, tangible or observable results. Funding is also often allocated in reaction to media, scandal and public opinion. Therapists are positioned to respond by justifying the work within this paradigm and thus, new integrations of therapeutic modalities are born as a cost-effective solution to the problem: the state's austerity. It may be, though, that a clinician's ethical practice transcends regulatory frameworks for an appreciation of the underlying dynamics at play. Indeed, such dynamics demarcate social groupings imbued with power, as Dalal asserts:

> Cultural practices consist of rules that are the means of policing not only the territory between 'us' and the 'them' but are also the means of sustaining and reinforcing the structures of power relations between different groupings within the culture. Among other things, cultural practices are rationales of domination and oppression.
>
> (2012: 79)

Implications for training

Ambiguity

How then, as andragogues, might we engage with training people in the endeavour (the art, craft or science) of being with others in a particular way, within the framework of therapy? First, we must look to ambiguity, to undoing that which is taken for granted or even going further – not only deconstructing but a total and embodied forgetting. Deleuze and Guattari argue that, while psychoanalysis asks the analysand to pause and 'find' themselves once more, we should instead seek to go further still in an endeavour to deconstruct ourselves. This deconstruction, they argue, is not an end point as it can never be reached. They also introduce the concept of a body without organs, which rather than being about the actual body, is presented as referencing our relationships, connections, affects and possibilities, which we often do not engage with but might involve the complete loss of memory. Discovering our body without organs also involves a sort of *re-engaging* with concepts in a novel, playful way:

> Is it really so sad and dangerous to be fed up with seeing your eyes, breathing with your lungs, swallowing with your mouth, talking with your tongue, thinking with your brain, having an anus and larynx, head and legs? Why not walk on your head, sing with your sinuses, see through your skin, breathe with your belly: the simple Thing, the Entity, the full Body, the stationary Voyage, Anorexia, cutaneous Vision, Yoga, Krishna, Love, Experimentation . . . Substitute forgetting for anamnesis, experimentation for interpretation. Find your body without organs.
>
> (Deleuze and Guattari 2004: 167)

From a postmodern perspective, the emphasis is on multiplicity and the interest is in ambiguity. In therapy, this might translate into a welcoming of fragmentation whereby the decentred subject is invited to *go further*. To provide a cohesive narrative, this perspective will be used to frame the implications for training and research in integrative therapy that follows.

Going further: deconstructing and dismantling

How do we, as practitioners, *go further* when facilitating learning in the context of integrative therapy from a postmodern perspective? Using the metaphor posited by Deleuze and Guattari, both in their conceptualisation of a rhizome as an organising principle and their description of a body without organs as a discursive tool to engage with the deconstruction of narrative and self, the implication for training is to co-create an environment whereby the learners can engage with this exploration. Specifically, in the first instance, it includes an exploration of values and interests embedded within the therapeutic paradigms, and the factors at play when the therapist engages in formulating their clients' 'presentations'. Deconstructing this is conducive to understanding how social worlds are represented and meaning is produced. The value of articulating these structures, both in the classroom and in clinical work, should not be underestimated. If the therapist is not aware of the inherent assumptions, not only within the approaches they are integrating, but also within therapy as an endeavour in and of itself, it would be difficult for the therapist to engage in this kind of dialogue with the client. Furthermore, if gone unnoticed, the therapist may be unintentionally replicating the value systems that disqualify or, at a minimum, give less importance to the client's sensory experience or subjective understanding. Indeed, it is one thing to have a difficult experience, it is another to have it disqualified (Laing and Esterson 1976). Sensing something, only to be told that it is not the case, is a maddening experience.

If a therapist were to draw on Deleuze and Guattari (2004), they might organise their practice around *a way of becoming*, whereby the therapist is attuned to *that which appears on the surface* and from there open the possibilities, moments of 'deterritorialisation' and 'lines of flight'. Training, then, should create spaces and opportunities for learners not only to conceptually (dis)engage with meaning-making systems but also experientially to process what it means to be radically open to possibilities, attuned, spontaneous, flexible and in-a-constant-state-of-becoming.

Going further: multiplicity

Pluralism, in ontological terms, denotes that reality consists of many modes of being. Under this umbrella are various philosophical positions that suggest multiplicity is the basic premise of human beings; an epistemology that posits there are several different, conflicting and equally-valid descriptions and perceptions in life; and an ethics promoting many, independent sources of value. Postmodernism is radically pluralistic. The implication for training is to provide spaces whereby the learner can engage with this multiplicity.

From a postmodern standpoint, there is less of a focus on the inner workings of an individual's mind and more of a focus on society and the relationships therein; less of a focus on an individual's subjective experiencing of the world as the basis for their understanding and more of an emphasis on deconstructing social processes (Shotter 1992). Fostering learners' appreciation for multiplicity could be aided by presenting many, varying paradigms – not only the dominant psychotherapeutic models that share philosophical assumptions on a macro level. Furthermore, to truly engage with human experience holistically, training programmes should cross-pollinate on content and delivery, for example, in a curriculum that includes sociologists, anthropologists or activists, as well as by employing the teaching practices adopted in these fields.

Going further: beyond words

We might either assume language shows us things as they appear in real life, or we can assume language has another function (it is symbolic, for example). If language is not assumed as showing us things as they appear in real life (Gergen 1985), then it is important to highlight the language that learners use to construct their worlds and the words of their clients. This language may manifest in their communications about their clients directly or the language they use to frame their clients' experience (perhaps in formulation), as well as when speaking about their clients with colleagues – in supervision or in class. Through attending to this language, the learner can attend to the ways in which they are co-constructing the relationship. Another point on communication: much of the way we co-construct our relationship with others is not through language but through non-verbal communication, and often we are unaware of this (Tantam 2018). These essential implicit communications are embedded within the therapist–client relationship and underwrite a secure environment, as Scaer describes,

> subtle variations of facial expression that set the tone for the content of the interaction. Body postures and movement patterns of the therapist . . . also may reflect emotions such as disapproval, support, humour, and fear. Tone and volume of voice, patterns and speed of verbal communication, and eye contact also contain elements of subliminal communication.
>
> (2015: 167–8)

Indeed, neurologists suggest therapists who engage the right hemisphere of the brain (linked with intuition, creativity and non-verbal communication) fare better in their clinical work, particularly when working with more complex presentations or clients in greater distress. Schore and Schore (2007) assert that skilled therapists (in particular when working with people who are severely distressed) depend more on the non-conscious, non-verbal part of the right brain, rather than the conscious, verbal, left-brain functions. Consequently, good outcomes in therapy are less about developing competencies in skills and more about developing non-conscious functions so that they can be expressed within the therapeutic relationship. These non-conscious functions range from body language to creativity:

> the ability to receive and express nonverbal affective communications, clinical sensitivity, use of subjectivity/intersubjectivity, empathy, and affect regulation. Neuroscience now indicates that the implicit processes of intuition . . . creativity . . . and indeed insight . . ., are all right, and not left, brain functions.
>
> (Schore and Schore 2007: 13)

The way we engage with others is an embodied co-creation, often silently communicated in ways that we are not overtly aware of. Drawing this to the learner's attention might help them think about what this dynamic interplay might look like for them and their client. But to go beyond a cognitive understanding of the non-verbal, trainers must provide opportunities for learners to relationally attune in this mode of being, aiding their learning and moving beyond cognitive processing.

Going further: the inter-relational self in construction

If we are to align ourselves with the fundamental assumption of a social constructivist standpoint, then we take for granted the notion that we are relational beings and, while intra-psychic dynamics might exist, behaviour and meaning are a consequence of interactional process, communication is a dynamic evolving process and the experience of 'self' is constructed as a result of being recognised by someone else within an interpersonal movement that takes place in a specific context (Faris and Ooijen 2012).

Here are some ways of applying this within an integrative framework (this is not an exhaustive list):

- Focusing on the client's resources (rather than lack thereof).
- Adopting an approach that leans towards understanding (depending on the needs of the client).
- Appreciating context.
- Adopting a curious attitude that allows an openness to what both client and therapist brings.
- Appreciating multiplicity (i.e. refraining from adopting linear or causal explanations).
- Attending to verbal and non-verbal communications, including body experiencing.
- Attending to language systems, noticing and sharing patterns and reference points.
- Giving primacy to 'being' over 'doing'.
- Using symbols and metaphors.
- Being particularly tentative of 'our own issues' as therapists, including how these might play out with the client (Faris and Ooijen 2012; Cooper and Dryden 2016).

The implications for training are to create environments where the learners can develop their skills, attitude and position in relation to these values and ways of being.

Underlying all of these is, of course, a sensitive and alert relationship with oneself. Programmes that require the learners to be in regular, personal therapy throughout the duration of their training might assist with this. Creating occasions to engage reflexively is also key, which would include opportunities to do the following:

- Identify blind spots.
- Notice biases and assumptions.
- Have a sense of what is meaningful and what is not.

- Be sensitive to personal 'trigger' points.
- Understand one's stance in terms of relational proximity.
- Build one's capacity to tolerate ambiguity, tension and paradox.

Going further: evidence-based practice

From a postmodern perspective, basing practice on research is seen within the wider context so that the whole is not reduced to the sum of its parts. An awareness of research findings relevant to the therapeutic setting (and not solely based on funding policies) is both part of an ethical practice that goes beyond slavishly adhering to guidelines and is a way of informing the work that recognises the many contributing factors of the therapeutic enterprise. For example, Cooper argues that research findings on the efficacy of therapy are not modality-specific and that 'there is evidence to suggest that different clients do better in different kinds of therapy' (2008: 59). Furthermore, Cooper demonstrates that rather than the therapeutic approach of the therapist, one of the most robust indicators of outcomes in therapy are client-related issues, including how committed they are, their expectations and their level of functioning. This is to say that when a client's expectations are hopeful but realistic, it is more likely that there will be a positive therapeutic outcome. Cooper (2008: 78) described these expectations in the following way:

- Expecting that their therapy will be beneficial (within reason).
- Being aware that therapy may sometimes be challenging and difficult.
- Being clear about what therapy is and why they are doing it.

Furthermore, better outcomes in therapy can also be expected of clients who have more developed functioning (in terms of psychological stability, their relationship with themselves or their relationship with therapy). Cooper (2008: 78–9) posed these assumptions the following way: the best clients are those who:

- Are not diagnosed with personality disorders.
- Have secure attachment styles and good interpersonal functioning.
- Do not have high levels of perfectionism.
- Are psychologically minded.
- Are ready to change.
- Have high levels of social support.

In terms of factors relating specifically to the therapist, research suggests that while the therapist's age or lived experiences do not appear to have an impact, their psychological health and the way in which they form relationships with clients do correlate with therapeutic outcomes (Cooper 2008).

As the way therapists relate to their clients appears, from the research, to play such a central role, it is worth unpacking. Research on 'relational factors' suggests that negotiation of goals, empathy, communication around inter-relational dynamics and self-disclosure are all central. Cooper argues that the kind of therapeutic relationship we have with clients is also a factor in therapeutic outcomes. Empathy, collaboration, self-disclosure, positive feedback and the capacity to repair ruptures in the relationship are all important factors. Therefore, creating learning environments that support developing these skills and attitudes is essential when training counselling psychologists and psychotherapists.

When clients come to therapy, one way of viewing their engagement is in the co-construction of the therapeutic relationship, where they have certain expectations, informed by their relational matrix and meaning-making systems, which in turn are formed by the context in which these come into being. Part of the client's position might seek to elicit a response in the therapist and therefore adopt a way of being that engenders this response. For example,

> if they expect rejection, they will make themselves worthy of rejection, if they expect to have their boundaries violated by being seduced, they will make themselves available for violation, act seductively and become angry whether you do or don't live up to their expectations.
>
> (Cozolino 2016: 111)

According to the evidence, it is the therapist's capacity to negotiate the client's expectations and perceptions through an articulation of process – a putting-into-words, an acknowledgement of the intersubjective, as well as a being-with the client in an emphatic, attuned coming-together within the therapy – which contributes to better 'outcomes' in therapy. This should be made explicit to trainee therapists, both in terms of the evidence and in terms of how they can continually inform their knowledge post-training and, of course, opportunities should be provided within the training to acquire and develop these qualities.

Going further: relational beings

If truth is a gesture that is subject to a time–space continuum, in that it only reveals itself or is realised in the context within which it is formed, then the process of teaching should be transitory, cautious, critical and radically reflexive. Engaging with the dynamic forces and interchanges, the multitude of meanings that thread learner-andragogue-education-politic-institute-culture-society-ecology might be deconstructed. These layers of meaning give rise to the classroom, a space that sees the event of these layers meeting minds and, if given the opportunity, unfold and transmute in different directions, take different forms and affect in different ways. Lapworth and Sills argue that the therapeutic relationship is central to meeting certain needs and the therapist's capacity to acknowledge and respond to these is key:

> These needs are identified as security, validation, affirmation and significance, acceptance by a dependable and protective other person, the need to

have an impact on the other person, confirmation of personal experience, self-definition, the need to have the other initiate and the need to express love. The therapist responds to these current needs of the client by providing a contact-orientated therapeutic relationship which is emotionally nurturing, reparative and sustaining, and employs the facilitative methods of inquiry, attunement and involvement.

(2010: 80)

Here, the therapist might attune themselves to what has been omitted, negated, disrupted, resisted, invited, struggled against or distracted by. Within the learning context, andragogues might seek to create conditions whereby the learner not only can conceptually understand self-other-world expressions but also can engage with self-other-world in an embodied, sensing mode of being.

As therapists, many of the people we engage with are distressed. In the learning environment, spaces need to be created where trainee therapists build their capacity for this sensing mode of being-in-relation-to-distress. To illustrate this, we might take the example of grief. Bowlby (1969) argued that 'suffering well' means expressing grief in a deep, embodied way, rather than simply trying to survive, endure or manage it. Grieving in this way can be a rich and informative experience, as besides the potential relief of accepting solace, there are opportunities for profound personal development. As Hillman articulates, there needs to be sufficient time and space to express feelings and, in so doing, we create the opportunity to be: 'if there is no time for grief, there is no time for soul' (2007, cited in Sunderland 2015: 17–18).

In contemporary learning environments, economic and political shifts have meant the university is a place to obtain a qualification that will feed into capitalist work-systems. This positions learners as customers and learning-facilitators as service-providers. Learning becomes commodified and both learners and andragogues are objectified. This environment, at times, is not conducive to creating spaces for learners to deconstruct assumptions and increase their capacity to tolerate anxiety, take responsibility and, perhaps most importantly, have time for the soul. Instead, the learning process in its entirety becomes reduced to outputs that can be measured in terms of their utility and often learners are put in the position whereby the totality of the process of becoming a therapeutic practitioner is reduced to accruing client hours on placement. Perhaps when considering training in integrative therapy, if the system cannot be challenged, both learners and andragogues must find better ways of negotiating this environment, or else training should happen outside of the institution to enable more freedom and congruence in fostering the craft.

Conclusion

So far in this chapter we have covered: the different types of integration; Deleuze and Guattari's theories and how these might provide a conceptual framework; and the contemporary context. We then considered how as trainers we might create the necessary conditions to facilitate the learning process in becoming competent integrative therapists, including: ambiguity; deconstruction; multiplicity; engaging with that which is beyond words; and evidence-based practice. We will now briefly look at how further research in the field might contribute to a knowledge base on integrative therapy.

Recommendations for further research

Beyond dominant epistemologies

Psychological and psychotherapeutic theories contain ideas drawn from many different disciplines: sociology, anthropology, neurobiology, medicine, even mathematics. Coherent integration occurs not only when a practitioner draws upon different therapeutic paradigms but also when the therapist draws on knowledge across different fields. To ignore these other spheres of wisdom is to do a disservice to the richness and depth of human experience. There are countless ways in which human beings have chosen to live. Ignoring that we are situated within a specific historical period and socio-cultural-political moment, positing a singular theory to explain or capture this is formulaic, reductionist, insufficient and often self-fulfilling. More research might be done into alternative possibilities. For example, most therapeutic approaches hold modernist values and objectivist assumptions. Developing approaches that begin with alternative philosophical underpinnings may provide other possibilities to the dominant narratives in psychology and psychotherapy, namely, therapies with constructivist epistemologies is one possible area for further research.

Philosophical underpinnings

Much attention is given, relatively speaking, in counselling psychology and some psychotherapy training programmes to the epistemological underpinnings of the therapeutic paradigms. However, often when learners are asked to integrate, for example, when completing doctoral research, they confuse which research method (with its epistemic assumptions) might be integrated with a particular clinical intervention (which comes from a specific paradigm with its own epistemic assumptions). Further research should be done in this area, so that there is more literature available relating to epistemology and psychology that can assist learners in grappling with the tensions and intersections within this domain. Furthermore, when considering therapeutic integration, the field would benefit from more of a focus on epistemology and how it features within integration. As Neimeyer wrote:

> from a constructivist perspective, many of the most popular forms of psychotherapy integration encounter serious epistemological obstacles [and without a rigorous and radical commitment to understanding these

tensions, overlaps and paradoxes amongst the psychotherapeutic paradigms, the therapist] risk[s] rendering the resulting synthesis superficial
or contradictory.

(1993: 113)

Beyond models of disease

Finally, modern psychology and psychotherapy tend to formulate clients' issues
according to a 'model' of disease; making deductive inferences about people's state
and therefore developmental processes often on the basis of behaviour. More
research needs to be done on alternative conceptualisations and approaches that
construct humans in relation to health (rather than illness) or, alternatively, a way
of engaging with the human condition that transcends this dichotomy. From a postmodern standpoint, humans are primarily sensing beings and thereafter are subject
to a host of constructs (for example, language and discourse) out of which existence
comes into being. The learning experience should first be an endeavour of *sensing*.
Thinking and *acting* should, therefore, not be given primacy. More research should
be done (focusing on both therapeutic training and practice) into honing this
pre-verbal mode of being whereby symbols, sounds and patterns are given primacy
over words, thoughts and behaviours.

References

Alexander, R. (2004) Still no pedagogy? Principle, pragmatism and compliance in
    primary education. *Cambridge Journal of Education*, 1: 3.
Bentall, R. (2004) *Madness Explained: Psychosis and Human Nature*. London:
    Penguin.
Bowlby, J. (1969) *Attachment and Loss*. Vol. 1: *Attachment*. New York: Basic
    Books.
Burr, V. (2015) *Social Constructionism* (3rd edn). Hove: Routledge.
Clarkson, P. (2001) *The Therapeutic Relationship*. London: Whurr Publishers.
Cooper, M. and Dryden, W. (eds) (2016) *The Handbook of Counselling and Psycho-
    therapy*. London: SAGE.
Cozolino, L. (2016) *Why Therapy Works: Using Our Minds to Change our Brains*.
    London: W.W. Norton.
Dalal, F. (2012) *Thought Paralysis: The Virtues of Discrimination*. London: Karnac
    Books.
Deleuze, G. and Guattari, F. (2004) *A Thousand Plateaus*, B. Massumi, trans. London:
    Continuum.
Faris, A. and Ooijen, E. van (2012) *Integrative Counselling and Psychotherapy:
    A Relational Approach*. London: SAGE.
Gergen, K.J. (1985) The social constructionist movement in modern psychology.
    American Psychologist, 40(3): 266–75.

Gergen, K.J. (2011) *Relational Beings: Beyond Self and Community*. Oxford: Oxford University Press.

Herman, J. (1993) *Trauma and Recovery: From Domestic Abuse to Political Terror*. New York: Basic Books.

Laing, R.D. and Esterson, A. (1976) *Sanity, Madness and the Family*. Harmondsworth: Penguin.

Lapworth, P. and Sills, C. (2010) *Integration in Counselling and Psychotherapy: Developing a Personal Approach* (2nd edn). London: SAGE.

Neimeyer, R. (1993) Constructivism and the problem of integration. *Journal of Psychotherapy Integration*, 3(2): 133–57.

Nuttall, J. (2008) The integration: A personal journey. *European Journal of Psychotherapy and Counselling*, 10(1): 19–38.

Orlans, V. and Gilbert, M. (2011) *Integrative Therapy: 100 Key Points and Techniques*. Hove: Routledge.

Scaer, R. (2015) *The Trauma Spectrum: Hidden Wounds and Human Resiliency*. London: Norton.

Schore, J.R. and Schore, A.N. (2007) Modern attachment theory: The central role of affect regulation in development and treatment. *Clinical Social Work Journal*, 36(1): 9–20.

Shotter, J. (1992) 'Getting in touch': The meta-methodology of a post-modern science of mental life. In S. Kvale (ed.), *Psychology and Postmodernism*. London: SAGE.

Sunderland, M. (2015) *Conversations That Matter: Talking with Children and Teenagers in Ways That Help*. London: Worth Publishing.

Szasz, T. (1976) *The Myth of Mental Illness: Foundations of a Theory of Personal Conduct*. New York: Harper and Row.

Tantam, D. (2018) *The Interbrain: Embodied Connections Versus Common Knowledge*. London: Jessica Kingsley Publishers.

UKCP (2018). *Ethical Principles and Code of Professional Conduct*. Available at: https://www.psychotherapy.org.uk/wp-content/uploads/2018/10/UKCP-Ethical-Principles-and-Code-of-Professional-Conduct.pdf (accessed 5 December 2018).

16 Coda

Reflection on integrative values

John Nuttall

Introduction

The chapters in this book explore postmodern perspectives on integration in psychological therapies and pose important challenges to ideas of a subject–object dichotomy within individual practice and the integration movement generally. The opening chapters trace the history of psychotherapy integration and present a framework for understanding the integrative quest as something inherently relational and reflexive – as something simultaneously, constructive, complicit and contiguous. It is posited as a personal journey for each integrative therapist and exhorts a view of integration as a pluralistic process of indeterminate end rather than an objective search for a grand theory. Such a view of psychotherapy integration places the notions of relationality and intersubjectivity at the heart of the therapeutic endeavour. We situate the therapist and client as relational beings who, through interaction, maximise the potential for emotional connection and depth, factors argued to bring about therapeutic change. Old ideas of therapists as objective, neutral observers who merely interpret transferences and bring psychological insight have been challenged by an integration movement in *statu nascendi*. An integrative approach views the therapy participants as agents whose subjectivities come together in collaborative efforts to understand through empathic affective connection with one another. Openness to a variety of therapeutic techniques and skills, as well as philosophical and theoretical viewpoints, makes this endeavour more likely. This postmodern *Zeitgeist* has not only led to the decline of the meta-narrative (Lyotard 1989) associated with single-school ideologies, but has led to the flowering of pluralistic inquiry that has revolutionised therapeutic practice, creating possibilities for profound change in the provision and delivery of psychological therapies to the community.

At the level of individual practice, integrative therapy involves actioning participant agency and *inter-personal relatedness* to create a therapeutic bond. This leads to *intra-personal relatedness* involving stages of participant self-reflection that produces a *self-relatedness* (see Chapter 3). This entails a process of deconstruction, like cracking open a nutshell to see its contents and understand its structure; a process analogous to the practitioner's quest for psychotherapy integration, which is characterised by questioning, reflexive analysis and critique. Other aspects of integrative therapy concern the kinds of techniques and skills used as psychological interventions; the professional aspects such as clear contracting; and factors that impact safety and trust such as confidentiality, data protection and referral procedures. As Horton expounds, 'personal integration is an individual construction that can be developed to reflect the thinking and practice of the individual therapist' (2000: 326).

One aspect of both thinking about and practising psychotherapy are the values we bring to the development of an integrated approach and to our engagement with clients. In concluding, we would like to present a Coda that addresses the issue of values in psychotherapeutic practice and the provision of psychotherapy to the community in need.

What do we mean by 'values'?

Values are those basic ideas and principles regarding what is generally considered good and evil in ourselves and the world at large. Values should not be confused with virtues, which can be more specifically defined as those attributes that represent moral excellence or righteousness, or indeed any admirable quality, feature or trait. Values encompass the continuum of what might be considered virtues and vices, and different societies and cultures have, and have had, different values or sets of values over the ages. Oscar Wilde, in *Lady Windermere's Fan* (1892), described a cynic as 'a man who knows the price of everything and the value of nothing' and, in recent times, monetary worth is the measurement by which most the population of the developed world assess their lives. The laws of economics and the system of New Public Management (NPM), which seem to control our lives and public services, now lead us to reduce the analysis of health and well-being to a monetary base so that comparative value judgements can be made about illnesses and resource allocation. No doubt, as discussed in Chapter 2, this drove the quest for integrative therapies with the aim of being more cost-effective and deliverable to a wide range of people in need. Paradoxically, the ascendancy of 'managed care' and the influence of evidence-based treatments are in danger of inhibiting integrative practice as both new and established manualised systems of therapy gain the limelight.

Wilde's adage raises the issue about how we value the provision of psychological therapies and the different sets or types of values that influence our judgement. We seem to place economic values ahead of those concerning the social, the aesthetic or the spiritual. Economic values are now arguably driving the very heart of our being as monetary reward becomes almost the only means by which we seek to satisfy our narcissistic hunger for recognition. Even our care services are riddled with incentives, bonuses and penalties that emulate and possibly evoke the internal world of object relations. It is a world that feeds some participants' greed to the point of being morbidly obese, while others are deprived of services to the point of starvation.

Gordon Allport (1961), one of the founding fathers of the Humanistic Psychology movement, distinguished six categories of life values – economic, aesthetic, social, political, spiritual and scientific. (He offered no judgement about the relative importance of one or another.) If universal, they probably have different emphases across cultural and historical divides. The issue has the potential of collapsing into a kind of anarchic relativism whereby no one set of values can be judged superior to another. No doubt each of Allport's categories has become figure or ground at some point in our lives, and perhaps the best we can do is accept the dialectic tension this evokes. We can take support for such equivocation from Jung who, after decades of self-reflection and deep confrontation with his unconscious, which he records in his autobiography, wrote the following moving and enlightening retrospective:

> The older I have become, the less I have understood or had insight into or known about myself. I am astonished, disappointed, pleased with myself. I am distressed, depressed, rapturous. I am all these things at once, and cannot add up the sum. I am incapable of determining ultimate worth or worthlessness; I have no judgement about myself and my life. There is nothing I am quite sure about. I have no definite convictions – not about anything, really.
>
> (1995 [1963]: 392)

Notwithstanding Jung's declaration, there have been attempts by philosophers to identify superordinate values throughout the ages. In ancient times, Plato, through the mouth of Socrates and Aristotle argued that all the virtues (such as the cardinal virtues of courage, wisdom, justice and temperance) needed to be pursued and mastered simultaneously – the so-called thesis of the unity of virtues. In more modern times, the US Constitution's concept of inalienable rights is a prominent working example of values legislation. In spite of these attempts, the task of finding some kind of unity of value categories seems questionable as they must, by definition, span gradations of good and bad, and often seem in conflict with one another. They are, at best, in some kind of dialectic tension.

The *coincidentia oppositorum*

Deciding on the relative importance of different value categories also presupposes that our rational abilities can override our instinctual nature, the part of ourselves Jung called the 'Shadow', a dominant archetype of the collective unconscious. He pointed out,

> There is an unconscious psychic reality which demonstrably influences consciousness and its contents ... We still go on thinking and acting as before, as if we were *simplex* and not *duplex*. Accordingly, we imagine ourselves to be innocuous, reasonable, and humane ... It needs only an

almost imperceptible disturbance of equilibrium in a few of our rulers' heads to plunge the world into blood, fire, and radioactivity.

(1970 [1957]: para. 561)

He is clearly referring here to the potential at that time for nuclear war; but it need not be limited to such major catastrophes – the current mental health crisis, the turn against gay rights, gender inequality are all examples of our cognitive capacity being subject to arcane, archetypal and unconscious influence. The new discipline of behavioural economics has highlighted how innate cognitive bias, particularly loss aversion, paradoxically induces further risky behaviours. Recent research with rhesus monkeys suggests that such biases have primordial 'archetypal' origins (Blanchard et al. 2014). Neuroscience suggests that our sense of right and wrong might be hardwired at birth – again suggesting instinctual or archetypal influence (Hauser 2006). Our 'duplex' nature is recognised in all the major religions and certainly is a characteristic of Western syncretism. Almost all the creation myths incorporate some kind of battle between good and evil at some stage. Heraclitus declared, 'War is the father of all and the king of all' (Fragment DK. B53). Empedocles posited that the four elements were held together by the forces of Love and Strife. We see parallels today in modern science in the concept of matter and anti-matter, dark matter and dark energy, and so on. Complexity theory now asserts that chaos has, at its core, *order*.

The psychologist, Erich Fromm, highlighted another dimension of our duplex nature. In *To Have or To Be?* (1976), he argued that there are two basic and opposing modes of existence. One is aimed at having and owning, and the other at being and living. This duality of our nature has been recognised in various traditions and its detrimental effect is perhaps manifest in the effect economic growth is having on our stressful lives and the environment. It is contained in the story of Eden where Adam's desire to *have* (knowledge) forfeited his right to *be* carefree and he was cast out 'to do' for himself. (The balance of these two dimensions was also sought by Prince Siddhartha, the Buddha, in his search for enlightenment.) In response, most of the world's religions espouse values associated with the absence of material possessions and desires. Fromm's response was a declaration, a call to transformation of the human psyche: 'For the first time in history the physical survival of the human race depends on a radical change of the human heart' (1976: 19). This admonishment is apposite in relation to the current rivalry between the desire for economic growth and the corollary of global warming, air pollution and mental ill health.

The need for reconciliation of this duplex nature was recognised as far back as the time of Lao Tzu and the *Tao Te Ching* (translated by Stefan Stenudd). Verse 29 reads:

> Conquering the world and changing it,
> I do not think it can succeed.
> The world is a sacred vessel that cannot be changed.
> He who changes it will destroy it.
> He who seizes it will lose it.

> So, among all things,
> Some lead and some follow,
> Some sigh and some pant,
> Some are strong and some are weak,
> Some overcome and some succumb.

Therefore the sage avoids extremity, excess, and extravagance.

These views suggest that value attribution is an essential part of our being, our soul, as well as having an effect in our behaviours. Understanding our own values and those of others and the resultant relational consequences might be the route to solving many interpersonal and international conflicts (see Verse 33 of the *Tao Te Ching*).

When attributing values to anything, there always seems to be an antagonistic point of view, or consequence; something alchemists referred to as the *coincidentia oppositorum* – the coincidence of opposites. The concept in the Western tradition is associated with Heraclitus and is a common axiom in many religious and philosophical traditions. One way of using this insight is to highlight the possibility that what one person considers good might well be considered bad by someone else or have unintended bad consequences. The great twentieth-century philosopher Bertrand Russell pondered this anomaly in an essay called 'The Harm That Good Men Do'. He argued that virtue does not always have desirable consequences and in a short satirical essay he debates the contextual definitions of 'good' and 'bad' and elaborates the kinds of activities that define a 'good' man (at least in the 1930s) and concluded that a good man is 'one whose opinions and activities are pleasing to the holders of power' (1935: 87).

We see this coincidence of opposites in the Roman Catholic Church's condemnation of contraception and the effect this has on the spread of HIV. Also, perhaps, in the provision of mental health care, the concept of 'managed care' presents an underlying contradiction in terms; its manifestation in the form of the Improving Access to Psychological Therapies (IAPT) scheme has arguably introduced a 'fetished target culture [that] simultaneously subverts the very care mandated' (Rizq 2012: 7).

Reflecting on our values

A number of aphorisms from different ages advocate reflection that acknowledges our duplex nature. For example:

- Heraclitus: 'Recognizing oneself and being of a sound mind are for all men' (Fragment DK. B116).
- The stoic, Marcus Aurelius: 'Look inward. Don't let the true nature or value of anything elude you' (Hays 2003: 77).
- The Sufi mystic, Rumi (1997):

The Guest House

This being human is a guest-house.
Every morning a new arrival.
A joy, a depression, a meanness,
some momentary awareness comes
as an unexpected visitor.
Welcome and entertain them all!
Even if they're a crowd of sorrows,
Who violently sweep your house
empty of its furniture.
Still, treat each guest honourably.
He may be clearing you out
for some new delight.
The dark thought, the shame, the malice,
meet them at the door laughing,
and invite them in.
Be grateful for whoever comes,
because each has been sent
as a guide from beyond.

(Re-used with permission from translator, Coleman Barks.
Original poem by Rumi 1991.)

The key principle that emerges from this understanding is that we must be willing to reflect upon our being and doing to gain self-knowledge and its corollary, autonomy. This is not the kind of autonomy that leads to wanton behaviour but the kind that springs from reflection, being self-aware, and being free from, and understanding the potential impact of, our shadow and our dark side. This brings the ability to be responsive to the present without the guilt associated with the past, or the fear of the future.

These are all relevant questions for contemporary psychotherapy. Despite the conviction of adherents to the various theoretical models of therapy, there is still no clear evidence that one therapeutic approach is more effective than another. Clarkson asserted, 'The bulk of research points to the fact that the most important factor in effective psychotherapeutic work is the relationship between the client and the therapist' (2003: xvi). Indeed, the fact that over 450 approaches have been identified and purport to have understanding of the human psyche and its vicissitudes clearly indicates that no single approach has the truth about how psychotherapy works (Polkinghorne 1992: 158). The duplexity referred to before and the resultant power struggle of values are exemplified in the term 'managed care', which, in the UK, manifests in the NHS's IAPT scheme. It has emerged from the dominance of economic, political and scientific values, as illustrated by David Clark's address at the British Psychological Society's (BPS) 2016 conference entitled, 'Developing and Disseminating Effective Psychological Therapies: Science, Economics and Politics'. The result has been the rise to prominence of so-called 'evidence-based practice', and of manualised systems of treatment for mental distress that are measured at every point for efficacy and effective delivery. These are supported by an edifice of bureaucracy that has more to do with containing the anxiety of its designers and managers than treating the nation's mental health. As one management guru pointed out: 'What is the major problem? It is fundamentally the confusion between effectiveness and efficiency that stands between doing the right things and doing things right' (Drucker 1993). In other words, efficiency is concerned with doing things right, while effectiveness is concerned with *doing the right things*, and, once entrenched, such edifices of power as seen in evidence-based practice might be efficient, but quite ineffective. The dominance of these values has upset the aesthetic, social and spiritual values arguably at the core of psychotherapy and has delivered what Rizq calls a 'virtual reality' in which attention to efficiency and measurement parameters of mental health provision has created a 'perversion of care ... used to mask the unbearable feelings of helplessness in the face of our limitations when trying to help those in psychological distress' (Rizq 2012: 7).

At the individual level, psychological research suggests that our experience of things or events is invariably comparative. Things are usually better or worse, more or less exciting, tasty or important to us than something else. The basis of these judgements might be determined by the value categories Allport identified, within which the innate antagonism is ironically illustrated by Wilde's adage. The implication is that we are constantly engaged in some kind of selection or prioritising process so that, as one stimulus becomes figure, others become ground in a never-ending cycle of *Gestalts*. Couple this with the psychoanalytic concept of transference and behavioural psychology's principles of operant conditioning and you have the perfect storm by which values are transmitted and sustained. The client brings preconceptions to the consulting room with associated selection criteria. These in turn can be reinforced or refuted by the therapist; either way values are communicated and received.

As individuals, or therapists, we influence and are influenced by others by selectively attending to only certain aspects of the encounter. How more significant is an intervention when it is the only one in the session? The communication is only implicit, but its effect is all the more charged when the transaction conveys 'ulterior' values (Berne 1974: 23), hidden from consciousness. Thus, relational psychology now considers a satisfying relationship to be the human's key motivational drive (Wachtel 2008). The developmental importance of relationship was pioneered in the UK by psychoanalysts Klein and Fairbairn, and in the USA by the humanistic psychologist Rogers, whose core conditions of empathy, congruence and unconditional positive regard are universally accepted interpersonal competences for 'any situation in which the development of the person is a goal' (Rogers 1990: 135).

Oscar Wilde aside, another source of ironic insight can be gained from the mythical Sufi figure of Mulla Nasruddin. Most of his allegories date from around the twelfth century and are based on humour yet are still studied by mystics today. It is thought that if you listen to seven Nasrudin stories consecutively, you will reach enlightenment (Shah 2007). One story concerns our ability to acknowledge the values of others:

> Suddenly [the Mulla] found himself in a carpenter's shop. 'What can I do for you?' asked the craftsman, stepping forward. Nasrudin said nothing. 'Perhaps you would like something made from wood?' 'First things first,' said the Mulla. 'Now, did you see me come into your shop?' 'Yes, I did.'

'Good. Now, have you ever seen me in your life before?' 'Never in my life.'
'Then how do you know it is *me*?'

(2007: *Nobody Really Knows*, 161)

Another story concerns where we should seek our values:

A neighbour found Nasruddin on hands and knees. 'What are you searching for Mullah?' 'My key.' Both men got on their knees to search. After a
while the neighbour says, 'Where did you lose it?' 'At home.' 'Good Lord!
Then why are you searching here?' 'Because it's brighter here.'

(de Mello 1982: *Searching in the Wrong Place*)

Do we find it easier to seek answers under the light of economic, political and scientific values, rather than look at home for more aesthetic, social or spiritual values?
In a historical review of the Kabbalah and its relevance to the twentieth century,
Hoffman emphasises the important principle of *cosmic interrelatedness*. He quotes
a Kabbalistic aphorism that says 'so, too, does the lower sphere affect the upper'
(Hoffman 1985: 35), meaning equally perhaps 'as within, so without'. As integrative
psychotherapists, we are challenged to resolve the problem of the hierarchy of value
categories by understanding what can emanate from within as well as what is
imposed from without. Hopefully, this book, and this Coda, will help identify qualities that assist with this process and lead to the development of an integrative attitude that will reverberate throughout your professional practice. Rumi believed:

> *Two kinds of intelligence*
> There are two kinds of intelligence:
> One acquired, as a child in school memorises facts and concepts from
> books and what the teacher says, collecting information from the tradi-
> tional sciences as well as the new sciences.
> With such intelligence you rise in the world. You get ranked ahead or
> behind others in regard to your competence in retaining information.
> You stroll with this intelligence in and out of fields of knowledge, getting
> always more marks on your preserving tablets.
> There is another kind of tablet, one already completed and preserved
> inside you. A spring overflowing its spring box. A freshness in the centre
> of your chest. This other intelligence does not turn yellow or stagnate.
> It's fluid, and it doesn't move from outside to inside through the conduits
> of plumbing-learning.

> This second kind of knowing is a fountainhead from within you, moving out.
> (Re-used with permission from translator, Coleman Barks.
> Original poem by Rumi 1991.)

The mystery of this 'other intelligence' is likened to Jung's idea of the psyche. In *Psychology and Alchemy*, Jung debates the function of the psyche and the soul and
asserts, 'It is yet to be understood that the *mysterium magnum* is not only an actuality

but is first and foremost rooted in the human psyche' (1970 [1944]: para. 13). Deep within the psyche he describes a soul in which 'supreme values reside' (1970 [1944]: para. 1) and are constructed as part of its innate function. In a similar vein, the Roman stoic, Seneca, argued that the single most supreme virtue was wisdom and that in the long run, the perfectly wise person would act in harmony with all the virtues. Reconciling and, on occasions, tolerating diverse values require a particular attitude that was advocated by Bertrand Russell in his critique of the 'superstitious reverence' (1946: 57) often bestowed on the early Greek philosophers. So, in studying the values of other people, cultures, religions, etc., we espouse the view that:

> the right attitude is neither reverence nor contempt, but first a kind of hypothetical sympathy, until it is possible to know what it feels like to believe in his theories, and only then a revival of the critical attitude, which should resemble, as far as possible, the state of mind of a person abandoning opinions which he has hitherto held. Contempt interferes with the first part of this process, and reverence with the second.
>
> (Russell 1946: 58)

Conclusion

This book aims to engender the questioning and reflexive attitude illustrated by Russell; and this Coda questions whether there are a set of qualities *sine qua non* that move from within to without that lead to beneficent values. But what might constitute 'beneficent values' in the practice of psychotherapy? As we argue, psychotherapy is a relational process (Clarkson 2003) with different facets of relationship. It is a developmental process that aims to be healing and to make people better. But the chapters in this book raise questions about what is meant by 'better', or 'good' development, and how our own values might impose on these meanings.

Not so long ago being gay was considered a developmental perversion that required psychological intervention to make people better, aversion therapy being one such intervention. Now the professions consider it unethical to even wonder if it has a psychological foundation. As mentioned earlier, values are constructs of one's era, culture, inheritance and the aim of this book and Coda is not to espouse any one set of values, but to propose a number of attributes or qualities that might help reflection on values and form the basis not of value-free psychotherapy, but of values-aware psychotherapists. Professionals who have seriously reflected on their beliefs, prejudices and biases and come to terms with their Shadow in order to avoid, as far as possible, imposing their values on their clients. Four qualities emerge:

- The first concerns *the process of individuation and the development of self-awareness, self-acceptance and autonomy.* It involves recognising disagreeable aspects of oneself and accepting them as thoughts and feelings that represent our often-denied Shadow. Thus we can avoid the derived behaviours that ultimately determine who we are. This allows the next quality to flourish with advantage.

- Aspiration leads to *self-direction and the capacity to choose our behaviours, goals and needs – our values*. This might be an organismic drive that engenders motivation, curiosity and creativity. Existentially, it situates us on the cusp of the future, where we can choose not to be determined by the past or present but be drawn towards our potential.
- The next is *solicitude*, a fundamental condition of being-in-the-world (Heidegger 1962). This involves love and care for ourselves and others. It brings the willingness to acknowledge and understand, if not always accept, the Shadow in others. This allows enjoyment in life and engagement with others; to have empathy for and understand the values of others without losing autonomy or aspiration.
- The fourth concerns *congruence* – a core condition of humanistic counselling. It involves feeling 'joined up' with the ability to be tolerant, hold ambivalence and paradox, and remain optimistic in the face of disappointment or challenge. This may involve adapting our values, objectives and relationships while maintaining autonomy, purpose and caring.

Notwithstanding these qualities, against all efforts we do impose, or at least transmit, our values on to our clients. The way we dress, decorate the room, speak, will resonate with the client's own duplex nature just as these things did in their childhood: 'You are complicit whatever you do in supporting or supressing values or value-clarification in yourself and your client' (Clarkson 2003: 183).

The *mysterium magnum* of values for integrative psychotherapy is still a work in progress. The exposition of views in this book is not an invitation for wild relativism or incoherent pluralistic practice. Instead, as Evans and Gilbert explain: 'Any model of integration [or integrative model of psychotherapy] needs to offer a coherent conceptual framework that reflects a consistency between philosophy, theory and practice' (2005: 149).

The ideas and examples presented, we hope, are an encouragement to abandon rivalry and the certitude of single-school approaches and not to lose sight of the one thing that research and experience tell us is the supreme unifying factor: the quality of the therapeutic relationship. Jung considered the soul to be the domain of unity and integration and so it is probably right to conclude that, for the integrative therapist, 'supreme values reside in the soul' (1970 [1944]: para. 14).

References

Allport, G. (1961) *Patterns and Growth in Personality*. New York: Holt, Rinehart & Winston.

Berne, E. (1974) *What Do You Say After You Say Hello? The Psychology of Human Destiny*. London: Corgi Books.

Blanchard, T.C., Wilke, A. and Hayden, B.Y. (2014) Hot-hand bias in rhesus monkeys. *Journal of Experimental Psychology: Animal Learning and Cognition*, 40(3): 280–6.

Clark, D. (2016) Developing and disseminating effective psychological therapies – science, economics and politics. Paper presented at Annual Conference, British Psychological Society.

Clarkson, P. (2003) *The Therapeutic Relationship* (2nd edn). London: Whurr.

Drucker, P. (1993) *The Effective Executive: The Definitive Guide to Getting the Right Things Done*. New York: HarperCollins.

Evans, K.R. and Gilbert, M. (2005) *An Introduction to Integrative Psychotherapy*. Basingstoke: Palgrave.

Fromm, E. (1976) *To Have or to Be*. London: Abacus.

Hauser, M.D. (2006) *Moral Minds: The Nature of Right and Wrong*. New York: HarperCollins.

Hays, G. (trans.) (2003) *Meditations of Marcus Aurelius*. London: Phoenix Paperback.

Heidegger, M. (1962) *Being and Time*. J. Macquarrie and E. Robinson, trans. Oxford: Blackwell.

Hoffman, E. (1985) The way of splendour: An introduction to the Kabbalah. *Yoga Journal*, March/April.

Horton, I. (2000) Principles and practice of a personal integration. In S. Palmer and R. Woolfe (eds), *Integrative and Eclectic Counselling and Psychotherapy* (pp. 31–56). London: SAGE.

Jung, C.G. (1970 [1944]) Psychology and alchemy. In *Collected Works 12*. London: Routledge.

Jung, C.G. (1970 [1957]) The undiscovered self. In *Collected Works 10*. London: Routledge.

Jung, C.G. (1995 [1963]) *Memories, Dreams, Reflections*. London: Fontana.

Lyotard, J-F. (1989) *The Postmodern Condition: A Report on Knowledge*. Manchester: Manchester University Press.

Mitchell, S. (trans.) (1999) *Tao Te Ching: An Illustrated Guide*. London: Frances Lincoln Limited.

Polkinghorne, D.E. (1992) Postmodern epistemology of practice. In S. Kvale (ed.), *Psychology and Postmodernism*. London: SAGE.

Rizq, R. (2012) The perversion of care: Psychological therapies in a time of IAPT. *Psychodynamic Practice*, 18(1): 7–24.

Rogers, C. (1990) *The Carl Rogers Reader*. H. Kirschenbaum and V.L. Henderson (eds). London: Constable.

Rumi, J. (1991) *One-handed Basket Weaving*. C. Barks, trans. Athens, GA: Maypop.

Russell, B. (1935) The harm that good men do. In B. Russell, *Sceptical Essays*. London: Unwin Paperbacks.

Russell, B. (1946) *History of Western Philosophy*. London: George Allen & Unwin.

Shah, I. (2001) *The Sufis*. London: Octagon Press.

Stenudd, S. (Undated) *Tao Te Ching* – Chapter 29. Available at: https://www.taoistic.com/taoteching-laotzu/taoteching-29.htm (accessed 25 April 2019).

Wachtel, P. (2008) *Relational Theory and the Practice of Psychotherapy*. New York: Guilford Press.

Wilde, O. (1892) *Lady Windermere's Fan*. I. Small (ed.). London: Bloomsbury.

Appendix 1 An integrative assessment model: client initial consultation

Full name: _____

Address: _____

Date of birth: _____

GP name, address and telephone no.: _____

Psychiatrist details (if relevant): _____

How referral was made: _____

Relationship to referrer: _____

Email: _____

Date of assessment interview and fee: _____

Presenting complaint and its history
*What is the problem? How long has it been going on for? Why are they here?
Have they identified any cause of the problem? Medicine/other therapy? Is
there any current suicidal ideation or intent? Risk assessment.*

Practical information
1. Occupation (state if currently in employment)

_____

2. Educational background (e.g. degree and type, where).

_____

3. Any previous therapy? How long for and client's experience of it?

_____

Psychiatric history
*Has the client ever been seen by a psychotherapist? Has the client ever been
seen by a psychiatrist? What was it for, when? Has the client ever made any
suicidal attempts? Ask client to elaborate. What other prescribed drugs are they
taking (relating to mental health)?*

Medical history
Is there any medical comorbidity that may be causing or contributing to the presenting problem's presentation?
No ☐ Yes ☐ (specify)

Family of origin history
Does anyone in the family suffer with any mental health difficulties?
Are there any major issues with other family members? Specify.

Alcohol and recreational drugs history
Do they drink; if so how much? Do they use any recreational drugs?

Current domestic situation
Where do they live and who with? What family support do they have? Do they work and have they any financial difficulties? Do they have a partner? How are they getting on? Any children?

What is your earliest memory as a child?

_____

Any traumas? Specify

_____

Family relationships (with parents, grandparents, siblings, extended family)

_____

Relationship with own children

_____

Sexual relationship history

_____

Client's expectations of therapy

_____

Therapist's feelings about the client
Brief formulation of client's difficulties and account of the session
Are there any obvious precipitating factors to the client's current problem? How does their personal history affect the way they are coping with the problem? What have you made of their story? What emotions are apparent in your client and in yourself? What sense have you made of the interaction between you and the client? To what extent did the client collaborate with you during the assessment? Any key observations and hypotheses on your part to help you formulate and decide on interventions?

Outcome plan for treatment
How receptive is the client to receiving therapy? What have you agreed with the client from here?

Any other relevant information

_____

Date of assessment and agreed future treatment plan:

Name of psychotherapist: _____

Signed by psychotherapist: _____

Date: _____

Model Two: An Initial Psychotherapy Assessment Model

Client name: _____

Client address and telephone no.: _____

Date of birth: _____

Ethnicity: _____

Languages spoken: (first language and other)

_____

Optional

Marital status: _____

Date of arrival in the UK: _____

Immigration status (Asylum Seeker, Refugee, British Nationality): _____

Address: _____

GP details: _____

Referred by: _____

Next of kin details: _____

Reason for referral and understanding of: _____

Presenting problems (please write three): _____

Carers involved: _____

Perceived risks (harming self or others): _____

General appearance (dress, postures, facial expression, over-active/under-active, irritability, withdrawn): _____

Behaviour (violence verbally or physically, cooperative/uncooperative):

_____

Speech and thought (rate, tone, quality, quantity, rhyming, preoccupied):

_____

Affect and mood (anxiety, range of feelings, tearful, laughter, elation, aggressive, verbal/physical abuse, suicidal thoughts, subjective/objective):

_____

Abnormal beliefs (over-valued ideas, psychosomatic presentations, religious beliefs):

_____

Persecutory ideas (guilt, worthlessness, self-esteem issues):

_____

Perceptions of hallucinations/delusions (auditory, voices, content, visual, flashes or flashbacks):

_____

Full circumstances:

_____

Cognitive state (orientation [time and place], attention/concentration, memory [short- to long-term]):

_____

Insight (level of understanding/awareness into the condition):

_____

Psychiatric history and current medication (if any):

_____

History of substance use:

_____

History of trauma (if any, where, when, why):

_____

Current daily living (social contact, living circumstances, finances, attitudes to others, employment, relationships, support system):

_____

Self-care and sleep (eating habits, fluid intake, grooming, hygiene, sleep patterns):

_____

Family history (brief family tree, psychiatric history, substance use, significant adaptations to):

_____

Personal history/Pre-school (birthplace/where grew up, developed significant memories, perceived relationships with parents/siblings):

_____

Education (enjoy school, level achieved, made friends; easily or not):

_____

Occupational interest (past/current plans):

_____

Sexual behaviour (first experience, current relationship, orientation, abuse, violence):

_____

Client's view/perception/expectations of counselling/therapy (how the process was explained to client):

_____

Brief summary (summary of main findings/presenting problems; symptoms in context of person, life and background):

_____

Initial psychological formulation:

_____

Assessed by: _____

Date: _____

Signed: _____

Appendix 2 Risk assessment template

Name of Patient:

Date of birth:

Gender:

Ethnic origin:

Date of assessment:

Current Mental Health Act status:

List of dependent children (include ages):

Name and information sources   Notes:
available/accessed in completing
risk history (i.e. GP, carer, relative,
other professional involved, other,
hospital notes):

Categories and level of risk identified (insert H [high], M [medium] or L [low] in relevant boxes)

Current risk		**History of risk**	
Aggression/violence to family	☐	Aggression/violence to family	☐
Aggression/violence to staff	☐	Aggression/violence to staff	☐
Aggression/violence to others	☐	Aggression/violence to others	☐
Suicide	☐	Suicide	☐
Abuse/exploitation of others	☐	Abuse/exploitation of others	☐
Deliberate self-harm	☐	Deliberate self-harm	☐
Severe self-neglect	☐	Severe self-neglect	☐
Accidental self-harm	☐	Accidental self-harm	☐
Abuse/exploitation from others	☐	Abuse/exploitation from others	☐

Risk to children	☐	Risk to children	☐
Road safety issue	☐	Road safety issue	☐
Substance misuse	☐	Substance misuse	☐
Non-compliance with treatment	☐	Non-compliance with treatment	☐

☐ Other risks/More information (please tick and specify below)

☐ No apparent risk (please tick). Proceed to signature

Indicate factors increasing risk (warning signs or trigger factors):

Indicate factors decreasing risk (protective factors):

Further Action Recommended or Required:

Discussion with psychiatrist ☐

Assessment by Specialist Team ☐

Discussion with GP ☐

Other (specify) ☐

Risk Management Plan:

Steps to be taken if patient fails to attend or meet commitments:

Send a further appointment ☐

Contact GP again ☐

Contact nominated relative ☐

Other (specify) ☐

Details:

_____

_____

Patient's view on Risk Management Plan:

_____

_____

Agreement of Patient to Risk Plan: Agree ☐ Disagree ☐

Risk Management Plan:

Steps to be taken if patient fails to attend or meet commitments:

Send a further appointment ☐

Contact GP again ☐

Contact nominated relative ☐

Other (specify) ☐

Details:

_____

_____

Patient's view on Risk Management Plan:

_____

_____

Agreement of Patient to Risk Management Plan: Agree ☐ Disagree ☐

Copies to:

GP: ☐

Psychiatrist: ☐

Relative (patient consent necessary): ☐

Client File: ☐

Signatures

Therapist Name: _____

Signature: Date: _____

Patient Name: _____

Signature: Date: _____

Appendix 3 Client therapy experience questionnaire/evaluation

Please help us to improve our service by answering some questions about the service you have received. We are interested in your honest opinions, whether they are positive or negative. Please answer all of the questions. We also welcome your comments and suggestions.

Please tick one box for each question	At all Times	Most of the Time	Sometimes	Rarely	Never
1 Did your therapist listen to you and treat your concerns seriously?	☐	☐	☐	☐	☐
2 Do you feel that the therapy has helped you to better understand and address your difficulties?	☐	☐	☐	☐	☐
3 Did you feel involved in making choices about your treatment and care?	☐	☐	☐	☐	☐
4 On reflection, did you get the help that mattered to you?	☐	☐	☐	☐	☐
5 Did you have confidence in your therapist and his/her skills and techniques?	☐	☐	☐	☐	☐

Please use this space to tell us about your experience of our service

Thank you very much. We appreciate your help.

Forename ....

Surname ....

Date of birth ....

Index